MW01056758

The Saga
of the
Johnstown
City Schools

The Saga
of the
Johnstown
City Schools
Echoes from
the Halls

Clea P. Hollis and Leah P. Hollis

Dear Frank & Rosella,
Thank you for inviting
me to be a part of your
life
As always,
Clea

Patllis Press
JOHNSTOWN, PENNSYLVANIA

Although the authors and publisher have made every effort to ensure the accuracy and completeness of information contained in this book, we assume no responsibility for errors, inaccuracies, omissions, or any inconsistency herein. Any slights of people, places, or organizations are unintentional.

Photograph on cover is by courtesy of Cover Studio.

First printing 2003

ISBN 0-9720260-4-5
LCCN 2002105279

ATTENTION CORPORATIONS, UNIVERSITIES, COLLEGES, AND PROFESSIONAL ORGANIZATIONS: Quantity discounts are available on bulk purchases of this book for educational, gift purposes, or as premiums for increasing magazine subscriptions or renewals. Special books or book excerpts can also be created to fit specific needs. For information, please contact Patllis Press, P.O. Box 5336, Johnstown, PA 15904; ph. 814-266-4835; e-mail patllis@aol.com; www.patllispress.com.

Table of Contents ❖

Grant • School Finance • Greater Johnstown School District–2001 • 2001 Cambria County Schools • 2001 Community Report Card Breakfast • Superintendent's Message • Safe Schools in a Safe City

Disclaimer ❖

The Saga of the Johnstown City Schools: Echoes from the Halls, is a reaction to many comments made to the authors about a complete history needed of the Greater Johnstown Schools. With the undertaking of this gigantic project, the authors found a full-flavored history paralleling the omnipotent mountains that surround the city of Johnstown. This rich history was flavored with the hardships of three terrible, consequential floods that devastated the city and its schools. Nonetheless, the authors attempted to include some of the issues in the school board minutes, many newspaper articles, notes from *Spectators,* countless interviews, and the extensive files of the late Dr. Levi B. Hollis, Jr. Although the project was elephantine, the task was relentless, with volumes of documents. Collected data also introduced multiple spellings of people's names, places, and buildings. The authors attempted to make adjustments or included the multiple spellings and/or changes. However, this study was controlled by available data.

Therefore, the authors present to you, the readers, *The Saga of the Johnstown City Schools: Echoes from the Halls,* with a few missing honors, some missing bricks from the many schools, and much missing data. However, we have attempted to capture highlights of some periods and look forward to sharing our findings with you, our readers.

Acknowledgments ❖

We acknowledge, with appreciation, the support of several organizations and many individuals who made *The Saga of the Johnstown City Schools: Echoes from the Halls* possible. Thanks to the Community Foundation for the Alleghenies who provided decisive grant support. Community leaders have also contributed to the writing, by providing yearbooks, photographs, and newspaper articles. We are indebted to you and the administration of the Greater Johnstown School District who opened their archives for research. Dorothy Thomas ('57) and the Johnstown Branch of the National Association for the Advancement of Colored People (NAACP) proudly endorsed the research and writing of this *Saga* in the rudimentary stage. Bruce Haselrig ('62), vice president of the association, is acknowledged for his major research contributions and his personal involvement at all levels of this project. Mr. Haselrig said, "Lee's [Dr. Levi B. Hollis, Jr.] extensive home library; his files of many documents, photographs and papers on his academic career sustained this research study." In essence this publication was started when Dr. L. B. Hollis became an administrator in the Johnstown Schools in 1975. (See appendix.) Therefore, as we offer our thanks to Mr. Haselrig, we must also recognized the collected data of the late Dr. L. B. Hollis. Attorney William L. Glosser is also recognized as a significant contributor to the collection of data.

When the study itself fell on troubled waters, Ms. Debra Crowder ('70), Secretary of the Board of Education of the Greater Johnstown Schools, voiced her concerns and disappointment. She made a plea for the project to be completed. We thank her for the encouragement. We also acknowledge the assistance of Mike Messina ('75) and Lorraine Bezy, owners of the Chameleon Bookstore. They opened the bookstore doors as a Johnstown gathering place to collect ideas and rare information. Among the rare books of the bookstore, pages of this manuscript unfolded with people knowledgeable about Johnstown.

Special gifted people provided the artwork, photography, and special features. Local photographers have been very generous providing photographs to capture past events and old school buildings. Photographs were provided by courtesy of Park Cover ('69) from Cover Studio and Judy Browne Photography. We debated about a cover that would best depict the new century for the schools. Recci Patrick answered with an inspired idea of the beloved Johnstown High School focused on Americanization, and Dr. Ralph Patrick finalized the tome with a photographic salute to the future. Kelly Ritgi made the historical photograph collection of Hoss's Family Steak and Sea House available to the study. The historical collection of the Johnstown public schools was a contribution of the Johnstown Area Heritage Association. Alice and Robert Hollis came forth with original formatting of the text and photographs and also created the website. For these people who gave of their special gifts, we thank you for the success of this publication.

Some members of the NAACP have served on the Board of Directors of the Greater Johnstown Schools and could visualize the need for this book as a community resource. In the early stages of the research, the National Organization for Women (NOW), the Unity Coalition of the Southern Alleghenies, the Greater Johnstown Minority Scholars Club, and First Cambria A.M. E. Zion Church also endorsed the study.

Other conscientious reviewers gave critical comments and detailed suggestions along the way. We are indeed indebted to you for your expertise, kindness, and guidance. They were Dr. Shirley A. Biggs, Daniel Gotwald, Jessica Hrabovsky, Claudia Jones, John Kovac ('67), Cora Jarvis-Redden, Armelia (Midge) Patrick, Herbert C. Weaver, and Dr. Gerald Zahorchak ('75). The endorsement of Dr. Zahorchak, superintendent of the Greater Johnstown School District, underscores our pride in producing *The Saga of the Johnstown City Schools*. Our greatest indebtedness is to the hundreds of people and organizations who provided materials and inspiration to tackle this two-hundred-year history of the Johnstown School District. Leora (Lee) Rager ('45), chairperson for the American Association of University Women's (AAUW) Annual Book Sale collected and held books pertaining to the Johnstown Schools for the study. As a result, the community's vision and support of this publication are indicators of the need for a book to cover the actions of the many school board directors, superintendents, and significant events that paradigmatically shaped the Greater Johnstown Schools. Consequently, people cited on the pages of this book played a role in the oral and written history of Johnstown.

The Saga of the Johnstown City Schools has been an enormous undertaking to capture the spirit of Johnstown School Boards as they moved the district and the community toward Americanization. However, the study cannot truly exhibit the many hours of research undertaken, including but not limited to the perusal of school reports, surveys, newspapers, board minutes, and interviews. Personal interviews provided a valued qualitative dimension to the study. This data engendered the *Echoes from the Halls,* that is, the halls of the Johnstown Schools. Therefore, the authors gratefully express appreciation for the cooperation of the Greater Johnstown School District's administrators, community leaders, and many educators.

As we completed the manuscript, Kweisi Mfume, President and CEO of the National Association for the Advancement of Colored People (NAACP), requested to peruse the manuscript. As documented history reveals, the NAACP has been involved with the development of the city of Johnstown and the schools. Consequently, Mr. Mfume offered to write the foreword. We count our many friends as blessings bestowed upon us.

Clea P. Hollis, Ed.D.
Leah P. Hollis, Ed.D.

Dr. Levi B. Hollis, Jr., *Courtesy of Cover Studio*

Dedication ❖

Levi "Lee" Berkly Hollis, Jr., Ph.D.
November 17, 1932–September 5, 1989

Change is inevitable; it is the direction that counts.
—Dr. Levi B. Hollis, Jr.

The Saga of the Johnstown City Schools: Echoes from the Halls, is dedicated to Dr. Levi B. Hollis, Jr., superintendent of the Greater Johnstown School District from 1984–1989. Two retired Greater Johnstown administrators made an appeal to the Johnstown Branch of the NAACP Executive Committee at a meeting in the summer of 2000 to write a history of the Johnstown Schools that would feature Dr. Levi B. Hollis, Jr. Dr. Hollis also served as the district's director of secondary education–assistant superintendent from 1975–1984, and they thought that his life of hardships could be likened to the growth of the Johnstown Schools. The Executive Committee of the Johnstown Branch of the NAACP acknowledged their request with a proposal written to the Community Foundation for the Alleghenies for funding.

Although this book features Dr. Levi B. Hollis, Jr., I should hasten to mention that the board of directors or controllers of Johnstown Borough and the Greater Johnstown School District have appointed an array of outstanding, distinguished superintendents over the last two centuries. Please note that in 2002 the boards have appointed nineteen Greater Johnstown School superintendents and sixteen Johnstown Borough School District superintendents.

Dr. Hollis' humble background symbolizes the growth of Johnstown and the school district. As the son of a cotton farmer and a coal miner, he worked himself through college to become superintendent of the largest school district in Cambria County, Pennsylvania. He was born in Sulligent, Alabama, as the older of two sons. Later in the 1930s, the Hollis family, motivated by western Pennsylvania's natural resource of bituminous coal, migrated to the Greater Pittsburgh area.

The Hollis parents had a great concern for their son's slight physique. Consequently, Dr. Hollis attended first grade later than expected because his mother kept him at home, hoping he would grow taller before experiencing formal education. Dr. Hollis was a member of the New Kensington High School (Ken Hi) class of 1952. Searching for a career, he sought assistance from his high school guidance counselor. The counselor told young Hollis he should be a plumber and not to waste money on college. Enrolled in the academic course of study, he loathed mechanical tasks. However, to earn his college tuition, he worked a year in the Allegheny Steel Mill before entering Duquesne University, Pittsburgh, Pennsylvania. He pursued a degree in English, vowing to make a difference in molding young minds.

Dr. Hollis' first professional teaching assignment was at Warren G. Harding High School, Warren, Ohio. He became the Chairperson of the English and Journalism Departments, the Yearbook Advisor, Executive Teacher, and Secondary Principal. *Echoes from the Halls* is a reflection of the *Echoes* Yearbook at Harding High School, where he was the yearbook advisor for more than ten years. His ambition led him to earn a Master's Degree in English from Ohio State University. Later as a Ford Foundation Fellow, he earned his Doctorate of Philosophy Degree at Kent State University, Ohio, in Curriculum and Instruction.

During his tenure at the Warren Schools, he was also an English Professor at Youngstown State University, Youngstown, Ohio. He motivated his high school students to aspire a degree in higher education. As an innovative educator, he established many academic programs in the Warren City Schools. With a federal grant, Dr. Hollis established the Focus Center, a magnate innovative elementary school with a high interest curriculum that focused on interactive reading and arithmetic programs. As his career matured, he longed to walk in the footsteps of his grandfather, who had been a superintendent of schools in Sulligent, Alabama. Among Dr. Hollis' keepsakes are inscribed books dated 1888 from his grandfather, who had attended Paine Institute in Augusta, Georgia.

In 1962, Dr. L. B. Hollis married the former Clea Patrick, a graduate of Har-Brack High School, Natrona Heights, and the School of Fashion Design, Art Institute of Pittsburgh, both in Pennsylvania. She was a freelance fashion designer with a trademark of Mar-Clee Fashions. The couple was blessed with two children.

In 1975, Dr. Hollis accepted the challenge of the Greater Johnstown School Board Directors to revitalize the curriculum of the district. He relocated to Johnstown to assist the spirited, charismatic superintendent of the Greater Johnstown Schools, Dr. Donato Zucco. Dr. Hollis saw an opportunity, as Director of Secondary Education, to make a difference, molding the youth of the school district. However, his dream to become superintendent of schools, like his grandfather, became a reality in 1984, when he was appointed by the Board of School Directors to serve in that position. Some of his accomplishments included the Phase I and Phase II Alternative Programs at all secondary schools, for dropout prevention. He developed the district's Long Range Plan that led to the district's K–12 Curriculum, Scope and Sequence. He involved the local community and state officials with his quest for quality education. Dr. Hollis was instrumental in the development of the Corporate Partnership Program and the district's Building Utilization Program. The West Side Elementary School of the Greater Johnstown School District was dedicated to him in 1991.

Beyond Dr. Hollis' responsibilities with the Greater Johnstown School District, he served the community on many executive boards. Some of the community boards were the Advisory Board of the University of Pittsburgh, Conemaugh Valley Hospital Board of Trustees, First Cambria A.M.E. Zion Church Board of Trustees, City County Clinic Board of Directors, East Hills Recreation Board of Directors, Chairperson of the 1988 United Way Campaign, Chairperson of the Education Section of the State Committee on Partnership, 1989 State Task Force on Special Education, American Red Cross Board of Trustees, the Greater Johnstown Enrichment School Advisory Board, the Greater Johnstown Minority Scholars Club, President of the YMCA Board of Directors, and Omega Psi Phi Fraternity. He and his family are Life Members of the National Association for the Advancement of Colored People (NAACP). In 1979, Dr. Hollis chaired the committee for writing the History of Cambria Somerset Chapter of the American Red Cross. Floyd L. Pillow was Executive Director of that Unit.

Levi Berkly Hollis, Ph.D., "Lee," died on September 5, 1989. His funeral commanded media coverage and attendance befitting a dignitary, and was recognized as a tribute to education in Johnstown. Flags were flown at half-mast. Although he was an accomplished school administrator, it can be said he was a teacher all of his life. He taught Sunday school from his teenage years, until death. After death, he continues to be credited with his great influence on education in Ohio, Pennsylvania, and particularly the Greater Johnstown community. He leaves the legacy of bonding the Hollis family, his wife, Dr. Clea Patrick Hollis, and his children, Dr. Leah Patricia Hollis and Robert Levi Hollis, to the progress of the Greater Johnstown Community. He is remembered for motivating parents to take interest in their child's education and accelerating student and academic programs in the Greater Johnstown School District.

Leah P. Hollis, Ed.D.
Rutgers University

Foreword ❖

The Saga of the Johnstown City Schools: Echoes from the Halls offers an obsessively detailed chronology of the growth, decline, and attempted resurrection of one American public education system. By examining the microcosm of a single small town, afflicted by natural disaster and political machinations, we can glean from this compilation of archived records and brief reminiscences the multifactorial nature of educational funding.

Hollis and Hollis track the system's evolution, from the earliest time when school was not available at all, through an era when it was made deliberately unaffordable to maintain class distinctions in a presumably classless society, past the separate and unequal years of segregation, and on to the present day.

Between the lines, beyond the lists of rules imposed on students, recitations of expenditures, and the recounting of systemic infighting, we use our own perspective to get past walls of brick and mortar, and bring meaning to the struggles of each age. *Echoes from the Halls* is a good step toward that full story, of those whose aspirations and dreams were alternatively swept away by flooding rivers and the too frequent missteps of a system that promised but seldom delivered equity and top quality. Some left to try to find freedom again—others stayed on this floodplain to forge it for themselves.

Our own admittedly selective perception makes more portentous than any new building or act of politics the successful organization of a multiracial "unity march" by a black student following the slaying of a white student by two African-Americans during an armed robbery. In an era where racial differences could have flared uncontrollably, that one wise communal act gives rise to the notion that together we can conquer hatred, ignorance and fear, despite all privation, lingering prejudice and the past.

With best wishes for the future and warmest regards, I am

Sincerely,

Kweisi Mfume
National Association for the Advancement of Colored People (NAACP)
President and CEO
KM/mp

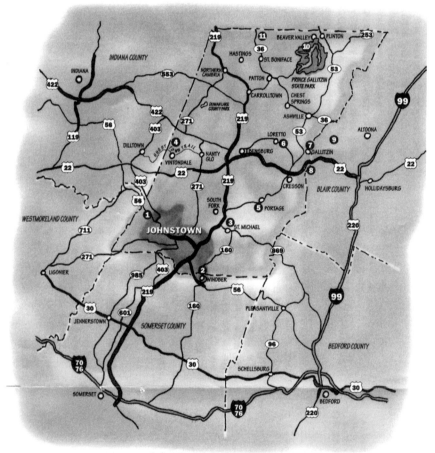

Johnstown, Pennsylvania
Courtesy of the Cambria County Chamber of Commerce

Introduction

The Saga of the Johnstown City Schools is an historical portrayal of the development of the school system in Johnstown, Pennsylvania. The history of the Johnstown City Schools in Cambria County was shaped by elected school board directors and their appointed superintendents. The progression followed revolutionizing laws of the commonwealth, with implementation of academic and social programs.

In 1790, the constitution provided a legal basis to establish a public school system in Pennsylvania. Nonetheless, only private schools were prevalent before the Free School Act of 1834. The Act enabled 987 public schools to be established, followed with management; that is, organizing school boards. Later, the constitution, in 1873, laid a solid foundation for the public school system stating that the General Assembly would provide for the maintenance of an efficient system of public schools. All children above the age of six were required to be educated in the commonwealth. In 1885, attendance for students was regulated to twenty days, monthly. Saturday classes were forbidden. An Act of 1887 increased the school term to a minimum of six months. The education attendance laws followed, in 1893, with a Compulsory Free Textbook Act. After the textbook law, a Compulsory Education Act was passed in 1895. School attendance became imperative for children between the ages of eight and thirteen.

In 1903, the Commonwealth of Pennsylvania regulated the minimum salary of public school teachers to $35 per month. An Act of 1921 lengthened the minimum school term to eight months. However, school districts like Johnstown, with a population of 50,000 or more, were able to hold classes for a term of nine months with 180 days per year. With the enforcement by state government, the Compulsory Education Act made school attendance free to students at the consideration of taxpayers.

At first, school laws were primarily concerned with basic elementary education, because secondary education was considered to be a private initiative. In 1836, an Act of Legislature established the Central High School in Philadelphia. In 1860, a quarter of a century later, there were only six public high schools in the commonwealth. However the establishment of high schools picked up speed. By 1866, the number of high schools had grown to fourteen. When the 1887 Act was passed to authorize the formation of public high schools in cities and larger towns, Johnstown had already established a high school in 1882, five years before the Act. Some families in small towns paid tuition for their children to attend high school in a nearby district. In 1893, legislation extended the law to include all towns. With government intervention, many changes and improvements in the public school system have marked the progress of public education in Pennsylvania.

In 1946, there were 2,500 school districts in Pennsylvania; in 1965 there were 1,600; in 1970, there were 504; and in 2001, there were 501. The 501 school districts in Pennsylvania are divided into 29 Intermediate Units. In essence, 2,500 school districts were reduced to 501 school districts, within fifty years. The Johnstown School District has been reduced to four schools.

In 1969, the Pennsylvania Department of Education (PDE) replaced the Pennsylvania Department of Public Instruction. The PDE is part of the Governor's Cabinet and brings cohesiveness to the various school districts. The Department regulates laws and financial support to local school districts and provides state grants. The Greater Johnstown School Board, with academic guidance of their appointed superintendent, has followed educational trends and abided by the laws of the Commonwealth of Pennsylvania, building public schools and changing curriculum to meet the needs of a changing community.

Thousands of high school graduates have memories of their days in Johnstown classrooms and in sports. Memories grew with graduates who gradually increased from seven in 1882, to a peak of 854 in 1940. When the senior class consistently totaled more than one hundred students, Superintendent Stockton proposed midyear graduations. Two graduation ceremonies were held between 1917 and 1933. In 1934, Superintendent McMaster reversed the graduation ceremony to an annual event. High school graduates, of course, declined with the population to 200 graduates in 2000.

Johnstown Public School District
High School Graduates from 1882–2000

Year	Number
1882	7
1887	10
1891	13
1895	13
1900	20
1905	34
1910	87
1915	135
1917	167

Beginning one-half year graduations

Year	Number
1917 ½	24
1920	173
1920 ½	62
1925 ½	18
1930	117
1930 ½	120
1932	261
1940	854
1945	58
1950	583
1955	619
1960	684
1965	738
1970	780
1975	570
1980	342
1985	252
1990	255
1995	21
1999	170
2000	200

Many graduates have remained in the Johnstown area; some have moved out of the area, carrying memories of their hometown school. Although most return to visit, some return to the area when employment opportunities are available. Other graduates return for retirement. Nonetheless, there are many Johnstown High School graduates living around the world.

Class of 1921 ½, *Courtesy of Hoss's Family Steak and Sea House*

1920–2000 Greater Johnstown High School Alumni
GJHS Graduates Living Around the World*

Alabama	43
Alaska	9
Arizona	227
Arkansas	15
California	698
Colorado	110
Connecticut	80
Delaware	79
District of Columbia	41
Florida	922
Georgia	148
Hawaii	9
Idaho	9
Illinois	134
Indiana	157

Iowa	12
Kansas	34
Kentucky	43
Louisiana	22
Maine	14
Maryland	681
Massachusetts	75
Michigan	213
Minnesota	23
Mississippi	15
Missouri	54
Montana	12
Nevada	67
New Hampshire	22
New Jersey	352
New Mexico	41
New York	370
North Carolina	232
North Dakota	5
Ohio	644
Oklahoma	27
Oregon	27
Pennsylvania	9,902
Rhode Island	13
South Carolina	112
South Dakota	5
Tennessee	54
Texas	315
Utah	15
Vermont	13
Virginia	684
Washington	64
West Virginia	81
Wisconsin	33
Wyoming	12
United States Military	5

GJHS Graduates Living in United States Territories and Possessions

Guam	1
Puerto Rico	1
Virgin Islands	1

GJHS Graduates Living Outside the United States of America

Australia	2
Bahamas	1
Canada	12
Denmark	1
Ecuador	1
Egypt	1
England	2
Finland	1
France	1
Germany	4
Ireland	2
Luxembourg	1
Netherlands	1
Poland	1
Russia	1
Spain	1
Sweden	5
Thailand	1

In 2000, 4,500 Greater Johnstown High School Graduates were reported as living in Johnstown.

* Data obtained from the Greater Johnstown Alumni Directory (2000).

Birth of the Johnstown Schools 1800–1890

Chapter II

Conemaugh Old Town

Johnstown, Pennsylvania, is the major city in Cambria County, strategically located about 70 miles from Pittsburgh and about 130 miles from Harrisburg. Johnstown, once known as Conemaugh Old Town, was developed by Native Americans of the Delaware tribe and settled by an Amish farmer, Mr. Joseph (Schantz) Johns. The first inhabitants consisted of about twenty Native American families with about sixty braves, who hunted, toiled, and lived on the land before 1730 (Robson, 1985, p.192). The Native American village, Kickenpawling's Town, was located at the junction of the Little Conemaugh River and Stony Creek (Buck & Buck, 1995, p. 29). The natives started navigating their canoes down the Conemaugh, Kiskiminetas, and Allegheny Rivers to the Ohio (Johnson, Giles, and Michaels, 1985, p. 214).

The land fell into the hands of many owners before Mr. Johns settled there in about 1800. Mr. Johns laid out lots and streets on a large plot of land and retained the name of the location as Conemaugh Old Town. Conemaugh Old Town became known as Conemaugh. The town was "[b]uilt on a nearly level flood plain at the confluence of two rivers, down at the bottom of an enormous hole in the Alleghenies" (McCullough, 1968, p. 24). The area was later named Johnstown, after its founder. Joseph Johns' initial town plan dedicated two lots numbered 133 and 134, situated on Market and Chestnut Streets in downtown Johnstown, for the purpose of erecting schools and houses of public worship. These dedicated lots were free and clear of any encumbrances. Later, the residents renamed Chestnut Street in the initial plan to Carr Street and then to Napoleon Street (Pawlowski, 1985, pp. 457–461).

Aerial View of the City of Johnstown, *Courtesy of Cover Studio*

Education, schools, and books were not household words of the families who lived in the settlement of Conemaugh Old Town. Most settlers came for the rich natural resources of the mountainous terrain on which they toiled from sunrise to sunset. At home, children were taught the art of toiling the soil for subsistence. "The early farmer and his wife were true partners, and the family closely knit, as everyone had chores to do, from the youngest to the oldest" (Himes, 1988, p. 24). However, one farmer had a vision to advance the culture through formal education. Mr. Joseph Johns had the foresight and interest to designate sites for schools in his initial plans, with hopes that Johnstown would be named the county seat. However, on March 29, 1805, by a

Special Act of the State Legislature, Ebensburg was chosen as the county seat of Cambria County. Shortly after, Mr. Johns left the settlement to retire in the nearby village of Davidsville (Pawlowski, 1885, pp. 547-459).

1854 Cambria Iron Works, *Courtesy of the Johnstown Area Heritage Association*

"Iron, steel, and coal have dominated Johnstown's economy and, therefore, its labor history nearly from the beginning" (Williams and Yates, 1985, p. 589). The first industry, flat boating was the process of floating iron down the Juniata River to Pittsburgh during the high water of spring streams. In 1810, the population had grown to about 50 people. The cost of land was about $10 an acre with an annual rental fee of $1. The availability of the natural abundant timber continued to provide the source of family income. The timber industry influenced a significant boating trade that also attracted many more settlers. By 1828, Johnstown was a village of 200 people with five general stores and two taverns. The completion of the Pennsylvania Canal in 1831 connecting Pittsburgh and Philadelphia brought prosperity and growth to the area (Williams and Yates, p. 590).

The new settlers built a one-story log schoolhouse on the northeast corner of Mr. Johns' designated sites for schools. The building, erected on Market and Carr Streets, later became the site of Johnstown High School. People in Conemaugh Old Town named the school "Old Blacky" because the building was weather-beaten but never painted. Subscription for attendance generated revenue for the mortgage. Until 1854, the building housed educational, religious, and community activities. From the beginning of Johnstown's history, records show the great importance of the inclusion of education in the planning. Education in Johnstown has always been one of the community's most significant investments.

Conemaugh Borough

On January 12, 1831, Conemaugh Old Town was chartered as Conemaugh Borough, with more than two hundred residents. In 1834, an Act of Assembly changed the name to Johnstown Borough to honor the founder, Mr. Joseph Johns. On April 1 of that year, the first act was passed authorizing the commonwealth's appropriation of $75,000 to assist boroughs and townships to educate residents in the common school system. The first Johnstown School Board of Controllers was organized in 1834 shortly after the authorization of the Act of Assembly. The board's primary responsibility was to manage the commonwealth's allocation for educating children. The School Board of Controllers also played a major role in hiring superintendents, administrators, and teachers to help establish school policies and programs. In essence, the School Board of Controllers shaped programs for the increasing student population. In a Rules and Regulations Release dated January 1, 1856, the School Board of Controllers signed the document as the board of directors. (See Rules and Regulations.) Controllers and directors were titles used interchangeably until about the early 1900s.

First School Board Controllers of the Johnstown School District, 1834

George Bheam	Adam Cover
Peter Levergood	Robert P. Linton
Edwin A. Vickroy	

Although Mr. Peter Levergood had been an opponent of the common school system, he accepted an appointment to serve on the first Johnstown Borough School Board of Controllers. Mr. Levergood had become the second proprietor, after Joseph Johns and was able to move the community in the direction that Mr. Johns had planned. "By 1840, Johnstown's population had increased to 1,000" (Burkert, 2000, p. 8).

The Board of School Controllers played a major role in the construction of school buildings, the appointment of superintendents, environmental catastrophe issues related to the Johnstown floods, and the development of an academic and social school system in the coming century. One of the stipulations of the free school system was the hiring procedure that required the board to interview or examine teachers. Therefore, new teachers were interviewed or examined by the board or someone employed by the school board. Leaders in the community, the clergy, and attorneys also accepted the responsibility to examine teachers to help select the "best" for the Johnstown Schools. More teachers were needed with the increased growth of the student population, with families moving to the area to work.

Considering the hinterlands and the mountainous topography, the first industry of the area was timber, which included the building of rafting and flatboats. Flatboats augmented the iron industry by transporting iron from the Juniata Valley to Pittsburgh (Burkert, 1985, p. 256). Of course, these industries attracted settlers. By 1850, the population of the borough of Johnstown was about 1,260 people. After the Cambria Iron Company was founded in 1852, the population grew to more than 6,000 by 1856. In the first half of the century, Johnstown was nurtured by flat boating and canal transportation and depended heavily on its agriculture. With its central location, Johnstown transformed from a small canal village to an important manufacturing center. In the second half of the 1800s, Johnstown was also nurtured by the iron, railroad, and coal industries. "By 1885, there were twenty-three [coal] mines operating in the county; production of that year totaled 1,107,965 tons" (Cooper, 1988, p. 16). Consequently, the spirit of the Johnstown School Board was influenced by environmental changes, cultural changes, and changing sources of livelihood for the residents.

Common Law Schoolhouses

Mr. Joseph Shaffer and Judge Easly built "Little Brick Schoolhouse" in 1836, under the Common School System Law of 1834. "Little Brick Schoolhouse" was also used for worship. A year later, in 1837, Judge Easly built the "McConaughy Schoolhouse" on the southwest corner of Walnut and Conemaugh Streets, at a cost of $2,000. The school board took action to place "McConaughy Schoolhouse" on Market Street between "Old Blacky" and "Little Brick Schoolhouse." Moving "McConaughy Schoolhouse" from Walnut Street to Market Street caused structural damages to the building. After the district repaired and painted the relocated schoolhouse, it took on a new appearance. Subsequently, the students renamed the building "Old Whitey." With the addition, three schools were located on Market Street.

With the growing school-age population, the board voted to build another schoolhouse at the head of Main Street. The distinction of this building was the little bell, located outside the front door, used to call students to class. Thus, the students referred to this building as the "Bell Schoolhouse." In 1855, "Old Blacky" was sold for $63 and "Old Whitey" was sold for $176. Data collected revealed neither the date of construction nor the sale of "Bell Schoolhouse." The "Little Brick Schoolhouse" was lost in the 1889 Flood.

1840 Tax Levy

In 1840, the school board increased the tax levy to $521 to adequately operate the schools, for four years, that is, until February 1846. With responsibility to provide students an adequate education, the school board took action on January 22, 1844, to appoint Mr. Charles Meegan as principal of the newly established public school. His annual salary was $145. The board also hired three female teachers, with an annual salary of $90 each, for a ten-month school term. On November 26, 1844, the board voted to open another school on the second Monday in December. Mr. R. West was appointed as a teacher at a salary of $20 per month, considerably more than the female teachers. In 1845, to produce the additional revenue to support the school personnel, the tax duplicate was 5 mils to produce $344.17. On February 12, 1846, the board voted to close the public schools until May 1 because of incompetent teachers. At the same meeting, the board directed the secretary to advertise for three male teachers and one female teacher on March 1, 1846. The deadline date for applications was April 10. On April 30, the board hired four teachers. The teachers' eight-month school term contract commenced on May 4, 1846.

1846 Teachers' Monthly Salaries

Mr. G. B. Breckenridge	$30
Mr. Sam Douglas	$25
Mr. W. H. Hitchcock	$25
Miss Angeline Vickroy	$15

On May 31, 1847, the board took action to appropriate the upper story of the schoolhouse on Main Street to a senior male schoolteacher, Mr. C. E. Richardson. The Brick Schoolhouse was appropriated to a senior female schoolteacher, Mrs. C. E. Richardson. At the same meeting, the controllers (directors) divided the Borough of Johnstown into three school districts.

Three Districts of the School System

District One started on Main Street between the alley of Fockler and Matthew Streets, and extended to Stonycreek. District Two's boundaries started on Main Street and ran to Zimmerman Street, north to the canal, including Platt and Ritter Streets, running along the borough line. District Three's boundaries were composed of areas that were not included in Districts One and Two. Even the board's strategic planning efforts were unable to overcome environmental and financial difficulties.

In February 1852, the board closed the schools due to scarcity of funds and inclement weather that caused poor attendance. That year, the board also secured benefits from the iron and steel mills' operative in town and ordered a tax levy of $1,200. The 1853 board minutes reported a total of 6 teachers and 333 students, with a student-teacher ratio of 1 per 55. For an eight-month school term, the instruction cost per student was 42 cents for school assessments to support the schools.

1900s Coal Mining, *Courtesy of Hoss's Family Steak and Sea House*

Paradoxically, the coal mines and steel mills also attracted many boys who left the school. Consequently, the school board found that the school buildings had too much space for the remaining students. With extra rooms, in 1854 the board granted the town permission to use a basement in the Main Street School to shelter a fire truck. The board also granted use of another building to John Cannon for his private school.

Disregarding the extra rooms in one building, on May 19 the school board requested bids for a school building to be constructed near Union Cemetery. The specifications detailed that the building was to be erected on a site 36 feet from Market Street and 36 feet from School Alley. The construction bids ranged from $2,675 to $4,500.

Union Schoolhouse Bids

Callan and Hannan	$3,395
Samuel Chrisman	$3,199
L. B. Cohick	$3,900
Joseph Kurtz	$3,323
Conrad Suppes	$4,500
Pringle, Rose, and Edson	$2,945
(The Honored Wesley J. Rose)	
* George Shaffer	$2,675
(Exclusive of cellar)	
(Exclusive of stone and brick)	
Valentine and John Varner	$3,300

* Awarded the contract.

Separate bids were submitted to complete the structure.

Stone and Brick Bids

Martin Hannan	Excavation and wall: $331
	Brick work: $999
John Hutzen	$2.25 per perk and 10 cents per yard
	for excavation
Henry Sutton	Masonry @ $2 per perk
	12 ½ cents per square yard for excavation
Charles Wilson	$2.12 per perk and $2.12 for excavation

The blueprints of the Union Schoolhouse specified 120 perks of masonry and 320 yards of excavation in the blueprints. The school board's minutes did not identify the contractor who was awarded the stone and brickwork contract. The board levied a 13-mil tax for building purposes, producing $1,976.41 and $817.02 for the school's operating budget.

When the Union School Building was completed, on November 22, 1855, controllers appointed Mr. Henry Ely as the Union School principal, at a monthly salary of $50. They appointed Mr. J. B. Ewing as Mr. Ely's assistant, at a monthly salary of $30.

School Climate in the 1860s

Chapter III

Conditions of the Schools

The conditions of schools in the surrounding boroughs and also throughout the county obscured the earnest attempt of Johnstown Borough School District Controllers to provide educational facilities. Low salaries, low taxes, and inadequate equipment angered the county superintendent, whose annual reports to the state superintendent detracted from the genuine interest held about public education by many teachers and parents. The northern part of the county claimed that the schools were poor because of the Democrats' and the Catholics' prevalence. However, in 1861, Mr. James Moor Swank, the county superintendent, chose to praise the patriotism of the rugged people of Cambria County, instead of focusing on the conditions of the schools, religion, and political affiliation. Mr. Swank said that all mountain regions produced men who knew how to fight for their country and also support the cultivation of the intellect for refinement of taste and to enable the whole man. He stated that the common school system flourished in our county because of competent teachers.

Negative Press

Mr. Swank stood alone in his defense of the Cambria County Schools. Subsequent superintendents did not shut their eyes to the county's school climate. A few years later, state school authorities requested information on the encouragement that churches gave to the free public schools. Mr. T. J. Chapman, county superintendent, de-

17

scribed the relationship in his report of the Superintendents of Common Schools in Pennsylvania for the year ending June 1, 1868, with sarcasm. Mr. Chapman argued: "[t]he pulpit is of about as much witness to our educational agency as are the moons to Jupiter. Not a single sermon in favor of education, so far as I know, has ever been preached inside a limit of the county. This is both shameful and astonishing. If I have done the sacred profession an injustice by making assertion. I regret it; but I am sure I cannot be far wrong, if wrong at all."

The Johnstown Schools could not escape the steady stream of denunciations. Administrative officers viewed all schools from one pattern. As an exception to the pattern, some boroughs, such as Woodvale, provided large playgrounds for its schools, but most did not. With continuous negative press, the *Johnstown Tribune* reported on February 18, with a follow-up story on June 19, 1874, that Conemaugh Borough closed its schools after a six-month term. They paid each of the four teachers $150 for the six months. Some citizens occasionally would trace existing hooliganism to conditions in and around the schools.

On January 15, 1887, the *Johnstown Tribune* published an article that illustrated conditions around the Prospect Borough School as a disgrace to civilization and an outrage to the unfortunate youngsters who attended. The *Tribune* stated that the school was a monument displaying the inefficiencies of those whose duties are to provide facilities for the children and correct training of the youth. However, the responsibility for correct training of the youth fell into the hands of sixteen Johnstown Borough superintendents. The board of controllers appointed superintendents as the academic leaders to reform the schools and to promote Americanization.

Superintendents of the Johnstown Borough School District, 1858–1895

A. H. Sembower	1858–1860
E. H. Mauck	1860–1861
S. B. McCormick	1861–1862
J. F. Condon	1862
H. Ely	1863–1864
J. W. Schwartz	1864–1865
A.C. Johnson	1865–1868
S. B. McCormick	1868
G. W. Cope	1869–1872
J. R. Hykes	1872–1873

B. H. Patterson	1873–1875
H. S. Phillips	1875–1876
N. N. Keener	1876–1879
A. S. Brubaker	1879–1880
W. E. Scheibner	1880–1881
T. B. Johnson	1881–1895

Before the appointment of a superintendent, the Johnstown Schools functioned for many years with a leading teacher assuming the responsibilities of a superintendent. Reverend John Meneely, builder of the first school, designated himself as the leading teacher in 1805. Not until 1858 did the school board appoint the first principal, Mr. Henry Ely, and an official superintendent, Mr. A. H. Sembower. On July 15, 1880, the school board appointed A. E. Scheibner as superintendent of the Johnstown Borough Schools at a salary of $120 per month for the school year.

Alleged Misconduct of Superintendents

Although sexual harassment was not defined for another century, the school board held a hearing for two complaints on April 9, 1881, regarding Superintendent Scheibner's alleged inappropriate behavior. Apparently, the board was cognizant of the ramification of the accusation. Although many other cases such as this surfaced, the courts did not include sexual harassment as part of sex discrimination until the 1980s. The decisions of the landmark case of *Meritor Savings Bank v. Vinson* (1986) upheld the concept that an employer can be held liable without further notice for acts of supervisors (C. Hollis, 2000, p. 21). Therefore, the Johnstown School Board advanced a century when they heard the first complaint of a teacher who accused the superintendent of kissing her.

Later, another female teacher filed a complaint about the improper behavior of the same superintendent. The board formed the opinion that the first teacher did not produce enough evidence to warrant disciplinary action. The board ruled after an investigation of the second complaint that the superintendent's behavior was not improper. Nevertheless, two months later, on June 20, 1881, Mr. Kress, president of the Board of School Directors, made a motion to hold a special meeting to appoint a new superintendent. That summer, Mr. T. B. Johnson was appointed superintendent of the Johnstown Borough Schools and served in that position until 1890. Johnstown Borough became the City of Johnstown; therefore, Mr. Johnson was the last superintendent of the Johnstown Borough Schools and became the first superintendent of the Johnstown City Schools.

On December 11, 1894, Superintendent Johnson's conduct was questioned. A committee of school board directors met to investigate charges against the superintendent, for "…using language unbecoming to his position." After testimony of the teacher and the student who was being disciplined, it was determined that the misconduct of the male student warranted discipline. However, in administering the punishment, the superintendent was unprofessional with using language inappropriate to the position of superintendent. The directors adopted a resolution that stated: "Resolved that the superintendent, principals and teachers be encouraged in their efforts to preserve strict discipline by all proper means, which does not include the use of abusive language or the display of a violent temper."

Johnstown Inclined Plane,
Courtesy of Cover Studio

The Inclined Plane Effects

Building of the Inclined Plane started after the 1889 Flood and was completed in 1891 to provide transportation for an escape if another water catastrophe occurred. At a grade of 71.9, it is the steepest vehicular inclined plane in the world. As a city school system, events that took place in the city also effected the city schools. The farmlands at the top of the hill began to expand and the growth took some of the student population from the Johnstown schools. However, the board was kept busy with internal problems.

Salary Disputes

On May 5, 1896, the Johnstown City Board of School Directors appointed Mr. Jacob M. Berkey of Berlin, Pennsylvania, as the school superintendent, for a three-year contract at a salary of $2,000 per year. On May 2, 1905, Mr. Berkey was retired by the board. The board of directors appointed Mr. James N. Muir to the position, with a vote of twelve to nine. According to the *Tribune*, the election was one of the most heated school board meetings in history. Mr. Enoch James charged the president of the school board, Mr. John Walker, with trickery. The controversy was caused by the perceived lack of knowledge of Mr. Muir's credentials. Apparently, all members of the board did not have the opportunity to view Mr. Muir's portfolio. Mr. Muir was thirty-three years old and a native of Tioga County, Ohio. He had attended the normal school of Mansfield and earned a Bachelor of Science Degree from the University of Pennsylvania. He had taught three years in Tioga County and was a supervising teacher in Waverly for three years. At the time of his appointment, he was employed by Ginn Publishing Company as an agent for school publications. In 1908, Mr. Muir was reelected for a three-year term, which he served until 1910.

Mr. J. N. Adee was appointed to begin the 1910 to 1911 school year. On Tuesday, April 9, 1918, Mr. Adee, the superintendent, and Mr. Herbert J. Stockton, the Johnstown High School principal, were nominated for the position. During the election, Mr. Stockton received six votes and Mr. Adee received three votes. A motion passed at the

Classroom of the Early 1900s, *Courtesy of Hoss's Family Steak and Sea House*

board meeting to make the election unanimous. Mr. Stockton was appointed and served as superintendent of schools until 1922.

On April 11, 1922, the Johnstown School Board voted to raise the salary of the superintendent to $7,000 per year. Five members voted for the increase in salary and four voted against. After the salary was set, the board voted for the superintendent's four-year contract, for the coming school year. The names of Mr. Herbert J. Stockton and Mr. Samuel J. Slawson were placed "on the table." Mr. Slawson received five votes and Mr. Stockton received four votes. A motion was made to make the election unanimous, but failed, because of the salary increase. Mr. S. J. Slawson from Bridgeport, Connecticut, was appointed superintendent at a salary of $7,000 a year. Seven years later, at a special school board meeting on February 19, 1929, Mr. Slawson was granted a leave of absence because of illness. Mr. James Killius was appointed as interim superintendent until Mr. Slawson was able to return. However, Mr. Slawson died in Roxbury, New York. On July 16, Mr. Killius was appointed superintendent for the unexpired term.

According to a report submitted on June 4, 1917, the Teachers' Committee recommended the adoption of a salary schedule for the 1917 to 1918 school term. The Teachers' Committee recommended that high school teachers' salaries should not be regulated by a salary schedule. The maximum salary was fixed at $1,500 for department chairpersons for a school term of nine months. The maximum high school classroom teachers' salary was $1,300 for the school term. High school substitute teachers were paid $3 per day.

Salaries of grade school teachers were established at a different rate. Apparently, more value was placed on high school teachers. School directors also directed the Business Office not to pay more than $80 per school month to any teacher who had taught in the Johnstown Public Schools for less than ten years.

1917 Grade School Teachers' Salaries

First year	$360
Second year	$405
Third year	$450
Fourth year	$495
Fifth year	$540
Sixth year	$585
Seventh and Eighth years	$630
Ninth, Tenth, and Eleventh years	$675
Twelfth and Thirteenth years	$720
Fourteenth and Fifteenth years	$765
Sixteenth and Subsequent years	$810

Grade school substitute teachers were paid $2 per day for teaching in the classroom. Kindergarten teachers were paid in accordance with the regular salary schedule of grade school teachers. Kindergarten became a reverse extension of the grade school in many respects, with more emphasis placed on preschool education. Although other teachers were not listed in the 1922 school directory, the kindergarten teachers were listed by name.

With the deviation in pay scale, teachers classified as secondary school teachers were elevated in prestige and compensation. Teachers' salaries in the junior high school were based on experience and individual merit. Teachers assigned to special education at the Opportunity Schools were paid $10 per month over and above the regular salary schedule. Principals', supervisors', and special teachers' salaries were tabulated on a different scale, followed by high school and grade school teachers. The salaries of all principals were established at the regular annual meeting for the appointment of teachers.

School Regulations

The Johnstown School Board of Controllers enacted regulations for schools in Johnstown Borough. The 1856 Rules and Regulations for the Borough of Johnstown proclaimed twelve articles of rules.

RULES AND REGULATIONS
For the Government of the Public Schools in the
BOROUGH OF JOHNSTOWN [sic]
General School Rules

1st—The school month shall consist of twenty-four days.

2d—From the first day of April to the first day of October, the schools shall open at 8 o'clock, A.M. and dismiss at 12 o'clock, noon; be again opened at 2 o'clock and close at 5 o'clock, P.M. And from the first of October to the first of April, they shall open at 9 A.M., dismiss at 12, noon; re-open at 1 o'clock and close at 4 P.M.

3d.—Recess may be allowed, not to exceed five minutes; provided, that only one school shall take recess at the same time.

4th.—From the first of April to the first of October, after the schools are dismissed, the doors are to be closed, until the schools re-open. And from the first of October until the first of April, one room may be left open for scholars to remain in; provided, one or more of the teachers remain with them, who should have a due regard to the preservation of the property.

5th.—All misconduct of pupils on their way coming to, or returning from school, shall be considered as if done in school, and the offender will be held accountable and punished according to the offense.

6th.—No pupil shall be permitted to go into any of the departments except the one which he or she is classed, unless accompanied or sent by one of the teachers.

Principal

7th.—It shall be the duty of the Principal, with his assistant, to take charge…furthest advanced male department, and devote his time therein; except so much as may be taken up in hearing a class in one of the other departments each day; to receive all the reports of the principal assistants, and assistants, and transmit the same to the board of directors; to consult and advise with the teachers on all subjects necessary for the well-being of the schools.

Principal Assistants and Assistants

8th.—The principal assistants and assistants are to have exclusive control in their respective departments, except where by these rules it is otherwise ordered. They shall, at the end of every month, report as required by law, to the principal; they shall also report to the principal any damage that may be done to the property in their departments, and the name of the person or persons by whom committed.

Teachers

9th.—The teachers shall place the scholars in their respective departments in classes, according to their capacities to learn, and shall bestow equal attention upon all the classes, and shall endeavor by mild and persuasive means to promote in all a disposition to receive instruction; they shall also preserve strict order in the schools, and teach the scholars the duty of obedience, of close attention to their studies, good behavior, and upright conduct.

10th.—It shall be the duty of the teachers to prevent as much as possible any damage to the chairs, desks, or other property of the schoolhouse, and in case of any damage done in any of the departments the principal assistant in that department will report to the principal the name of the person injuring said property, who shall report the same to the directors in writing, that the parents or guardians may be charged with the same. And in case said principal assistants or principal, as the case may be, shall neglect or refuse to make report within two days after they ascertain the offender, the said principal assistants or principal shall be held responsible for such damage.

11th.—It shall be the duty of teachers to keep regular lists of the scholars according to their classes, stating their sex, their names, and the time of their attendance at school, and make return to the principal at the end of each month, who will forthwith transmit the same to the Secretary of the Board.

Punishment

12th.—The law of kindness in reproving must first be exhausted before the "rod" is resorted to. The rod as a punishment must be administered with humanity. In the event that neither persuasion nor the rod will subdue the pupil, the same shall be reported to the board, who will suspend or expel in their judgment seemth [sic] right.

By order of the Board of Directors.

JOHNSTOWN, Jan. 1, 1856.

1856 Article of Rules for School Attendance

The 1856 regulations stipulated that students should attend school twenty-four days during the month, from 8:00 A.M. to 12:00 P.M. and from 2:00 P.M. to 5:00 P.M., between the months of April and October. For the remainder of the year, school sessions ran from 1:00 P.M. to 4:00 P.M. with a recess not to exceed five minutes. Administrators may have factored in the weather on the new school regulations. Students walked home for lunch and returned for afternoon classes. Whatever the rationale, the regulations of 1856 changed from those of December 13, 1837, that proclaimed seventeen articles of rules. The first of the 1837 article stated [sic]: "The school quarter shall consist of twelve weeks. No school shall be kept up on every second Saturday in the county and every Saturday afternoon in Johnstown and on Christmas Day. No 'barring out,' as heretofore usual will be permitted."

The article also stated that all children above four years of age should be admitted to school. Teachers were required to sweep the classroom once a day and make fires early to keep the building warm. Each scholar had to attend classes with books according to the following classification: *Cobb's Speller, Goodrich's History of United States, Kirkham's Grammar,* and *Olney's Geography.* A reader and an arithmetic book were also required. For students whose parents or guardians requested religious instruction, the Old and New Testaments were required. The teacher was directed to disallow students from using anything except good paper and quills. The teacher or one of the leading scholars had to read deliberately and "distinctly" a portion of the Holy Word every morning and afternoon at the opening and closing of the school day. The afore-mentioned articles of rules and regulations were read in the classroom every Monday morning. Student attendance was sporadic, at best, until compulsory school laws were passed.

Compulsory School Laws

The Commonwealth of Pennsylvania did not enact the compulsory school attendance law until 1895. This law required students to attend school from ages eight to seventeen. The Commonwealth of Massachu-setts was a forerunner in progressive education and was the first state to enact a Compulsory School Attendance Law in 1852. Other states fol-lowed with different mandatory age ranges for school attendance and restrictions for withdrawal before high school graduation. The board of controllers of the Johnstown School District was proactive with plan-ning schools for children in the borough before the laws.

State Compulsory School Attendance Laws*

State	Enactment	Age Limits
Alabama	1915	7–16
Alaska	1929	7–16
Arizona	1899	6–16
Arkansas	1909	5–17
California	1874	6–18
Colorado	1889	7–16
Connecticut	1872	7–16
Delaware	1907	5–16
District of Columbia	1864	5–18
Florida	1915	6–16
Georgia	1916	7–16
Hawaii	1896	6–18
Idaho	1887	7–16
Illinois	1883	7–16
Indiana	1897	7–18
Iowa	1902	6–16
Kansas	1894	7–16
Kentucky	1896	6–16
Louisiana	1910	7–17

Maine	1875	7–17
Maryland	1902	5–16
Massachusetts	1852	6–16
Michigan	1871	6–16
Minnesota	1885	7–18
Mississippi	1918	6–17
Missouri	1905	7–16
Montana	1883	7–16
Nebraska	1887	7–16
Nevada	1873	7–17
New Hampshire	1871	6–16
New Jersey	1875	6–16
New Mexico	1891	5–18
New York	1874	6–16
North Carolina	1907	7–16
North Dakota	1883	7–16
Ohio	1877	6–18
Oklahoma	1907	5–18
Oregon	1889	7–18
Pennsylvania	1895	8–17
Rhode Island	1883	6–16
South Carolina	1915	5–17
South Dakota	1883	6–16
Tennessee	1905	7–17
Texas	1915	6–17
Utah	1890	6–18
Vermont	1867	7–16
Virginia	1908	5–18
Washington	1871	8–18
West Virginia	1897	6–16
Wisconsin	1879	6–18
Wyoming	1876	7–16 *

* Data obtained from Department of Education, National Center for Educational Statistics—August 1994.

High school graduation supersedes the age requirement in states with a compulsory age over sixteen.

Livelihood of Residents

A school system reflects the changing culture and economic status of the community. The steel and coal industry in the Johnstown vicinity attracted newcomers to seek livelihood from the plants. Johnstown became a city of diversified industries of various mines, with steel and coal dominating the workforce. Bituminous coal was the most plentiful natural resource and the workforce mined more than 40,000,000 tons of soft coal annually. The former Cambria Iron was the bread and butter of many homes and became the forerunner for innovations. Johnstown was first in the nation with many inventions and steel undertakings.

1870 Mill, *Courtesy of Johnstown Area Heritage Association*

Johnstown's First Steel Ventures

Year	Inventor/Venture	Product
1852	William Kelly	Steel converter
1855	Cambria Iron	Rolled first 30-foot iron rails
1857	John Fritz	World's first three-story high rolling mill
1867	Cambria Iron	Filled first commercial steel rails orders
1867	Cambria Iron	First in US to use retort coke oven
1870	Cambria Iron	Installed Battery of Belgian type ovens

About 1852, William Kelly invented the steel converter. The converter, the first in the United States, was used in Cambria Iron Works in 1861. By 1873, the Johnstown Plant was the largest iron and steel plant in the nation. About 75% of the town's labor forces, mostly men, were manual workers. About 67% of these workers were employed at Cambria and Bethlehem mills and coal mines. School administrators adjusted programs and curriculum to correspond with industry. With innovations and the growing reputation of the Johnstown area as a coal and steel Mecca, many more talented and skilled workers migrated to the area. Children were educated about the culture and their parents' employment through the schools.

However, the Johnstown area provided minimal opportunities for women. In 1900, only 11% of women over 15 were gainfully employed. Girls were needed at home to help with chores and only daughters of affluent fathers could afford to be educated. An edu-

9 inch Rolling Mill 1950s, *Courtesy of Johnstown Area Heritage Association*

cated woman was also a threat to a man. Often females became teachers with the realization that they would not be sought for marriage. The culture of the early 1900s dictated that women were homemakers.

Cultural Communities

Although an influx of new immigrants came before World War I, the community also maintained a large and stable population of native-born Americans. Mixed with people of West European origin, the groups were strongly conscious of separateness and superiority of other groups (Morawska, 1985, p. 501). Immigrants usually settled in a section of town with relatives or others from their country. These cultural communities, or ghettos, were foreign colonies. "Newcomers tended to settle…into established neighborhoods of similar ethnic backgrounds, creating 'English Streets,' 'Polish Streets,' and 'German Hills' in many turn-of-the-century [Twentieth] mining towns" (Cooper, 1988, p. 17). Except for work, these groups were isolated in their communities with little or no communication between groups. Often these groups maintained their own language and mores and found security and comfort within the group. Only men who went to work and children who attended neighborhood schools gained an English-speaking language. Since very few women, mostly single, worked outside the home, boarders were common. According to the census, 51 % of Johnstown households had boarders. Children were the third source of income, and they worked at jobs such as shining shoes or selling produce from their family gardens. Many family members arrived by rail to seek employment and help with the family survival.

Johnstown Train Station, *Courtesy of Recci Patrick*

To perpetuate the lifestyle of an ethnic culture, organizations developed such as the National Association for the Advancement of Colored People (NAACP), Slovene Benefit Society, Ukrainian National Society, United Lutheran Society, Sons of Italy, and the B'nai B'rith Lodge, and others. Some of the organizations published their own newsletters and taught their children group solidarity. Some of these cultures also established places of worship, where much education took place within the group structure. School buildings were used for both the purpose of education during the weekdays and worship on Sundays. In February 1874, Reverend M. W. Knox organized Cambria Chapel A.M.E. Zion

Church in Dibert Street School with eight charter members (C. Hollis, 1997, p. 3). While the school was under construction in the spring of 1873, religious services were held in the loft of the Tannery in Woodvale. The Tannery "...was owned and operated by William H. Rosenstell, an African American," who was affiliated with the Underground Railroad (Blockson, 2001, p.166). Mr. Rosenstell also recruited workers from the South and was one of the chartered members of the church. About 1877, Reverend C. H. Rogers moved the church to the corner of Haynes Street and Menoher Boulevard.

The Pennsylvania Historical and Museum Commission recognized Cambria Chapel A. M.E. Zion Church as the oldest black church in Johnstown. The Bureau of Archives and History, Division of History, presented an Historical Marker to First Cambria A.M.E. Zion Church (Cambria Chapel) on May 10, 1997 (C. Hollis). Since establishment, the church served a dual purpose: for worship and as a meeting place to discuss issues pertaining to equality and unity in the community. Over the years, the NAACP and Johnstown students have met in Fellowship Hall of the church. The marker is a reminder of the partnership of the Johnstown Schools and the church, with promoting the Americaniza-

Cambria Chapel A.M.E. Zion Church Historical Marker (First Cambria A.M.E. Zion Church), *Courtesy of Recci Patrick*

tion paradigm. Cambria Church has remained a church that welcomes academic reform. Many forums, school events, and voting for elected officials take place at the site.

Education was partially provided by all ethnic communities. With economic insecurity, large families needed to survive. In early years, education was valued for moral and religious purposes. The clergy and selected males in the neighborhood were delegated as the "learned men," with command of the English language. Within their ethnic community, they held respect as leaders for rational reasoning for their group. Some religious groups thought that their children would lose their ethnic identity and religious beliefs in the public school system. Therefore, parochial schools became popular. More students attended parochial schools than public schools. The parochial schools placed more emphasis on moral, religious, and national education. The public school emphasized American values.

The second generation of immigrants usually remained at home or near their parents in the same neighborhood. The same cultural mores were perpetuated. High school was not viewed as upward mobility for professional careers. Often professional career positions were lower paying than jobs in the coal mines and steel mills. Consequently, strong work ethics were emphasized and the rate of college enrollment rose only slightly between the 1920s and 1930s. Families moved to the Johnstown area for prosperity and work was plentiful. Even with large families and profitable jobs in the mills, families had to prepare for the constant strikes. The regular strikes took the family's small savings and people were always starting over to buy a home or to try to have a better life. Many company strikes or layoffs occurred at holiday time; therefore, many families, accustomed to celebrating, were depressed. Steel mill families related to Charles Dickens' popular short story *A Christmas Carol;* Ebenezer Scrooge was symbolic of the steel mill or the coal mine who took away their Christmas. The schools attempted to educate these students who came from insecure and troubled homes.

1937 Steel Mill Strike, *Courtesy of the Johnstown Area Heritage Association*

Lineage of the Johnstown Schools

Chapter IV ❖

Stonycreek Township Schools

Shortly after the earliest settlement, before Stonycreek Township incorporated, a schoolhouse was built on the corner of the current Penrod and Bedford Streets, on the property of Ludwig Wissinger. The school was a log structure with a window on each side of the building. The villagers covered the windows with greased paper to slow down the soaking process from rain and snow. They constructed the floor of half-logs with the flat side placed upward for surface walking, and heated the building by burning wood in an open fireplace. Flat boards were attached with pins to the walls for student desks, with benches made of wooden slabs.

The first teachers, mostly men, received a salary of $25 per month. Compared to the salaries of $20 for men and $15 for females in Conemaugh Old Town, Stonycreek teachers were well paid for working an eight-hour day and a twenty-four-day month. Teachers were provided room and board for a charge of $2 per week. Their teaching responsibilities also included janitorial duties such as sweeping and making the fire.

The school building was not fully utilized because school law made provision only for educating children whose parents were unable to pay. Therefore, a tuition charge of $2 per quarter or 3 cents per day was required for students to attend class. Many families would not admit that they could not afford to pay tuition; therefore, their children did chores at home. Some names appearing on the school roster were Wissinger, Vickroy, Slick, Stutzman, and Wertz.

Although the first school in Stonycreek Township was a subscription school for those who could afford tuition, education in the township continued to be a top priority. The second school in the township was built about 1834 as the Harshbarger Von Luren School. The first teacher is believed to have been S. W. Dripps, followed by Captain West. The school was located in the Maple Grove section of town, close to Sam's Run Stream. Students attended Johnstown's subscription school from the Fourth Ward to the city limits of Cambria County, including Walnut Grove. In 2001, the area is Upper Yoder Township.

Mr. Jacob Trefts, a Stonycreek school teacher, in 1851, provided much information about the Stonycreek Township Schools, including his class roster. The surnames included Jacoby, Horner, Wertz, Constable, Wissenger and Harshbargar. Among the students, two females were identified as Sarah Vickroy and Sarah Harbison. Mr. Trefts stated that degrees were not required; the most important attribute was the desire to instruct students. Some teachers were well liked and remained as teachers for more than one term. Nevertheless, many left after the first year. The turnover of teachers did not provide consistency in instruction from year to year. While employed, some teachers had the willingness to instruct students beyond the regular requirements of a school day. A spelling contest indicated that students competed beyond the disciplines of reading, writing, and arithmetic.

In 1859, a school was built in Walnut Grove, near Bedford and Solomon Streets. (See Maple Park.) The school was approximately 9 feet in height and 16 feet wide, with three small windows on each side. A long desk was nailed on each side of the interior walls of the building. Four benches were made and two were placed in front of each of the desks, for older students. For smaller children, two

Early Class, *Courtesy of Hoss's Family Steak and Sea House*

more benches, theater-style, extended the length of the room. A coal stove sat in the middle of the room. The school had a picturesque setting, with huge rocks among the forest of trees and the rhododendron-bordered bank of Solomon Run. An abandoned orchard was on the opposite side of Solomon Run; students often enjoyed the fruit from the grove. The Village of Walnut Grove continued to expand; the school law that required all persons over the age of four to be admitted to school strained the existing building. Students of that era were expected to dress in appropriate attire, often considered their "Sunday Best." Therefore, parents were overburdened with the expense of making clothing and providing their children with necessary school supplies such as books, paper, pencils, and the very popular quill and ink. Good penmanship was a skill that emphasized mastering the quill.

As Walnut Grove Village continued to grow, a new four-room school was built in 1884, at the cost of $3,000. Four years later a fifth room was added to the building because the student population continued to accelerate. However, the student population came to an instant decline in 1891 with Dale Borough's charter. Dale Borough created its own school with former Stonycreek students. Although the growth of Walnut Grove was impeded with Dale Borough's formation, the student population grew into a six-room schoolhouse by 1906. The Highland Park School was also built by the Stonycreek Township School District in an area know as Hogback. This building consisted of two rooms.

The Walnut Grove villagers maintained an interest in promoting good schools. As early as 1893, they organized "The Walnut Grove School Library Association." Mr. George M. Wertz, secretary of the Association, created a card catalog for the library. The catalog contained the by-laws and membership of the Association. The aforementioned data about the Stonycreek Schools and neighboring village schools were obtained from the catalog. The Stonycreek Township School District maintained its identity until 1915, when the township school merged with the Johnstown City School District.

Cambria Iron Company–Millville Borough Schools

Millville, a small school district of blue-collar workers, built large schools, kept them better equipped than most other schools, and paid their teachers higher wages than neighboring districts and boroughs.

Millville's act of generosity was enabled by the commonwealth public school grant. Public schools received funding from state appropriations, taxes levied to local residents, and taxes levied on the iron and steel mills located within the district. Millville Schools had the advantage of having the Cambria Iron Works located in the borough; thus the tax wealth manifested into better schools. The Cambria Iron Company, founded 1852, had replaced some smaller iron furnaces and was the precursor of Bethlehem Steel Company.

Blast Furnace, *Courtesy of Johnstown Area Heritage Association*

Millville Borough, the Minersville section of Johnstown, opened a school in 1872. The school was named Benshoff because it was located on Benshoff Street, formerly High Street. (See Benshoff School.) On September 24, 1872, the *Tribune* reported that the term of school districts, required by law, was a minimum of five months in high school; the term in grade schools was six to nine months. At that time, Millville and Woodvale were the only districts that offered a nine-month school term. Millville's largest expenditure was the employment of teachers for more than the required months. Millville also paid the highest average teacher's salary in Cambria County. Schools were comfortable for students and for professional staff.

In 1873, the Millville Borough School Controllers retained a teacher for night school. (See Evening School.) The Benshoff School withstood the Johnstown Flood of 1889. Following that environmental catastrophe, the school board designated the school as a morgue. In 1890, Millville Borough was annexed to the Johnstown School District. The Johnstown District closed Benshoff School during the 1933–1934 school year. The site is a playground in 2002.

English and Classical School

Location: Locust Street

On February 26, 1878, Cambria Iron Works opened the English and Classical School for the children of their officials. They thought that this school offered better instruction than other private schools, church schools, or public schools, because of the strong financial source. Although tuition was $30 to $50 per term, the school opened with an enrollment of only eleven students. Mr. Columbia Howe, a primary teacher, was hired to assist Principal L. A. Burr. Dr. Helen Magell also taught in the English and Classical School. "The *Johnstown Tribune* for June 12, 1879, records Florence Dibert as one of the participants in closing exercises at Professor Burr's English and Classical School" (Clifton, 1988, p. 176).

On September 18, 1886, the *Johnstown Tribune* reported that a Coopersdale Academy opened to accommodate students who lived too far from the English and Classical School. The school enjoyed good patronage until it was destroyed by the 1889 Flood.

Subscription School

Location: Vine Street and Park Place

Only affluent families could afford education for the first half of the nineteenth century. Schools were classified as subscription because parents paid tuition for their children to attend. In other words, they subscribed to attend school. Although Mr. Joseph Johns designated a site for schools in his plan, the first school was a parochial subscription school. Reverend John Meneely built a log structure in 1805, as the first institute of learning in Johnstown. The dimensions of the building were 18 by 20 feet, located at the northeast corner of Vine Street and Park Place. Reverend Meneely was also the teacher. The tuition was a monthly fee of 50 to 75 cents per student for six days per week of instruction. Very few residents could afford to send their children to the school.

With the passing of Pennsylvania's Act for Free Common Schools, dubbed the "Pauper School Act of 1809," children of low-income families could now afford to attend public schools. County commissioners paid tuition for students from the public treasury, if parents would sign an affidavit stating that they did not have adequate family income to pay tuition for schooling. The villagers were very proud people, who labored for their subsistence and were not of the culture to accept handouts. As a result, the commissioners paid very little tuition money from the public treasury. Because of the board of directors' diligence to provide better schools, they made constant demands for more money. These public demands left the steel mill workers, whose sons also worked in the steel mills, apathetic toward the advantages of public education. The grade school fees averaged 50 cents or more per month, per student. Tuition, however, did not reach a dollar per student, per month before 1889. Even with reasonable tuition for public schools, private schools continued to recruit area students.

Female Select School

Location: Near Main Street

In 1851 the Johnstown Female School, a propriety school for girls, opened. The school held etiquette classes in a building behind the Old Presbyterian Church on Main Street. (At various times, two different theaters occupied the site. The theaters were the Nemo and the Embassy. In 2002, the Lincoln Office Complex occupies the site of the Old Presbyterian Church.) A Johnstown Gymnasium School was started to compete with the girls' etiquette school. The concept of the Gymnasium School originated in Germany. The mission of the school was to prepare students for higher education, that is, colleges and universities.

Morrell Institute

Location: Main Street

About 1878, the Morrell Institute was established as a private school on Main Street. The building had been the home of Daniel J. Morrell, a partner in Wood, Morrell and Company. Administrators of the school offered spring and summer sessions in six departments. The departments were art, music, commerce, language, methods, and typewriting and shorthand. Except for the school of methods, departments were open for ten months. The faculty consisted of ten professors who taught thirty different classes. Pedagogic methods courses were offered in all subjects for three-week sessions. The school was closed after the 1889 Flood (Strayer and London, 1964, p. 35). The Morrell School was private, with a tuition requirement.

Evening School

The first documentation of a night school occurred in 1847. On November 15, the board of controllers approved a request for the establishment of an evening school. Ten years later, in 1857, Cambria Iron Company started a night school for employees, before sponsoring day school classes. From 1860 to 1899, the company sponsored three-to-five nights of instruction, free to employees. Nonemployees paid tuition of $3 for a course of study that included mathematics, drawing, mechanics, and metallurgy.

The Johnstown School Board arranged night classes for those who could not attend the day school classes. Many boys who worked in the mills exercised the option of night school as a gateway to formal education. School board action permitted the use of the school buildings for evening school. Evening school classes were canceled after the Great Flood.

On November 16, 1891, the Johnstown School District reopened its evening school classes. The school board minutes, January 14, 1892, stated that evening classes were held in various school buildings and a few churches. The school board agreed to admit persons over twenty-one years of age to the evening school, from outside the city limits. The tuition for nonresidents of the city was $1.50 per month, payable in advance. Superintendent Berkey released a directive by the board of school controllers relative to evening school regulations.

Evening School Regulations

1. For the convenience of all pupils who may desire to attend evening schools, the city has been divided into six districts.

Evening School Districts

First District	Wards 18, 19, 20, and 21.
Second District	Wards 14, 15, and 16.

Third District	Wards 1, 2, 12, and 13.
Fourth District	Wards 3, 4, 9, 10, and 11.
Fifth District	Wards 5, 6, and 7.
Sixth District	Wards 8 and 17.

2. Schools will be organized in each of the six districts provided twenty-five or more eligible pupils apply for admission. If a less number applies, or if the average attendance shall fall below twenty after the school has been opened, the board of controllers reserves the right to provide for the pupils of such district or school by admitting them to the school of an adjoining district.

3. In accordance with the law governing evening schools, no pupils will be admitted who are under thirteen or over twenty-one years of age, who are in attendance at any day school, or who are not regularly employed during the day at some useful labor.

4. The regular sessions will be held from 7:30 to 9:30 P.M. of each day upon which the City Public Schools are in session.

5. Unless otherwise ordered, the schools will open Monday Evening, November 4, 1901, and continue with the Public Schools four consecutive months, or longer as may be determined.

6. Textbooks and school supplies will be furnished free upon the same conditions and regulations as apply to the day schools.

7. Competent teaches will be employed to instruct in these schools, preference being given to the Principals of the ward schools.

8. The course of instruction, methods of teaching, discipline, and general management will be under the official supervision of the City Superintendent and subject to the control of the school board.

9. Attendance at these schools must be punctual and regular, and in case of necessary absence or tardiness written excuses will be required.

10. The evening schools are not intended for any pupils who do, or possibly can, attend the day schools. They are only for such as are necessarily and regularly employed during the daily school hours, and who attend yet earnestly desire a better common school education. They will prove a great benefit to those who attend them with an earnest and steadfast purpose to go regularly and study well. Only such should apply for admission.

All applications should be placed in the hands of the ward Principals not later than Friday Evening, October 4th, and by them reported on the same date to the City Superintendent. Later applications will, of course, be considered, but all should be filed promptly, that the Board might determine the number and location of the evening schools to be organized.

By Order of the Board of School Controllers

J. M. Berkey

Superintendent

Committee on Evening School

G. W. Rose

David Barry

P. Connelly

Ellsworth, Kunkle

September 25, 1901

With demands of parents for their children to work in the mills or farm during the daytime, the interest in night school increased. On August 23, 1915, the Morrellville Parent Teacher Association presented a petition to the Board requesting that night school classes be opened in Morrellville. Since the directors took no action, the Association made the request again at the school board meeting on December 20, 1915. The Board acknowledged and granted the second request. On March 15, 1917, the principal, Mr. S. D. Elrick, submitted a report to Superintendent Mr. J. N. Adee and the board of directors. The report encompassed nineteen weeks on the progress of night school. The night school enrolled 683 students who engaged in forty-two different courses of study. The nineteen nationalities represented in night school illustrated Johnstown as a diverse city in the early 1900s. In his report, Mr. Elrick dubbed night school as a school for foreigners. With this observation, he recommended to the Board that the school district should seek authorization to issue a certificate for citizenship. Early in the history of the Johnstown Schools, the Americanization paradigm was emphasized.

At the November 27, 1917, school board meeting, night school teachers requested a salary increase. On December 4, 1917, the superintendent and the board released a letter to all night school teachers that the salary increase could not be granted. The teachers rescinded their unified letter to resign immediately, but stated that for consideration of the students, they would remain in their teaching positions until the end of the term. Data do not reveal a resolution on the controversy salary issue.

On December 17, 1917, the director of vocational education reported to the school board that he started classes in Mechanical Drawing, Blueprint Reading, Radio, and Buzzer work. These classes were offered under the auspices of the Federal Bureau of Vocational Education and organized by the U.S. Army Signal Corps. All classes were conducted in the night school program.

On September 26, 1921, the committee on night school recommended to the school board that the high school should be the only center established for night school. Special work could be offered at the Casino Vocational School. The committee also recommended that Americanization Centers be opened at Woodvale School and at a Cambria City School. During 1922, evening classes were held in the Woodvale School building. The Board later ordered demolition of the building.

Night school attendance continued to increase from 1919 to 1924. The highest enrollment for Evening School was 1,505 students. The largest number of students was enrolled in the Americanization Course.

Night School Attendance

Year	Total Enrollment	Average Attendance
1919–1920	1,104	391
1920–1921	1,105	415
1921–1922	1,198	422
1922–1923	1,337	501
1923–1924	1,505	590

In 1924, the administration of the Johnstown Public Schools stated that the work in Americanization would continue to be the most important phase of the Evening School Program for Adult Education. School administrators' primary efforts emphasized the need for socializing masses of foreigners in Johnstown.

Wards of the Borough

The Great Johnstown Flood of 1889 has been classified as the most devastating flood known to the United States. After the environmental catastrophe, May 31, 1889, the Johnstown Schools closed. Twelve teachers lost their lives in the flood. With the loss of professional staff and damaged buildings, the board was not able to reopen the schools until September 30, for an indefinite period. Consequently, the catastrophe also caused an economic upheaval in the city; therefore, the board did not levy a school tax for that year. The greater community worked together to expedite recovery from the flood by consolidation with other boroughs and surrounding villages.

When Johnstown Borough received its charter as a city in 1889, the Village of Moxham was annexed as the Seventh Ward. By a court decree, in 1891, the Seventh Ward became the Seventeenth Ward. The Village of Morrellville, annexed in 1897, became the Eighteenth, Nineteenth, and Twentieth wards. In 1898, Coopersdale became the Twenty-first ward. Roxbury Borough became the Eighth Ward and Walnut Grove became the Seventeenth Ward (Pawlowski, 1985, pp. 460–461).

"Johnstown became a third class city by consolidation of the boroughs of Johnstown, Grubbtown, Conemaugh, Woodvale, Prospect, Millville, and Cambria, upon a favorable vote by the citizens in each of those boroughs, November 5, 1889" (Berger, 1985, p. 710). From 1899 to 1910, the city of Johnstown showed a population growth of approximately 489 people. In one year, school records show an increase of 350 students in the high school. With the additional students came the additional funding source of taxation from the Cambria Iron Company. Of course, decisions were made by the board of directors to immediately provide education for the increased student population. Therefore, the school board had representation from all wards.

1897 Board of School Directors (Controllers)

J. M. Berkey, City Superintendent

Fred Krebs, President	Dr. J. W. Hamer, Fourth Ward
W. A. Cochran, Secretary	Fred Krebs, Fifth Ward
B. F. Speedy, Treasurer	George Mellinger, Sixth Ward
Francis Griffith, First Ward	Thomas C. Stone, Seventh Ward
Thomas E. Morgan, Second Ward	John N. Horn, Eighth Ward
Fred W. Stammler, Third Ward	P.M. Smith, Eighth Ward

From 1889 and subsequent to the time the United States entered World War I, the Johnstown School Board built, renovated, or leased several buildings to use for classes.

According to the Herald Directory, 1899, the population of the city of Johnstown was 40,000, with twenty public school buildings. The number of students enrolled in the twenty public schools was 5,500. The 1900 general statistics of the schools documented the population was 35,036, with 5,663 students enrolled in twenty-two school buildings. The population decreased, while the student enrollment increased. Parents may have left the area to find employment, leaving their children with extended family. We can assume that either the *Herald* was an estimate or the population decreased in one year. For a point of reference, the General School Statistics are given.

1900 General School Statistics

Population of city	35,036
Number of wards	21
Number of Public School buildings	22
Number of schoolrooms 144	
Number of unoccupied schoolrooms	11
Whole Number of teachers employed	134
Number of Primary Grade Teachers	50
Number of Intermediate grade teachers	46
Number of Grammar grade teachers	23
Number of high school teachers employed	8
Number of Special Supervisors	3
Number of Substitute Teachers	4
Numbers of pupils enrolled	5,633
Average number of students per teacher	44
Assessed city valuation, 1899 approximately	13,000,000
Total value of school property	495,000
State appropriation, 1898	25,071.66
Number of teachers holding college degrees	6
Number of teachers holding State Normal diplomas	46
Number of teachers holding State certificates	19
Number of teachers holding professional certificates	20
Term enrollment in High School, 1898–1899	141
Number of beginners admitted to school during term, to date 784	

Average attendance	123
Graduates, 1899	18
Class of 1900	22
Date of opening of schools	September 3, 1900
Approximate date for closing of term	May 31, 1901
Length of school term	9 months

Although the various annexations of boroughs increased the student population in the Johnstown Schools, the graduating classes remained small. The senior class did not reach one hundred graduates until 1912. That year, 110 students graduated from high school. Before 1926, the largest class had 196 members. Between 1900 and 1926, 3,445 students graduated from the high school. In 1914, the student population had continued to grow with 141 students in the senior class. The junior class was smaller with 118 students. The sophomore class reported 231 students and the freshman class 486 students. With increased student enrollment, the principal implemented schedule changes.

Radical High School Class Schedule

In 1910, the people thought that the principal's class schedule changes were radical in the high school. Morning exercises activated only on Friday was a change from everyday exercises. The principal scheduled classes in sessions of four, forty-five minute periods from 8:45 A.M. to 12:00 noon. Two forty-five minute periods were scheduled for the afternoon from 1:15 P.M. to 3:00 P.M. The study period was the last half hour of each day. Progressive development advanced societal values for the growing demographic changes (C. Hollis, 2000, p. 60). The societal values included survival programs.

Early Intermediate Class, *Courtesy of Hoss's Family Steak and Sea House*

School Garden Program

Location: Eighth Ward

According to the school board minutes, May 21, 1917, the School Garden Program was an integral part of the curriculum. The school board approved a motion that the available ground in the rear of the Suppes Plot, Eighth Ward, be granted to any citizen who desired garden plots, and that such arrangement may be made through the Office of the Secretary. Many families raised much of their produce and canned food for the winter months. According to the Supervisor of the School Garden Program, the students of some school garden sites plowed, harrowed, and scored the planting lots themselves. Under the management of a supervisor, students removed large rocks, stumps, and stones. Teachers and women of the community often prepared the buds and seeds for planting. In some cases, students were paid to work in the Garden Program.

Renovations and Additional Elementary Schools

Chapter V ❖

The Board of School Directors responded to the growing student population by renovating and building schools. Schools were also devastated by flood waters and a response to that situation involved students' being assigned to different buildings and districts. The trend of moving from neighborhood schools to school technical communities, with information highways, also began to eliminate smaller neighborhood schools that inhibited the growth of technology. School boards, with the direction of the appointed superintendent, reacted to the needs of the city students for the good of the community. The schools are listed in the order of their date of erection.

Peelor Street School

Location: Peelor Street—
Prospect Section

Peelor Street School was built in 1883 in the Prospect section of Johnstown. It served as an elementary school until the 1921–1922 school year. The district abandoned the building. The last students would be about the age of eighty and they still

Possibly Peelor Elementary School–
Prospect Section, *Courtesy of Johnstown
Area Heritage Association*

47

remember their elementary days at the school. They walked to school and went home for lunch.

Benshoff School

Location: Benshoff Street—Millersville Borough

Benshoff School opened its doors in 1872, on Benshoff Street in Millersville Borough. Later Benshoff Street was renamed High Street. In 1890, Millersville became a part of the city of Johnstown. Conse-

quently, the Johnstown School District assumed ownership of the building. However, the board of directors closed the school at the end of the 1933–1934 school year and sold it to the city of Johnstown in 1948. Back in the hands of the school district, the building was demolished in July 1975. This site is a playground in 2002. As a play-

Benshoff School, *Courtesy of Johnstown Heritage Association*

ground, the grandchildren and the great grandchildren play on the grounds, often mentioning that their grandparents went to school there.

Coopersdale School

Location: Boyer Street—Coopersdale Borough

Coopersdale School was built in 1890 on Boyer Street in the borough of Coopersdale. The loan to build the school was exempted from taxation with the exception of state purposes. With the aforementioned stipulation, the Deputy Secretary of the Commonwealth approved a loan on June 24, 1873. He authorized the school board directors of the borough of Coopersdale to borrow money on the credit of the borough. The purpose of the loan was to erect a new schoolhouse at a cost not to exceed $2,000, and to issue bonds payable within ten years. On March 24, 1898, Coopersdale became the Twenty-first Ward of Johnstown. In 1922, a new school building was constructed on the same site.

Mrs. Mary Louise Wagner ('34) remembered in "Memories about Johnstown" attending Coopersdale in the first first-grade class. She mentioned that the teachers lived in the community and misbehavior was reported to the parents and to the principal. Superintendent Slawson came around each month for special education and testing. Penmanship was stressed. She mentioned that the school was part of the community. The Community Club held meetings and special events at the school. The community also used the gym for basketball. The playground was used for all kinds of sports throughout the summer.

Coopersdale School was closed as an educational facility on June 4, 1983. The school district and the housing authority used the building jointly for storage, before demolition, in August 1997. A playground and many memories like Miss Wagner's occupy the site in 2002.

Park Avenue School

Park and Forest Avenues—Seventeenth Ward

Park Avenue School was built in 1891 on Park and Forest Avenues in the Seventeenth Ward. Mr. Henry Leventry was the contractor for school with a cost of $22,323. The Smead Wells Company was awarded the contract for heating. The Board also took action to furnish the classrooms with single desks and Hills' sliding window blinds. A seating contract was awarded to Archeua Company. In the fall of 1892, when the eight-room school building was ready for occupancy, six teachers were appointed.

First Teachers of Park Avenue School–1892

Teacher	Grade	Monthly Salary
Mr. S. J. Bierly	Second Intermediate	$65
Miss Hattie R. Woodward	First Intermediate	$50
Miss Mary E. Gageby	Third Primary	$50
Miss Mary Kauffield	Second Primary	$45
Miss Mary P. Kinkead	First Primary	$45
Miss Ida Robinson	First Primary	$45

Although the building remained an eight-room school, crowded conditions from the increased population necessitated provisional classroom arrangements. World War I restricted building operations, but the population in Moxham continued to increase. With student population concerns, the board implemented a half-day school program to accommodate families with children who could attend school for only one-half of a day. In 1909, the board took action to rent a room in the Church of the Brethren located on the corner of Grove Avenue and Bond Street. Miss Belle Marshall's second-grade class was moved to the church. In 1915, the board of directors authorized a comprehensive school–building program. This program added more classrooms to relieve student congestion in the Seventeenth Ward and other parts of the district.

In 1917, three rooms on the first floor of the Park Avenue School were divided by 7-foot beaverboard partitions, to make six classrooms. The principal's office was also used for a classroom. During the construction, more than one hundred students were assigned to two of the divided rooms. To relieve the crowded conditions, Miss Gwen Stroup and Miss Belle Marshall were assigned as recreation teachers to teach one-half of the student body, each hour in the hallway. Two single portable buildings were brought to the Park Avenue School grounds and the partitions were removed in the school building. The student enrollment continued to grow.

In the 1900s, the Park Avenue School was considered to be one of the most up-to-date, beautiful school buildings in the Johnstown School District. The spacious rooms with large cloakrooms and cupboard space made the rooms desirable for students and teachers. Although the building did not undertake major interiors alterations, the playground was replaced with brick and a concrete wall was made around two sides. The exterior renovations included an iron fence that enhanced the beauty of the building and was an eye-catcher in Moxham. In 1934, the building interior had been repainted and plasterwork mended under the Civil Works Administration. The concrete was replaced by a stone wall and iron rail.

Park Avenue Elementary School, Courtesy of Johnstown Heritage Assoc.

The beauty of the school and its stability in the Moxham community has been attributed to Mr. W. A. Cochran. Mr. Cochran was a school board director from 1892 until 1917. As a representative from the Seventeenth Ward, he promoted and defended the interests of the district. In the December 11, 1894, school board minutes, Mr. Cochran made the following motion: "Resolved—that the Secretary be directed to call the attention of the Mayor and City Council to the conditions of the walks in the Seventeenth Ward and ask these officials of property owners or by the city, that should Mayor and Council neglect to this matter, we will hold them responsible for any damage that may result to pupils of our schools." The motion was adopted.

Until 1901, the Park Avenue School was the only building that had all elementary grades and was dubbed the grammar garden. However, when the Cypress Avenue Building was completed in 1929, the portable classrooms were discontinued.

With the building of Cypress Avenue and Village Schools, Park Avenue was reorganized to offer only first through fifth grades. The school served many different programs. The first kindergarten and the first opportunity school in Moxham were opened at Park Avenue School. Miss Ella Wilt was the first teacher to teach in the Park Avenue Opportunity School. The building was closed on February 3, 1991, and demolished. Parents and grandparents in the neighborhood have many memories as their children still enjoy the playground that is on the site in 2002.

Horner Street School

Location: Horner Street—Hornerstown Section

Horner Street School was built on Horner Street near Poplar Street. On April 6, 1934, Horner Street School celebrated its fiftieth anniversary. The speakers for the event were Mr. James Killius, superintendent of schools; Mr. J. D. Rutledge, president of the school board of directors; Mr. Calvin T. Jones, a member of the board of directors; and Miss Mary Jane Cooper, former supervisor of primary grades. The neighborhood was proud of their school located in the Hornertown section of town. However, the building was closed on November 22, 1967, and sold to Leitenberger's Cars for $10,000. As parents and former students shop for a used car, they recall the education that took place on the site.

Osborne Street School

Location: Akers Street

Osborne Street School was built in 1894 on Akers Street. The school had eight rooms without a gymnasium or auditorium. During the summer of 1919, summer school was held for fifth graders from the Roxbury area students. For fifth and sixth graders from the downtown area, summer school was held at Somerset Street School. Sixth graders from the West End attended summer school at Bheam School. At the end of the 1966–1967 school year, students who attended the Osborne School were assigned to Meadowvale School. The

Osborne Street School, *Courtesy of the Johnstown Area Heritage Association*

Practical Nursing Program occupied the building for a number of years. The building was closed in 1967 and sold to John Chiodo. On March 18, 1979, the *Johnstown Tribune* Newspaper featured Osborne School being razed. A high-rise apartment for the elderly occupies the site in 2002. Many residents who attended school there before television can now enjoy watching television on the site.

Chestnut Street School

Location: Chestnut Street and Fifth Avenue

Chestnut Street School was built in 1894 at Chestnut Street and Fifth Avenue. The original building was replaced at Chestnut Street in 1922. As late as June 1931, the Board of School Directors granted the use of the old building to the Cambria County Association for the Blind. This school was not listed as a school in the school directories after the 1961–1962 school year. During the 1970s, Superintendent Zucco and his administrative staff had offices there. However, the Board gave a

First Chestnut Street School (1894), *Courtesy of Johnstown Heritage Association*

directive that the gymnasium and the playground would be retained for public use. The neighborhood continued to enjoy recreational activities at the site.

During the week of October 17, 1983, Superintendent Zucco and the administrative staff relocated to the third floor of Meadowvale School building.

Meadowvale classroom space was converted into office space. However, the school district did not seek approval from the Pennsylvania Department of Education or the Department of Labor to convert the classrooms. Several years later, the conversion of the office space was reversed back to classrooms. Consequently, since the district neglected to get approval for the initial conversion, the commonwealth did not reimburse the school district for the expense involved in the changes. The Chestnut Street School was used as a storage building. According to school board minutes, March 4, 1985, the Chestnut Street School property was sold to B.C.D. Associates for $25,000.

Chestnut Street School (1922), *Courtesy of Judy Browne Photography*

Since the building was in public school use in the early 1960s and is still standing today, many former students, teachers, staff, and administrators drive by the building with thoughts of events and activities that took place.

Dibert Street School

Location: Dibert and Napoleon Streets

Dibert Street School was built in 1872 and expanded with additional rooms in 1894. The building contained six classrooms, without a gym or auditorium. Cambria Chapel A.M.E. Zion Church was organized in the school. (See Cambria Chapel.) According to the April 15, 1915, school board minutes, directors purchased land adjacent to the

school for $27,000. After the 1936 flood, the school was closed for a period of time and reopened. The school was again closed on November 22, 1967, and used by the district for storage purposes. The building was demolished and a car-undercoating garage occupies the site in 2002.

Dibert Street School 1872, *Courtesy of Johnstown Heritage Association*

Morrell School

Location: Barron and D Streets

Morrell School was built in 1895 at Barron and D Streets; the building was called the D Street School until 1913. The school was closed June 11, 1956, and used for the school district's storage. The Board of School Directors sold the school to St. Francis Congregation on December 13, 1971, for $5,000. The church occupies the site in 2002.

Morrell Elementary School (1895), *Courtesy of Johnstown Area Heritage Association*

Washington Schools

Location: Ebensburg Road—Twelfth Ward

Washington School Number One, built in 1897, had an addition constructed in 1909. The school, located on Ebensburg Road in Prospect, was known as the Twelfth Ward School. In 1922, Washington School Number Two was built. In 1970, the Pennsylvania Human Relations Commission (PHRC) informed the school district that Washington School had a higher than 70 % black student enrollment. The school was one of eight in the state classified as a black school. To rectify this issue, the school district submitted two plans to PHRC, one for desegregating and one to close the school. The school district closed the school in 1971. However the local NAACP, with Mr. Charles Collins as president, filed a petition in the Pittsburgh Federal District Court for an injunction to stop the closing of the school. The injunction was denied and Washington School remained closed (Johnson, 1985, pp. 564–565). The building was used as a community center before demolition in 1988. The site is a memory box for many as their children and grandchildren use the playground.

(Old) Washington Elementary School, *Courtesy of Johnstown Heritage Association*

Maple Park–Walnut Grove School

Location: Bedford and Solomon Streets—Stonycreek Borough

Maple Park—Walnut Grove School was first built in Stonycreek Borough near the corner of Bedford and Solomon Streets (Walnut Grove) in 1859. Walnut Grove was annexed to the city of Johnstown in 1912. The ground was originally purchased from Peter Jacoby for $10 and Jacob Jacoby built the school for $139. The first addition was built in 1884 and another addition was built in 1922. On February 17, 1918, the Johnstown School Board of Directors approved sketches for a new building. However, on March 16, 1918, the plans were destroyed by fire in the office of J. E. Adams, the architect. The first two buildings were built on Bedford Street. The last building, 1922, located on Jacoby Street was named Maple Park. The school contained sixteen rooms, eight upstairs and eight downstairs. The Johnstown School Board directors sold the building to Chapple Brother Contractors for $51,000. The Veterans Association owns the building in 2002. (See Stonycreek Township Schools.)

Maple Park School, *Courtesy of Bruce Haselrig*

During the Depression, the game of horseshoes was very popular in Walnut Grove. Adults and students were interested in this sport. Students played horseshoes before school and on their lunch hour. The Walnut Grove Horseshoe Court Club was organized, with dues at 25 cents a month. The club competed with Conemaugh, South Fork, Cover Hill, and other areas. The game of horseshoes may have had its start in the Johnstown area at Walnut Grove. This sport is still exercised in backyards and at family gatherings in the Johnstown area.

Hudson Street School

Location: Center Street—Conemaugh Borough

Hudson Street School was built in 1895, with an addition in 1924. The building was formerly called the Conemaugh Borough School and was located on Center Street, extending to Railroad Street. The Pennsylvania Railroad purchased land on the south side of Center Street for $20,000. The railroad permitted the school district to use the property until 1896. This purchase made Conemaugh Borough School unsuitable and dangerous for students to attend. The school's property was on Hudson Street, bordered by Delvin Street, and the alleys are named Lucas Place and Cardboard Alley in 2002. The building was sold to a private contractor and closed in 1971, which returned the building to the school district. This building was destroyed by fire on Sunday, November 20, 1994. Fire officials reported that the fire was caused by arson. People in the neighborhood have mixed thoughts about the school and about what happened.

Woodvale Elementary School

Location: Maple Avenue—Eleventh Ward

Woodvale Elementary School was built on Maple Avenue in 1901. The June 1, 1896, school board minutes report that a special tax of one mil on the dollar was levied on the assessed valuation of $256,565 for the Eleventh Ward of the City of Johnstown. The indebtedness was for the Woodvale School District. At a school board meeting on December 11, 1900, a director reported that the school building in the Eleventh Ward was in dangerous condition. The Board took action to construct a new building to be ready for occupancy at the beginning of the 1901 School Term. At the February 12, 1901, school board meeting, the board took action to build a school in the Eleventh Ward. They decided that the building should be four rooms, similar to the Seventh and Seventeenth Wards Schools. At a February 26, 1901, meeting, the board took action to initiate dialogue with officials of the Cambria Iron and Steel to discuss the advisability of exchanging the existing site in the Eleventh Ward for a more suitable school location. At a special meeting, on April 2, 1901, the board received sealed bids for the construction of a new school in the Eleventh Ward.

Bids for Eleventh Ward School

George Krneger *	$12,844
Edward Overdorf	$13,788
Christopher C. Hornick	$13,830
Saly and Lucas	$15,235

* The contract was awarded to George Krneger, the lowest bidder. The action of the Board called for an approved bond in the sum of $8,000 for faithful performance.

At a special meeting on June 12, 1906, the board of directors levied a special tax of one mil on one dollar on the assessed valuation of the properties in the Eleventh Ward. The taxation was for the interest on the bond indebtedness of $1,000 and created a sinking fund for the liquidation of the school bond. At a board meeting on January 15, 1917, the Grounds and Building Committee reported that it had submitted a proposal to Cambria Steel Company. The proposal requested an exchange of school property on Maple Avenue, Eleventh Ward (Plot 260 x 154 feet), for a plot of ground (350 x 133 feet) on the opposite side of Maple Avenue, owned by George B. Glenn. The proposal included that Cambria Steel Company would pay $10,000 to the school district. In addition the Cambria Steel Company reimbursed the school district for expenses incurred to move the present school building to the new site, including excavation of the foundation.

Woodvale Elementary School (1901),
Courtesy of Johnstown Area Heritage Association

Meadowvale Schools
(East Side Elementary School)

Location: Wood Street

Meadowvale School building Number One was built on Wood Street in 1900, with additions in 1902. Meadowvale Number Two building was built on Wood and McMillen Streets in 1908 with additions in 1912. The building was demolished in 1971 for the construction of a new Meadowvale School Building with open classrooms. Mrs. Gwynne Fetsko ('59) recalled her elementary school days at Meadowvale School, which she attended from 1947 to 1952. She remembered lining up, single file, to enter the building. The line had to meet the teacher's or principal's approval. One of the events in Miss Geiger fourth-grade class was that on a certain day all students brought an apple to school. At a designated time, the students took the apples out and rolled them to the front of the room. Miss Geiger accepted the gesture as a token of love, picked up the apples, and took them home. From Meadowvale, Mrs. Fetsko went to Cochran and then to the high school. In her twelve years of education in the Johnstown School, she never rode a school bus (Fetsko, 1998, p. 216).

The building was the only school in the district that experienced teaching and learning in an open classroom environment. Unfortunately, the 1977 flood damaged the first floor of the building that included the swimming pool, gym, nurse room, storage rooms, cafeteria, administrative offices, and elevators. Consequently, students had to attend classes on the second and third floors during the 1977–1978 school year. Maple Park School was closed due to flood damage and students were assigned to Meadowvale. Conditions were crowded; moving students to other parts of the building, plus additional students, added an extra strain on all students and teachers.

Meadowvale continued to be plagued by inconvenience. In June 1982, the building was tagged for asbestos removal and closed for one school year

Meadowvale (1900), *Courtesy of the Johnstown Heritage Association*

(1982–1983). The building was to undergo pool repairs, asbestos removal, heating, ventilation, and air conditioning reconstruction. Later, on June 5, 1995, school directors took action to remove all asbestos at the Meadowvale Building. At a following meeting, the board voted to completely remodel the Meadowvale Building, to convert the open classrooms for regular classrooms. At the July 1, 1995, school board meeting, the board assigned Meadowvale students for the 1995–1996 school year to different schools. The Johnstown Catholic Schools were very cooperative. First graders and Chapter I students were assigned to St. Caesar Catholic School on Power Street in Cambria City. Kindergarten and second-grade students were rescheduled to attend classes at St. Mary's Catholic School on Fifth Avenue and Chestnut Street in Cambria County. Third and fourth Grade students were rescheduled to attend classes at St. Columbia School in Cambria City. Fifth grade students were rescheduled to attend middle school at Garfield Middle School. Again, student movement strained other schools and participating teachers.

Renovations on Meadowvale School were completed in December 1996. The school was renamed East Side Elementary School. East Side Elementary School was dedicated on August 23, 1997. Many students have memories of the many faces of Meadowvale or East Side Elementary, as the community experienced a school in the process of changing for a changing society.

East Side Elementary School (Meadowvale), *Courtesy of Judy Browne Photography*

Cypress Avenue School

Location: Cypress—Nineteenth Ward

Cypress Avenue School was built in the Nineteenth Ward at the cost of $11,980. The Board of School Directors approved the plans for the school on March 2, 1900, and purchased land from the Von Lunen Estate for a four-room building. The school was built on Von Lunen Street and Cypress Avenue. Mr. George Wilde, the architect, designed the rooms to allow expansion as needed. Overdorf Brothers used money from the sinking fund to finance the construction. Mr. James K. Boyd was appointed by the school board to act as superintendent of construction at a monthly salary of $90 per month. At midnight, February 14, 1901, the secretary of the board, David Berry, accepted the building.

Cypress Avenue School, *Courtesy of Johnstown Heritage Association*

Mr. M. D. High was appointed principal of Cypress School, at an annual salary of $950. His credentials included a degree from Franklin and Marshall College, two years of experience in the academic department of Rome College, and five years in the public schools. His teaching staff consisted of three teachers.

1901 Cypress Avenue Teachers

Miss Maude Boucher	First grade and Intermediate Grades
Miss Martha E. Davis	Second Grade
Miss Georgia Kyle	Third Grade

Miss Mora Miller was appointed as the first substitute teacher of the Nineteenth Ward. In 1902, Mr. S. E. Ream was appointed as principal of the Cypress School. Miss Ida Bash replaced Miss Boucher, who was transferred to another building. Mr. W. J. Miller, the janitor, spoke about the crowded conditions in the new four-room building. A report of the minutes of December 10, 1901, concurred with Mr. Miller. The report stated: "Owning to the rapid increase in population in the Seventeenth Ward more school room is needed." After an investigation by a special committee, on March 25, 1902, the board took action to build a four-room addition. As the lowest bidder, Mr. C. C. Hornick was awarded the contract for the amount of $9,366 and completed the building for the fall term.

At the June 19, 1902, board of directors meeting, Mr. G. A. Ricketts was appointed principal to succeed Mr. S. E. Ream. A staff of six teachers was also appointed.

1902 Cypress Avenue Teachers

Miss Ida A. Plotts	Miss Lizzie Yoder
Maggie Dresser	Miss Ida Bash
Miss Carrie Porter	Miss Ruth Adair

The building was soon filled beyond capacity. The board bought additional lots with double houses. The homes were sold for a nominal fee and moved away. The site of the houses was back-fielded and covered to grade level with asphalt to make a city playground. The school board of directors approved additions to the building in 1906 and 1929. Eighteen classrooms were added in addition to a gymnasium. The gymnasium was built to serve as an auditorium with a seating capacity of 600. The school enrollment totaled more than five hundred students with a staff of fourteen teachers. The third floor was not used.

Kindergarten Centers were established earlier, but the kindergarten classroom within a school building had its beginning in the Cypress Avenue School, in September 1926. The lumber storage room for manual training was renovated to house the first kindergarten classroom. Miss Ruth Richardson was the first kindergarten teacher in this basement classroom. The kindergarten classroom was later moved to a first floor, partitioned classroom. On the other side of the kindergarten classroom, a first-grade class was taught. In 1929, Miss Grace T. Elliott, the appointed teacher, enrolled the largest class of five-year-old students for the kindergarten classroom. Many kindergarten classrooms were started in the basement of school buildings. Research did not uncover the rationale. Kindergarten classes may have been placed at the bottom of first grade to show the growth of the student or perhaps the basement was the only vacant space in the building. Cypress School had the largest elementary student enrollment until 1945.

Cypress School Principals 1900–1922

M. D. High	1900–1901
S. E. Ream	1901–1902
G. A. Ricketts	1902–1904
L. J. Lehman	1904–1905
J. Ross Horne	1905–1911
A. G. Ober	1911–1922
W. F. Grunizer	1922

Bheam School

Location: J Street and Fairfield Avenue—Morrellville

Bheam School, built in 1906, was located on J Street and Fairfield Avenue, in Morrellville. The building was closed on June 4, 1976, and demolished July 28, 1979. Mr. Frank E. Farrell of Morrellville wrote a letter to the Secretary of the Johnstown School Board, Mr. Charles H. Meyers, on January 16, 1915. The letter stated that several students from Morrellville and Cambria City had expected a half-year promotion. Mr. Farrell requested a response about why none of the students were promoted that year and only two the preceding year. He asked: "Do you know or can you suggest any reason for this apparent discrimination? Is the fault with the Scholars or the Teachers?" Other citizens of Morrellville accompanied Mr. Farrell. Superintendent Adee stated that he would investigate the situation and invited residents to the next regular school board meeting to hear his response. The response is unknown.

However, a former student, Mrs. Jessie Crawley-Grigsby ('47), remembered returning to school after summer vacation to find that some of her friends were demoted to their last grade. Apparently, they had not retained enough grade-level knowledge over the summer.

Bheam School, *Courtesy of the Johnstown Area Heritage Association*

In "Memories of Bheam School," a former student, Miss Nancy C. Hoover ('67) wrote about her experience as a student in the 1950s. She remembered that the grades at Bheam School were from kindergarten to sixth, with art and music classes taught only once a month. The art teacher and the music teacher taught these classes about once a month because they taught all of the other elementary schools in the school district. She remembered the principal, Miss Patch, as the discipliner, who paddled students who went beyond the classroom teacher's control. Miss Hoover talked about the wide slate steps that led from floor to floor with four classrooms on each level. The principal's office was on the second floor and the library on the third floor.

Students walked home for lunch, stopping for penny candy before they returned to afternoon classes. Recess was held once in the morning and once in the afternoon, outside in good weather. Fire drills were actually conducted on the fire escape steps. Students had to walk in an orderly fashion onto the outdoor metal fire escape stairs. Of course all holidays were celebrated. Teachers led the students in costumes through the neighborhood for the Halloween parade and a Christmas play was presented before winter break (Hoover, 1998, pp. 212–213). A playground occupies the site of Bream School in 2002.

Village Street School

Location: Forest Avenue—Seventeenth Ward

Village Street School was built in 1908, with additions in 1910. With the rapid growth of the Seventeenth Ward, the board purchased seven lots facing Forest Avenue and extending from Village Street to Wheat Street on December 12, 1905. The lots located in the Moxham District were purchased from Mrs. Henrietta Von Lunen Woodruff. One of the lots was purchased from Frank C. Rager. On June 12, 1906, the board took action to place the schools in debt for $100,000 to erect and equip a new school building in the Seventh, Seventeenth, and Eighteenth Wards. Issued bonds were redeemable in thirty years. On July 1, 1906, Mr. Eckles, the school architect, was presented with plans and specifications for the building. After the approval of the building committee and on the motion of Mr. Kunkle, the secretary was directed to advertise

Village Street School, *Courtesy of the Johnstown Area Heritage Association*

for bids. The bids ranged from $36, 470 to $44,362. With the advice of the school solicitor, the contract was awarded to the lowest bidder, Mr. George Krneger. The building was closed February 3, 1971; a playground occupies the site in 2002.

Roxbury School

Location: Sell and Franklin Streets

Roxbury School was built in 1908 on Sell Street near Franklin Street. Auditorium and gymnasium additions were built in 1913. On September-

ber 16, 1917, the board of directors took action to permit the Memorial Hospital to use the cooking room to teach second year nurses.

During the 1994–1995 school year, the principal and the faculty created a new program called micro-society that received board approval. The program be-

Roxbury School, *Courtesy of Bruce Haselrig*

came controversial, because several board members questioned the management and the financial report. Barnes, Saly and Company, Certified Public Accountants, audited the books and recommended that proper guidance and policies be established by the school district before approval of new programs. The building closed in 1997 due to declining enrollment, and was sold in 2000. Students from Roxbury School were sent to other schools in the district. The school still stands as a reminder of many school adventures. Nearby Roxbury Park was used for many athletic events.

Iron Street School

Location: Iron Street and Walnut Street

Iron Street School, built in 1872, was located on Iron Street near Walnut Street; it was used as a morgue for the 1889 Flood. The Iron Street School property was sold to the Penn-

Iron Street School, *Courtesy of the Johnstown Area Heritage Association*

sylvania Railroad Company for $34,000, as reported in the school board minutes, May 17, 1915. The Railroad Company demolished the building shortly after the 1915–1916 school term ended. There are still a very few memories left of Iron Street School. It is one of the many schools that the board built to accommodate academic programs for the city children.

Oakhurst Old School

Location: Dorothy Street—Harold Avenue

Oakhurst Old School, built in 1915, was located on Dorothy Street and was abandoned in 1953. The Johnstown School Board Minutes, May 12, 1919, reported that the Borough of Oakhurst was annexed to the city of Johnstown. Oakhurst's new school had been constructed at 475 Harold Avenue; therefore, the Johnstown Schools assumed the debt of $12,546.45. The Dorothy Street School was not used after the 1951–1952 school year. The Harold Avenue Building was not used after the 1975–1976 school year. The building was demolished on March 26, 1980. A playground occupies the site of many memories in 2002.

West Taylor School

Location: 511 Cooper Avenue

The West Taylor School District built West Taylor School at 511 Cooper Avenue, in 1913. The West Taylor School District became a part of the Johnstown School District during the 1957–1958 school year. Although the school was closed after the 1957–1958 school year, memories of the West Taylor students live on.

Chandler School

Location: Garfield Street

Chandler School was built on Garfield Street in 1917. The school was Garfield Junior High School until 1927. In September 1927, school board directors

Chandler School, Garfield Junior High School 1917–1927, *Courtesy of the Johnstown Area Heritage Association*

designated the school as an elementary school. The board also took action to close the elementary school after the 1991–1992 school year.

Zion Lutheran Church

Location: Jackson and Locust Streets

Zion Lutheran Church, located on Jackson and Locust Streets, was the home of the Andrew Jackson School from 1917–1923. The Johnstown School District leased the space for $150 a month. The *Johnstown Tribune* reported on October 12, 1922 that the Johnstown School Board awarded a contract to Gilpatrick–Dawson of Pittsburgh to construct twelve rooms as an addition to the Hudson Street School, for a bid of $64,690. The students from Andrew Jackson School returned to Hudson Street School. In 1977, the Johnstown School District, again, leased classroom space from Zion Lutheran Church, for the Alternative School. This program continued until most of 1990.

Zion Lutheran Church,
Courtesy of Recci Patrick

Riverside School

Riverside School, a one-room building, housed students from first to eighth grades. When students graduated from the eighth grade they had the option of attending Ferndale High School or Johnstown High School. A new two-room school was built in 1921 and several years later two more rooms were added. The school continued to expand in 1926, with two more rooms and an auditorium. The first Riverside PTA was organized before 1925.

West Side (Westwood) Elementary School

Location: Westgate Drive

Westwood Elementary School was built on Westgate Drive in Lower Yoder School District in 1959. The school consisted of twenty classrooms and a cafeteria. The Lower Yoder School District joined the

Johnstown School District. In 1990, according to the Building Utilization Plan, the additional rooms were added–a new gymnasium, a new cafeteria–with a complete renovation of the older building.

West Side Renovation Team

Architect	Patrick Ditko
General Contractor	Model, Inc.
Electrical Contractor	Murdock Electric, Inc.
Plumbing Contractor	Joseph M. Hazlett, Inc.

The Dedication Program was held on Sunday, November 8, 1992, officially changing the name to West Side Elementary. The new school was dedicated to the late Dr. Levi B. Hollis, Jr., for his Utilization Plan, which included planning the building. His family attended the dedication ceremony.

West Side Elementary School 2001, *Courtesy of Judy Browne Photography*

The school became more of an integral part of the school system. The new gymnasium at the school became the home court of the Johnstown High School basketball team. For the first time in almost twenty years, since 1974, home games were played in the schools. Prior to the renovations, the team had played its home games at the Cambria County War Memorial Arena. Many students will share the memories of the transition of the new technical building. The West Side School was the last building to be built in the Johnstown School District and the last one to complete its renovations, as of January 2002.

West Side Elementary School Marker,
Courtesy of Recci Patrick

Ms. Carpenter's Fifth Grade Class

West Side Elementary had great interest in connecting with the community. Mrs. Rita Redden, the assistant principal, often initiated community programs. At the request of Mrs. Redden, Ms. Connie Carpenter and her Fifth Grade Class participated in a Write, Read, and Write Program with the American Association of the University Women (AAUW). The fifth-grade girls wrote letters to Mrs. Anne Fattman, president, and other members of AAUW about their interests, hobbies, and career plans. AAUW members read the letters and purchased books of interest for each student. AAUW members also responded with motivational letters to the girls. Five members of AAUW presented the books to fifteen students on December 18, 2001.

West Side Elementary School, Mrs. Carpenter's Fifth Grade Class and AAUW Members

1939 Decline in Enrollment

Although more schools were under construction, enrollment began to decrease in the late 1930s. For example, from September 1939 to September 1940, the student enrollment decreased from 12,524 to 11,967. These figures indicate that 557 students withdrew from the public schools in the Johnstown School District. Data on the enrollment of students in the Johnstown School District during the 1939–1940 school year illustrate the loss of students in one year. Data on the student enrollment in neighborhood schools indicate gains or losses between 1939 and 1940.

Elementary	September, 1939	September, 1940	Loss or Gain
Bheam	305	324	19 Gain
Chandler	461	434	27 Loss
Chestnut	474	440	34 Loss
Coopersdale	169	159	10 Loss
Cypress	336	306	30 Loss
Dibert	192	183	9 Loss
Horner	254	241	13 Loss
Hudson	453	408	45 Loss
Maple Park	300	306	6 Gain
Meadowvale	428	410	18 Loss
Morrell	173	124	49 Loss
Oakhurst	298	260	38 Loss
Osborne	243	245	2 Gain
Park	162	133	29 Loss
Rosedale	26	27	1 Gain
Roxbury	323	327	4 Gain
Somerset	354	372	18 Gain
Union	255	230	25 Loss
Village	300	278	22 Loss
Washington	356	327	29 Loss
Woodvale	431	385	46 Loss
Elementary Totals	6293	5919	374 Loss
Aggregate	12,524	11,967	557 Loss

The students in Johnstown were educated in more than fifty schools from 1810 to 2001. The elementary schools are listed below in the order of construction date. A review of the secondary schools appears in the next chapter.

Johnstown Elementary School Buildings

Elementary Classrooms

School	Location	Built	Abandoned/Closed
Old Blacky (Blackie)	Market & Chestnut (Carr, Napoleon)	About 1810	1855
Little Brick	Market & Chestnut	About 1834	Lost 1889
McConaughy (Old Whitey)	Walnut & Conemaugh Market Street		1837 1855
Bell	Main Street	Unknown	Unknown
Union	Market Street	1868	
	& School Alley	1855	1889 Fire
Adams	Adams Street	1870	1933
Dibert Street	Dibert Street	1872	
	Addition	1894	1968
Benshoff	Benshoff Street	1872	1934
Iron	Iron Street	1872	1915
Walnut Grove	Bedford Street	1880	
		1884	1922
Maple Park	Jacoby	1922	1977
Peelor	Peelor Street	1883	1922
Horner	Horner Street	1883	1971
Union	Union Street	1886	1961
Coopersdale	Boyer Street	1890	1922
		1922	1983
Park	Park Avenue	1891	1971
Somerset	Somerset Street	1891	1961
Chestnut	Chestnut Street	1894	1963
		1922	
Osborne	Akers Street	1894	1967
Morrell	Barron & D Street	1895	1956
Hudson	Hudson Street	1895	1971
	Addition	1924	Fire 1994
Washington # 1	Ebensburg Road	1897	1922
Washington # 2		1922	1983

School	Location	Built	Abandoned/Closed
Meadowvale # 1	McMillen Street	1900	
	Addition	1902	1971
Meadowvale # 2	Addition	1912	1971
Cypress	Cypress Avenue	1900	1995
	Addition	1903	
	Addition	1929	
Johnstown College		1946	1967
Woodvale	Maple Avenue	1901	1968
	Addition	1909	
	Moved	1917	
	Addition	1928	
Rosedale	Hinkston Road	1905	1948
Beam	J & Fairfield	1906	1971
Roxbury	Sell Street	1908	1997
	Addition	1913	
Village	Village Street	1908	1971
	Addition	1910	
Oakland	Penrod Street	1910	
	Addition	1925	Fire 1973
West Taylor	Cooper Avenue	1913	1975
Chandler	Garfield Street	1914	1992
Garfield Jr. High		1918	1925
Oakhurst	Dorothy Street	1915	1952
Andrew Jackson	Jackson Street	1917	1922
	(Lutheran Church) (leased)		
Casino Vocational	Somerset &		
	Napoleon Street	1917	1924
Oakhurst	Harold Avenue	1919	1976
South Ward	Decker Avenue	1919	1924
Robertson Store	Fairfield Avenue	1919	1927
	(leased)		
Oakland	Penrod Street	1910	
	Addition	1925	Fire 1973
Riverside	Riverside Street	1922	1969
	Addition	1926	
Highland Park	Highland Park Road	1925	1967

School	Location	Built	Abandoned/Closed
Westwood	Westgate Drive	1959	
(Westside)	Addition	1990	
Grove Methodist	Grove Avenue Church (leased)	1946	1951
St. Mary's Catholic School	Fifth Avenue & Chestnut Street	1995	1997
St. Casmier's Catholic School	Power Street	1995	1997

Evolution of the High School

Chapter VI

Population Growth

From 1899 to 1910, the city of Johnstown had a population growth of approximately 48 % that reflected an increase of 350 students enrolled in the high school. Needless to say, schools were in need of additional classrooms and new academic programs. According to Superintendent Herbert J. Stockton, the high school building did not meet the standards of current education. He stated that modern education should consider the cognition of all children of all people. In Mr. Stockton's opinion, the modern high school should appeal not only to the "novitiates" of the learned profession, but also to skilled trades, and agricultural and commercial pursuits. In addition, it should make ample provisions for the health training of its students. Mr. Stockton asked all students in the district to urge their parents and neighbors to vote for the passage of the bond issue for the building of a new high school, a new junior high school, and a number of new elementary buildings. He said that additions could also be added to the existing buildings. Mr. Stockton's philosophy, in the early 1900s, appeared to be futuristic. He believed in educating the whole student body to prepare them for their choice of work after high school. He also thought that he could reach the voters through students; in many cases, parents were the voters.

In 1914, with a continuous influx of student enrollment, additional rooms were built at the south and north wings for Johnstown High School. Some new features were a student lunchroom and a domestic science room in the south wing, and a large gymnasium in the north wing, with additional classrooms. Additional renovations included removal of walls in Rooms 107 and 109 for a wood shop, and removal of walls in Rooms 110, 111, and 112 for a machine shop. A plumbing shop occupied Room 113. Teachers taught English, math, and science in Room 108.

According to Morawska, between the 1920s and the 1930s, "[t]he Johnstown high schools, to judge from the contents of school bulletins and commencement speeches recorded in the graduation yearbooks, and from…interviews with former students and their teachers, did little to promote further education" (1996, p. 178). Teachers did not discourage extraordinary talent, nor did they encourage professional careers, but stressed perseverance and work ethics.

Nonetheless, extensive renovations to various buildings continued. School directors also took action on June 25, 1917, for a $2,000,000 bond issue to erect new schools. The bond issued provided for a new high school building, a complete junior high school system, and several new grade schools. The elementary schools that were under construction with the junior high school were Chestnut Street School in Cambria City, Washington Street School on Ebensburg Road in Prospect, Maple Park School on Jacoby Street in Walnut Grove, and Coopersdale School on Boyer Street. In support of the bond issue, Superintendent Stockton wrote an article for the October 1919 *Spectator*.

In the article, he said, "The present high school building on Market Street served its purpose well in its day, but now belongs to a past era. In the first place it is crowded beyond all reason. The conversion of every possible room into a classroom had largely served to shave off the initiation of a new building operation."

He further stated that two assembly rooms were gained by equipping the physics and chemistry lecture rooms with desks. Three assembly rooms were gained by arranging for seating in the biology laboratories, and three basement assembly rooms in the original building were gained by removing the manual training rooms area to the new south wing. Superintendent Stockton had a great influence on building the Greater Johnstown High School.

Student Enrollment

Secondary	September, 1939	September 1940	Loss or Gain
High School	1824	1778	46 Loss
Cochran	1393	1346	47 Loss
Garfield	1568	1470	98 Loss
Joseph Johns	1446	1454	8 Gain
Totals	6231	6048	183 Loss

The Johnstown Board of Directors was instrumental in building, renovating, or closing high schools.

Union Schoolhouse

Location: Market Street and School Alley

The Union Schoolhouse was dubbed a high school, because the curriculum was designed for higher-grade levels. The building was ready for student occupancy on January 1, 1856. The two-story structure measured 60 feet by 42 feet. Two rooms on each floor had 12 feet high ceilings. Seven windows in each 24 feet by 30 feet room provided light. Two furnaces located in the basement heated the building. The rooms were equipped with ventilators and furnishings of the era that included desks and seats. A portico covered the two main entrances in front of the main partition.

Graded Classrooms

Until 1855, students attended ungraded classrooms. The spirit of the board visualized a more progressive educational system and voted to classify students according to grade levels. Teachers were examined and appointed by the school board for Union School.

First Graded System Teachers

Miss Amelia E. Clippinger	Principal Assistant.
Miss Mary Swank	Teacher
Miss Louise E. Vickroy	Teacher
Miss Mary E. Shaffer	Assistant Teacher
Miss Virginia Roberts	Assistant Teacher
Miss Hortense Kooken	Assistant Teacher

High school classes were not co-educational, although female teachers taught the classes.

First High School

Location: Franklin and Canal Streets

Mr. S. B. McCormick organized the first high school in Johnstown. The building was erected on a lot at Franklin and Canal Streets. (In 2002, Canal Street is named Washington Street.) The board purchased land from Cambria Iron Company. The board appointed Mr. A. C. Johnson as teacher and principal. In the Washington Street Building, a high school division was started in 1868; however, the school had remained one-room, with one teacher teaching a few advanced subjects.

1868 High School Courses

Reading	Writing
Arithmetic	Grammar
Philosophy	Physiology
Botany	U.S. History
Algebra	Geometry
Physics	Music
Civil Government	

The German Language was introduced into the course of study as an elective, because of the large German-speaking population. At first, Latin was not included; however, several students studied and recited the language after school hours. In 1875, Latin was added to the curriculum.

The school board moved the high school to the Adams Street building in 1880; one year later it was moved to the Union Street School. The board sold the Washington Street Building to the Somerset and Cambria Branch of the Baltimore and Ohio Railroad, which used the building for a passenger and freight station. The Washington Street Building withstood the 1889 and the 1936 flood waters. The building served as a morgue after the 1889 Flood and was demolished in December 1936.

Adams Street Elementary School
Senior High School (1875–1881)

Location: Adams Street

The school board contracted to build the Adams Street School for a cost of $17,500. The two-story building had four large classrooms and four smaller classrooms. The board designated the Adams Street School as the high school from 1875 to 1881. The board appointed Mr. N. N. Keener as principal and later promoted him to the position of superintendent. The board then appointed Mr. A. A. Brubaker to the principal position. According to the school records, the Honorable Anderson H. Walters, Mr. John A. Kramer, Mr. Gomer Walters, and Mr. Henry Douglas were members of the senior class.

The Johnstown School Board's 1881 minutes reported that Mr. J. Frank Condon was granted use of a room to teach shorthand writings. After 1881, Adams Street School was used as an elementary school until the early 1920s. According to the school board minutes, December 20, 1915, the board established a Continuation School with programs in many buildings. They decided to put the Continuation School under one roof.

Adams Street Elementary School, Johnstown High School 1875–1881, *Courtesy of Johnstown Area Heritage Association*

Adams Street School Continuation Program

The Adams Street School Building was designated as the Continuation School Program. Teachers assigned to the program taught civic and vocational studies to increase the students' general education and enhance their daily occupations. They also taught the process of critical thinking to help students function in their practical daily lives. General education was provided for both girls and boys between the ages of fourteen and sixteen who dropped out of regular school. These teenagers were required to attend Continuation School for eight hours each week when regular day school was in session. The Continuation School provided continuation of education for about five hundred students per year. Student conferences and group discussions with faculty were utilized to provide an understanding of complex daily problems. Fundamental teaching pointed out the need for essential skills for daily living.

Continuation School Subjects

Practical Arts	Cooking
Sewing	Woodwork
Metal Work	Electrical Construction
Painting	Salesmanship
Office Skills	Social Customs
Leisure Reading	Practical Problems

The course of study was taught with the knowledge that students would implement those skills immediately. The Continuation School was a living school with actual workday conditions that relieved students of the pressure of being in school. The afternoon lesson on preparing food was often repeated in the home the same day, in family dinner preparation. The lesson in electrical construction was implemented at the students' homes for electrical problems and also provided necessary skills for employment consideration in electrical stores. Dressmaking provided the girls with a new wardrobe and the learned skill could be used in the home to help make other things. In essence, the Continuation School helped teenagers to do better the things that they were required to do. The standards used to evaluate the students were the usefulness of the subjects. The board abandoned the Adams Street School building as a school during the 1933–1934 term. The building was sold to Swank Hardware Company on June 14, 1946, for $33,900.

Reasons for Drop-outs (1926)

	% Boys	% Girls
Help family financially	68.3	18.3
Death of Parent	11.7	9.0
Work	6.7	–
Help at home	5.0	72.2

Reality of Drop-Outs (1926)

Boys' Percentage		Girls' Percentage	
Industry	38.7	Home Helper	38.6
Sales	27.0	Industry	17.8
Messenger	16.0	Clerk	16.0
Delivery	12.4	Domestic service	14.9
Paper Carrier	4.1	Office Work	4.9

The Continuation School enrolled 390 students. The purpose of the Continuation School was to make all instructions practical and vocational. To prepare students for volunteer fire fighting, Truck Co. No. 1 members of the Fire Department instructed one class.

On June 5, 1924, the former students of the Adams Street School had a Golden Jubilee. Although the first principal of the school was Mr. N. N. Keener, the administration had changed to Ms. Katherine Baumer at the time of the Golden Jubilee.

Adams Street School Opportunity Room

In the late 1920s, the board of directors used motion power to establish an Opportunity Room in the Adams Street School. The Opportunity Room was planned for students with academic or physical problems, that is, speech problems, for children who could speak but not hear. Students assigned to the Opportunity Room received special individual academic instruction as an attempt to alleviate physical defects. Many of these students were able to return to their regular classrooms. (See Special Education.)

Union Street Elementary School (1891–1961) Johnstown High School (1881–1890)

Location: Union and Lincoln Streets

Union Street School was built in 1881, on Union Street near Lincoln Street. The building was used as a high school until 1891, when the board of directors designated it as an elementary school. The Johnstown School Board minutes, 1881, report that Mr. J. Frank Condon was granted one room to teach shorthand writing. The board also permitted the German Language to be introduced as an elective.

The first graduating class in 1882 consisted of seven girls. According to Mary J. Cooper, a member of the graduating class, the first commencement exercises were depicted as an affair of civic importance. The girls wore short gloves with one button, and fancy dresses. Everyone was invited to partake of a dish of ice cream and homemade cake at Fend's Ice Cream Parlor. However, the following year, 1883, the graduating class was co-educational with four boys and four girls. In 1888 only one female graduated.

Union Street Elementary School, Third High School, *Courtesy of Johnstown Area Heritage Association*

At the Union Street School, Superintendent Johnston adopted the three-year high school course of study. In 1884, the four-year course of study was introduced, adding classes in philosophy and higher mathematics. The Union School located on Market Street was destroyed by fire approximately a week after the 1889 Flood. The Johnstown School Board received $5,357.75 from fire insurance for damages to the building. The 1889 Flood also destroyed the school buildings in Woodvale Borough and Conemaugh Borough. The Union Street School, serving as a high school, closed after the 1889 Flood. The school reopened as an elementary school in 1891. The Union Street School was closed on June 7, 1961; the Pennsylvania State Employment Building was constructed on the site.

Somerset Street Elementary School (1892–1898) High School (1892–1898)

Location: Somerset and Dibert Streets

Somerset Street School, built in 1891, was located on Somerset Street near Dibert Street. This school served as a high school between 1892 and 1898, after the 1889 Flood. The board appointed Mr. H. J. Johnson as principal. Miss Amanda Brixner and Miss Polly Horrocks served as high school teachers. The graduating class included Earl Warden, (Dr.) Edward Kress, Jacob Horner, Myrtle Waugh, Myrtle Walters, and Ivy Walters (Mrs. Fred Waterman). In 1898, the Board of School Directors converted the building to an elementary school. The school was closed on November 22, 1967, and demolished at a later date. In 2002, the site is used as a playground of memories for the Kernville section of town.

Johnstown College

Location: Johnstown Central Senior High School

Somerset Elementary School, Fourth High School, *Courtesy of the Johnstown Area Heritage Association*

The Johnstown College, now known as the University of Pittsburgh at Johnstown, was housed at Johnstown Central Senior High School from 1927 to 1946. John Wilson shared his memories of Junior Pitt from 1942. He said that the University of Pittsburgh occupied the first floor of one wing of the high school located on Somerset Street. He mentioned that Mrs. Viers Adams, head of the Johnstown Center, and the faculty objected to the term "Junior Pitt" used by the community, because the course offerings and the requirements were the same as University of Pittsburgh. The only thing "junior" about the offerings was the Center's offering only two years of work. High school students used the Napoleon Street Entrance to the building and the Junior Pitt students used the Somerset Street doors.

Mr. Wilson said that many college students had attended high school in the same building the year before. Extracurricular activity classes were taken at the YMCA. The policy of the all-male YMCA was to swim in the nude. Girls took swimming instruction at the YWCA. On Fridays, the extracurricular activity was a marathon that began at the YMCA and ran up Easy Grade Road (Menoher Boulevard) to the top. The students were checked off by an instructor before returning to high school via Millcreek Road.

Mr. Wilson remembered that one of his teachers over forty years of age was drafted into the U.S. Army. Between 1942 and 1943 he and other male students were drafted. Few were able to continue their two-year college program. He included that the faculty was knowledgeable and approachable (Wilson, 1998, pp. 218–219).

Asphalt Campus

Location: Cypress Elementary School

In 1946, Johnstown College was moved into the Cypress Avenue Elementary School building and was dubbed the Asphalt Campus. In 1958, the College was renamed the Johnstown College of the University of Pittsburgh. In 1967, the College was relocated to suburban Johnstown, in Richland Township. The college was also renamed the University of Pittsburgh at Johnstown (Blackington, 1994, pp. vi, vii). In 2002, it is a four-year undergraduate college of the University of Pittsburgh. People from the Greater Johnstown Community, students of the Asphalt Campus, and graduates of Greater Johnstown High School have given generously to the campus. The Pasquerilla Performing Arts Center was donated by Sylvia and Frank Pasquerilla ('44).

Pasquerilla Performing Arts Center—PPAC, *Courtesy of Judy Browne Photography*

Miss Elvina J. Owen ('27) attended the Johnstown Center and received her baccalaureate degree in secondary education from the School of Education at the University of Pittsburgh in 1932. She returned to Johnstown High School to teach, motivate, and guide thousands of high school students. She believed in continuous learning; therefore, she made a generous donation to the library at the University of Pittsburgh at Johnstown. In 1992, the Library was named the Owen Library in honor of Miss Elvina J. and her sister, Mrs. Sara Jane Owen Torquato ('35). Mrs. Sara Jane Torquato also attended the Johnstown Center and graduated from the University of Pittsburgh in 1939.

After students completed two years of undergraduate studies at the Johnstown College, they transferred to the main campus in Pittsburgh to complete requirements for a bachelor's degree. They usually traveled round-trip seventy miles to Pittsburgh several times a week by bus or by train. A commuter train was scheduled between Johnstown and Pittsburgh three times a day. A former student of the Asphalt Campus said that her travel time was longer than her class time. In 1967, when community leaders established a four-year college in the Greater Johnstown area, Johnstown High School students and the community appreciatively took advantage of the opportunity to acquire a degree.

Owen Library–Lower Level, *Courtesy of Bruce Haselrig*

In the 1960s, the Asphalt Campus' future became uncertain. Mr. Walter W. Krebs, the late publisher of the Tribune-Democrat, launched a multimillion dollar campaign to keep the campus in Johnstown (Tribune, 2002, p. C8). In 2002, the University of Pittsburgh at Johnstown is a residential, undergraduate college of the University of Pittsburgh. Twenty-eight campus buildings are aesthetically arranged on 650 suburban acres, about 7 miles from its Asphalt Campus and about seventy miles from the Pittsburgh main campus.

Many faculty members and administrators moved to the township site, bridging the gap between a two-year campus and a four-year campus. Dr. Lowell Shaffer and Mr. Michael Flynn ('54) were transitional administrators who retired as vice presidents of the campus. Dr. Shaffer was one of the founders and the first president of the Asphalt Campus Club.

Johnstown Central High School

Location: Market and Carr (Napoleon) Streets

Johnstown Central High School, built in 1899 on Market and Carr Streets for $136,000, had five floors. Two hundred twenty-four students received diplomas in 1899.

According to school board minutes:

November 11, 1896—The Building Committee, in conjunction with the President, Secretary, and Superintendent, was [sic] instructed to prepare specifications for competitive plans for a High School Building to be erected on the vacant lot on Market Street.

January 27, 1897—The Board advertised for competitive plans in accordance with specifications and sketches submitted by the Building Committee.

April 6, 1897—The plans for the High School Building were unanimously adopted. The plans proved to be by Architect George Wild, of Johnstown. Revised specifications were presented to the Board.

Revised Specifications for the High School Building [sic]

The Board of School Controllers of the City of Johnstown, Pa., will receive competitive plans for a High School Building, until 12:00 A.M., April 6th, 1897.

Said plans must be forwarded in a sealed envelope, through Express Company, to W. A. Cochran, Secretary School Board, Hannan Building and endorsed "Plan for High School Building."

A descriptive letter must accompany the plans, with the amount of fee required for architect's services. This letter must be marked with a motto or cipher for identification of the author.

The author's name is to be delivered in a plain envelope, securely sealed with sealing wax, in such a manner that the name cannot be read without opening the envelope.

In case the lowest bid of a responsible contractor exceeds the successful architect's estimate, the architect will forfeit his plans to the School Board, and will receive no remuneration for his plans and services rendered.

All plans and elevations are to be drawn to a scale of 1/8 of an inch to the foot, on heavy white paper, with a 4" margin. No shade or color is to be used, except the filling in of walls or plans.

Drawings must consist of basement, floor plans, and two elevations. All unsuccessful plans will be returned to the respective authors, and no distinctive features of any rejected plans will be used without the consent of the authors.

The purposed building is to be located on a lot fronting 135 feet on Carr Street and 262 feet on Market Street.

The building was to face Market Street.

The building shall consist of basement and three stories, and material used in its construction shall be stone, wood, brick, terra cotta and steel, preference being given to material that can be obtained in Johnstown vicinity.

The basement shall be well ventilated and well lighted, so that a large part of it can be used for playrooms or for manual training school purposes.

The building shall contain at least 16 classrooms, offices for Superintendent, Controllers and Teachers, book storage room with a fireproof vault, an assembly room on second floor with a meeting capacity of 1000 to 1200.

The classrooms shall be large enough for 50 desks, must be well lighted and ventilated, and to have cloak rooms.

The heating and ventilating shall receive special attention, and must conform to the best modern practice.

The attached sketch gives a general idea of school facilities desired, but any other arrangement giving the same general result will receive consideration.

The entire cost of the building, including heating, ventilation, plumbing, and electric fixtures, blackboards, and architect's fees, shall not exceed $75,000.

The Board reserves the right to reject any or all plans.

April 13, 1897—Board unanimously agreed to proceed to erect a High School Building, according to plans adopted.

May 13, 1897—Mr. L. E. Jordan employed as Mechanical Engineer to supervise heating and ventilation of building.

June 18, 1897—School lot surveyed and building located.

August 3, 1897—Complete plans and specifications by Architect Wild and competitive bids from contractors advertised for.

August 26, 1897—Proposals from contractors opened and contact awarded to Keenan & Co., of Altoona, Pa. for $73,850.

September 14, 1897—Bond of Keenan & Co. for $50,000. Accepted.

September 20, 1897—Formal contract closed with Keenan & Co., and the early building of foundation walls authorized.

September 28, 1897—Special contract entered into with Keenan & Co. for sub-foundation of concrete to secure solid foundation. The cost of this item alone was $4,477.

February 8, 1898—Bids for $100,000 four per-cent school board bonds advertised for.

April 12, 1898—One hundred thousand dollars four-per-cent. 3–30 year bonds were sold to the Penn Mutual Insurance Co., of Philadelphia, for $100,763.46.

April 26, 1898—Contract for heating and ventilating building awarded to McGinness, Smith & Co., of Pittsburg[h], Pa. for $7,060.

January 31, 1899—Contract supplying the school and office furniture for the building awarded to the Grand Rapids School Furniture Co., and the Baker Specialty Co., for a sum approximating $3,500.

February 17. 1899—Extras on building by Keenan & Co., amounting to $2,101.71 were approved.

Contract for hand-shaved slate blackboards for building awarded to M. I.R. Hedges, Pittsburg[h], Pa., for $850.

Contract for library, book rooms and laboratory cases awarded to William Lloyd & Son for $525.

March 28, 1899—Contract for light fixtures awarded to Johnstown Supply House for $830.

Contract for paving and grading school lot awarded to Theil & Co., for $850.

According to the school board Minutes:

May 9, 1899—Building accepted and settlement with Keenan & Co., as per contract ordered, subject to final approval.

Insurance for $50,000 on the High School Building and $8,500 on the contents.

The board awarded other contracts as following:

Temperature Regulation—Johnson Electric Service Co., No. 91 Diamond Street, Pittsburg[h], Pa.

Electrical Contractors—Altoona Electrical Engineering & supply Co., Altoona, Pa.

Gas Engine—Backus Water Motor Co., Newark, N.J.

Water Closets, Urinals, Etc.—American Foundry & Furnace Co., Bloomington, Ill

Hot Air Pipes, Deflector, Etc.—F. A. Joy & Son, Johnstown, Pa.

Sanitary Fixtures and Glass—Swank Hardware Co., Johnstown, Pa.

Gas and Electric Fixtures—Johnstown Supply House, Johnstown, Pa.

Hardware—Reading Hardware Co., Reading, Pa.

Bricks and Steel—Cambria Steel Co., Johnstown, Pa

Alpha Cement for Concrete. Basement, Floors, and Walls—Chas. E. Pope & Co., No 421 Wood Street, Pittsburg[h], Pa.

Cumberland and Potomac Cement, in Mortar for Foundation Walls and Brick Work-Cumberland & Potomac Cement Co., Room No. 201 Builder's Exchange, Philadelphia, Pa.

Slate Roof and Copper Work—W. F. Overly, Greensburg, Pa.

Steel Beam Fireproofing—Martin Hannan, Johnstown, Pa.

Salamander Fireproofing—American Fireproofing Co., No 166 Devonshire Street, Boston Mass.

Ornamental Iron Stair Work, Wire Window Guards, and Wardrobes,—Taylor & Dean, No. 201 Market Street, Pittsburg[h], Pa.

Rolling Partitions—James G. Wilson, No. 74 West Twenty-third Street, Cor., Sixth Avenue, New York City.

Slate Blackboards—I. R. Hedges. No 203 Water Street, Pittsburg[h], Pa.

Window Shades—John Thomas & Sons, Johnstown, Pa.

Wardrobes and Interior Finishing Lumber—W. J. Rose & Sons, Johnstown, Pa.

Book Room, Library, Drawing Room, Chemical and Biological Room Fixtures—William Lloyd & Son, Johnstown, Pa.

According to the media, in 1899, the newly built Johnstown High School building was, beyond doubt, the most important edifice in the city and one of the finest buildings in the state. The corner of Market and Carr Streets (Napoleon Street) was a very desirable one. The campus was almost in the center of the city, yet far enough from the business section to afford the quiet necessary to promote teaching and learning. The exterior design of the high school building emphasized the well-proportioned lines, rather than the decorative details. Emphasis on the main entrance doorway and the cupola on the roof accentuated other prominent points. Although the proportions and details were colonial lines of architecture, the structure exhibited its own style.

Johnstown Central High School (1899–1926), (Became Joseph Johns Junior High School in 1926), *Courtesy of Cover Studio*

In the shape of the letter "H," the school consisted of two buildings, united by a central wing. A fireproof staircase hall attached each end, with a stairway in the central part. The complete structure was 204 feet long and 100 feet deep. The main entrance hall had a vestibule 17 feet wide on the first floor, with corridors 12 feet wide running the entire length of the building on each floor. The building, constructed with twenty-one classrooms, included drawing and commercial rooms, physics and chemistry laboratories, a library, and study rooms. Eight additional basement rooms were used for manual training. Other rooms on various floors were designed for the controllers, city superintendent, principal, teachers, and book supplies. The auditorium, with a gallery and seating capacity of about nine hundred people, occupied the second and third floors of the building's southern wing. The building was approximately four stories high. The basement totaled 12 feet high, with eight of the feet above ground level. The concrete foundations extended down to river gravel, with heavy masonry walls up to grade level. Above grade, the basement walls, built of native blue quarry stone, were laid in level courses with rock face. The base course, windowsills, and keystones were buff limestone from the town of Bedford, Indiana. The terra cotta trimmings and valance had paneled copper cornices. The cupola on the roof was also constructed of copper conductors.

All stairways were built of steel, with slate treads and balusters of ornamental iron, topped with oak handrails. Stairways were described as of ample width, well lighted, and easily accessed from all rooms. Special construction was given to designing three flights of stairs. Above the base course, three stories were built from the local Cambria Iron Company's repressed red brick, laid in red mortar with a hollow joint and Flemish bond. The roof was of colorfast green slate with red terra cotta heap and ridge rolls. Finished entirely in red oak, the building had Georgia hard pine plastered with patent cement on metal. Interior walls were fireproof brick, with the first floor built of steel beams. Other fireproofing consisted of concrete between the steel beams, with embedded twisted bars suspended on the beams. Salamander fireproof composition, used on the second and third floors, was made of yellow pine. The composition helped to contain the spread of a potential fire or water damage through the floors. Yellow pine was also used for the framing of the roof. The auditorium design prevented heavy traffic and allowed the room to be emptied, if necessary, without complications.

Considering teachers and students, attention was given to their health and comfort with well-ventilated classrooms, lighted from the left and the rear. Ventilated wire wardrobes with racks for umbrellas and rubbers were connected to the classrooms. Wardrobes regressed from both the room and the corridor. Foot warmers were also provided on the first floor. Drinking fountains and standpipes were installed on all floors for fire emergencies. Toilet rooms, as well as rooms for teachers, superintendent, and other professional and support staff were supplied with hot and cold water. Sanitary appliances were installed. Each floor had a custodial closet equipped with an enameled slop sink, with hot and cold water.

Wall switches controlled lighting for both gas and electrical systems. In the auditorium, two rows of lights were installed on a frieze near the ceiling around the entire room. The frieze had numerous sidelights. A row of lights along the top of the stage was arranged to be invisible from the front. Lights were provided with reflectors, controlled by wall switches from the stage.

Return call bells and telephone lines in each classroom connected to the principal's office. Both bells and gongs rung in each classroom to designate the time to change classes and also to start and finish the school day. The sound system was also used during fire drills or for unannounced emergencies.

A double-blower, hot blast furnace system heated and ventilated the building. The system supplied not less than 35 cubic feet of air per minute for each student and exhaust of equal amount at velocities not to exceed six feet per second. Large flues from a point 30 feet above the ground took in fresh air. Air was then forced over steam heat coils by means of powerful blowers through brick flues to the schoolrooms. Steam heat entered the rooms through registers placed eight feet above the floor line. Foul air was taken out of the room at the floor line through flues by underground ducts, and driven out of the building by means of exhaust blowers. Ventilating stacks of flues extended ten feet above the highest part of the roof. The building was heated by indirect steam that supplied two horizontal steel boilers. The entire apparatus was of sufficient capacity to heat the building at 70 degrees Fahrenheit in any weather, not to exceed twelve pounds of pressure. A gas engine supplied power.

A Johnson System regulated the temperature of the building and consisted of a thermostat with a thermometer placed in each room. The thermostat could be set at any temperature and could accurately adjust to operate at a variation of one degree. Operation of the temperature was through a system of concealed pipes, with double dampers used for heating. With this heating system, teachers were freed of the responsibility of heating or cooling the classroom.

1899 Building Status Statistics

Number of perches of masonry	800
Number of cubic yards' foundation concrete	1,400
Number of square yards' fireproof concrete	1,400
Number of square yards cement floors	1,400

Number of pressed brick	150,000
Number of common brick	1,600,000
Number of buff brick	120,000
Number of cubic yards Indian limestone	1,500
Number of square yards plastering	12,000
Number of squares of green slate	250
Number of outside double doors	11
Number of inside doors	100
Number of rolling partitions	2
Number of windows	283
Number of square feet of blackboards	3,600
Number of square feet of flooring	56,000
Number of chairs in assembly hall	850
Number of 80 horsepower boilers	2
Number of 72-inch fresh air fans	2
Number of 72-inch foul air fans	2
Number of 45 horsepower gas engine	1

Rooms and Sizes

8 manual training rooms	25x33x12
14 classrooms	25x33x12
3 classrooms	18'6x2
1 study room	33x52x13
1 commercial room	33x52x13
1 drawing room	27x38x13
1 physical laboratory	20x27x13
1 library	20x27x13
1 Principal's room	17x27x13
1 Superintendent's room	20x27x13
1 Controllers' room	20x27x13
1 book room	18'6"x27x13
1 teacher's room	18'6"x27x13
1 assembly hall with stage	52x90x30
2 lavatories	18'6"x27x12
2 lavatories	20x26x13
2 blower rooms	18'6"x26'6"x12
1 boiler room	19'6"x26'6"x20
1 coal room	16x28x20

The new Johnstown High School officially opened doors for students, with Dedicatory Exercises held on Thursday evening, June 1, 1899.

Administration–1900

J. M. Berkey	Superintendent
Fred Krebs	President, board of directors
William L. Long	Principal

First High School Graduating Class–1900

Francis B. Hamilton	Eva B. Blauch
Edith Conser	Rena Cohn
Carrie B. Dick	Elfrieda Krieger
Carolyn Kugel	Pluma Longshore
Margaret E. McLain	Blanche K. McMillen
Katie Stroup	Elizabeth T. Watkins
Grace V. Dresser	Merrill Baker
Caroline Edwards	Lyda Fearnley
John F. Henderson	Robert A. Judy
Jacob J. Kramer	Carl Resley

1918 Johnstown High School Class, *Courtesy of Hoss's Family Steak and Sea House*]

Although the high school included a library, many students and teachers continued to use the facilities at the Carnegie Library located in downtown Johnstown, on Walnut and Washington Streets. The Johnstown Public Library was one of the buildings destroyed by the 1889 Flood. The new building was rebuilt by Andrew Carnegie and dedicated in 1892.

1891 Johnstown Public Library (Carnegie) (Johnstown Flood Museum),
Courtesy of Judy Browne Photography

In 1911, the addition to the high school was completed with a domestic science (home economics) suite. The art of cooking was emphasized, with golden rules for the kitchen.

Golden Rules for the Kitchen

1. A place for everything and everything in its place
2. A good cook wastes nothing.
3. A thing that is worth doing is worth doing well.
4. An hour lost in the morning have to run after all day.
5. Clear up as you work; it takes but a moment then and saves time afterwards.
6. A time for everything and everything on time.
7. Do not make unnecessary work for others.
8. Much depends on starting right.
9. Without cleanliness and punctuality good cooking is impossible.

10. Leave nothing dirty, clean and clear as you go.

11. An attractive table makes even plain food palatable.

12. Far greater skill is shown where, with small material, there are good results.

13. A good cook is a good taster and no waster.

14. Love lightens labor.

15. Anything, which has to rise in the oven, should be placed on the floor of the oven.

16. Cultivate the habit of opening and shutting the oven door quickly but gently.

17. Look at things as they are baking and turn and watch then until you are sure they can be left alone.

18. Learn the hottest and coolest places in the oven.

The 1912 kitchen did not have electrical equipment or appliances. Preparing meals was time-consuming. Nonetheless, great pride was taken with presenting labored meals.

On January 5, 1920, new students enrolled at Johnstown High School totaled 250, with 37 students from Morrellville Junior High School. The student enrollment for the term was 1,562.

Term I Courses

Normal Preparatory	College
Technical	Industrial
Two Year Commercial	Four Year Commercial
General	

According to excerpts from the *Spectator*, in 1922, Mr. J. D. Ripple was appointed principal. His slogan was "cooperation." Cooperation and acceptance were personality traits that prevailed in the freshman class displayed in the school climate. On February 19, 1922, the Junior-Senior reception was held in the school gymnasium. Most of the freshmen class was not permitted to attend because of their 9:00 P.M. curfew. However, most freshmen accepted the restriction and became of age in March to participate in school activities that ran after 9:00 P.M. On May 4, 1923, the graduating class of Central High School hosted the Junior-Senior Prom, with Funk's Ambassador Orchestra providing the music.

Joseph Johns Junior High School

Johnstown Central High School became Joseph Johns Junior High School in 1926. To reduce the congestion of the newly built Cochran Junior High, Central High School became a junior high school, with the completion of Greater Johnstown High School. With the influx of workers for Cambria Iron Works, the mergers of outlining districts, and enforcement of the compulsory school laws, the student population continued to expand. The schools were neighborhood schools and students walked to school and home for the lunch hour.

In 1967, the student population was on a decline. Therefore, the board took action to officially close Joseph Johns High School on December, 11, 1967, and agreed to conduct classes there until June 1970.

The board's solicitor petitioned the Orphans' Court Division of the Court of Common Pleas of Cambria County for approval of the sale of Joseph Johns Junior High School to the Redevelopment Authority of the City and to determine the portion of proceeds of said sale. The sale was based on the value of lots numbered 133 and 134 of the plan for Conemaugh Old Town as dedicated on November 3, 1800, by Joseph Johns. The junior high school was closed in June 1970. According to the *Tribune Democrat,* January 28, 1970, the board made arrangements to transfer 653 students from Joseph Johns Junior High School to other schools at the beginning of 1971. The transfers were necessary because the board had sold the building to Johnstown Redevelopment for $850,000. A high-rise apartment occupies the site in 2002.

1970 Faculty of Joseph Johns, *Courtesy of Cover Studio*

1962 Class, Joseph Johns Junior High School, *Courtesy of Cover Studio*

Junior High School Reading List
Seventh Grade—Nonfiction

Spirit of Youth in the City Streets	Addams, Jane
Book of Ruth	Bible
Birds Every Child Should Know	Blanchan, N.
Book of Stars	Collins, A. F.
Stories of Great Americans	Eggleston, Edward
Wonderbook and Tanglewood Tales	Hawthorne, Nathaniel
American Citizenship in Pennsylvania	Maltby
Boys Life of Lincoln	Nicolay, Helen
Book of Woodcraft	Seton-Thompson, Ernest
The Great Peacemaker	Watson, H. C.

Seventh Grade—Fiction

Little Men	Alcott, Louisa M.
Little Women	Alcott, Louisa M.
The Last of the Mohicans	Cooper, James Fenimore
Alice in Wonderland	Dodgson, (Lewis Carrol)
Stories of Sherlock Holmes	Doyle, Sir Arthur Conan
The Call of the Wild	London, Jack
Anne of Green Gables	Montgomery, L. M.

Merry Adventure of Robin Hood	Pyle, Howard
Black Beauty	Sewall, Anna
Swiss Family Robinson	Wyss, Johann David

Eighth Grade–Nonfiction

Joan of Arc	Alden
Bible	Book of Daniel
Life of "Kit" Carson	Burdett, Charles
Our Little Roman Cousins of Long Ago	Cowles, Julia D.
George Junior Republic	George, Henry
Life at West Point	Hancock, H.I.
Nights with Uncle Remus	Harris, Joel Chandler
Pennsylvania Trees	Illick, Joseph
The Travels of Marco Polo	Knox, T. W.
Heroines in Service	Parkman, Mary F.

Eighth Grade–Fiction

Jo's Boys	Alcott, Louisa M.
Master Skylark	Bennett, John
A Christmas Carol	Dickens, Charles
The Hooster School Master	Eggleston, Edward
Just So Stories	Kipling, Rudyard
Two Little Savages	Seton-Thompson, Ernest
Tales	Poe, Edgar, A.
Heidi	Spyri, Johanna
20,000 Leagues Under the Sea	Verne, Jules
Mother Cary' Chickens	Wiggins, Kate D.

Ninth Grade–Nonfiction

Story of the Plants	Allen, Grant
Book of Esther	Bible
The Wit of the Duck	Burroughs, John
Insect Adventures	Fabre, Jean Henry
Tales From American History	Lodge and Roosevelt
Travels in Alaska	Muir, John
Village Life in America	Richards, Caroline
Ranch Life and the Hunting Trail	Roosevelt, Theodore
Being a Boy	Warner, Charles D.
Life of Washington	Wilson, Woodrow

Ninth Grade–Fiction

Pilgrim's Progress	Bunyan, John
Story from the Odyssey	Church, Alfred, J.
Huckleberry Finn	Clemens, S. L.
The Red Badge of Courage	Crane, Stephen
The Adventure of Sherlock Holmes	Doyle, A. Conan
The Little Shepherd of Kingdom Come	Fox, John
Uncle Remus, His Songs and Sayings	Harris, Joel Chandler
Stories of Tennessee	Morris, William
Story of King Author and his Knights	Pyle, Howard
Red Men and White	Wister, Owen

Tenth Grade–Nonfiction

Book of Judges	Bible
An American Citizen	Brooks, J. G.
Handy Guide for Beggars	Lindsay, Nicholas, Vachel
A Minstrel in France	Lauder, Harry
Black Sheep	MacKenzie, Jean
Red Cow and her Friends	McArthur, Peter
Heroes of Progress in America	Morris, Charles
The Charm of Fine Manners	Starrett, Helen
Marco Polo	Towle, H. M.
Daniel Boone, Wilderness Scout	White, Stewart E.

Tenth Grade–Fiction

The Little Minister	Barrie, J. M.
The Sky Pilot	Gordon, C. W.
Robinson Crusoe	Defoe, Daniel
Best American Humorous Short Stories	Jessup, Alex, (Ed.)
Little Citizens	Kelly, Myra
The Day's Work	Kipling, Rudyard
Put Yourself in his Place	Reade, Charles
Russian Short Stories	Schweikert, H. C. (Ed.)
Rob Roy	Scott, Sir Walter
The Riverman	White, Sewart E.

This is a partial reading list for students in seventh through tenth grades at Joseph Johns Junior High School. Some of the titles reflected the lack of empathy or insensitivity of the 1920s. Biblical Books are recommended on every grade level. The List (1927) was provided by the Department of Public Instruction, Harrisburg, Pennsylvania, for English Courses.

1962 Class, Joseph Johns Junior High School, *Courtesy of Cover Studio*

1962 Class, Joseph Johns Junior High School, *Courtesy of Cover Studio*]

Cochran Junior High School

Location: Central Avenue

Cochran Junior High School's foundation was started in 1917, two years after the board of directors approved the purchase of two Suppes lots in the Eighth Ward for $96,000. The academic and heating units were completed in 1921. While the junior high school was under construction, the Johnstown School Board of Directors contracted to have five new elementary schools built, Chestnut Street, Washington, Maple Park, Walnut Grove, and Coopersdale. The student population was growing rapidly.

On January 14, 1946, years later, the board of directors purchased additional lots at the rear of Cochran Junior High School for $28,000. The school board was of the opinion that junior high facilities would recognize differences in children and would provide for varying ages of progress so that students may advance as rapidly as their abilities permitted. The junior high facilities permitted various educational vocational exploration courses. The junior high school relieved the congestion from the elementary and high schools. In April 1924, the gymnasium was completed and the auditorium followed in October. The approximate cost of the building's original plan was $1,250,000 and included land acquisition. Henry Hornbostel of New York City was the consulting architect and furnished the design for the initial building. Architects, J. E. Adams, J. Emmett Lucas, and George Wilde executed the drawings. J. E. Adams was the supervising architect for all construction. Major Henry Hornbostel was the architectural consultant. The Major was known for his bold mastery of large, massive architectural forms. He was well known for numerous Pittsburgh landmarks, such as Carnegie Mellon University campus, the University of Pittsburgh scheme, and the beaux-arts styled Soldiers and Sailors Memorial Hall.

The school board directors named the new junior high school the William A. Cochran Junior High School, in honor of a former member of the school board. The initial Cochran Junior High School consisted of six buildings, an academic building with manual and domestic art wings, an auditorium, and the plumbing shop. The shop was equipped with current tools to train students to become apprentice plumbers. Students could complete many fine intricate designed cabinets in the woodworking shop with modern woodworking machinery. Students learned the practical work of electricity in the electric shop. The domestic science dining room and toilet were also located on the first floor. In addition, the first floor also housed two drawing rooms, two classrooms, two storerooms, two toilets and washrooms, and two football rooms. The cafeteria (the size of six classrooms), included a kitchen and a cafeteria store. It was located on the Napoleon Street side of the building and had the capacity to seat five hundred students. A vestibule and a lobby occupied the first floor. Space under the auditorium was utilized as a general storeroom and as a book room. The second floor was composed of teachers' rooms; ten classrooms; two laboratories; one health room; one auditorium with a seating capacity of 1,200; two gymnasiums; two showers, with locker facilities; one vestibule; one lobby; and two toilets.

Before completion of the Cochran Junior High School building, the school directors compiled a list of possible honorees. This list consisted of men well known in their field.

Cochran Junior High School Honorees

Chopin	Polish Composer and Pianist
Edison	United States Inventor
Homer	Greek Poet
Mann	United States Education Reformer
Michaelangelo	Italian Sculptor and Poet
Pasteur	French Chemist and Bacteriologist
Raphael	Italian Painter
Taft	Chief Justice and President of the United States

The renowned list of honorees made it difficult to make a decision to display only one. Therefore, the school directors gave a directive that all aforementioned names should be etched in concrete in the auditorium wall facing Central Avenue. According to the November 1924 *Spectator*, the beautiful new Cochran Junior High School auditorium was informally opened on October 24, 1924, with the public invited. Mr. Baldwin, the musical director, rendered several pleasing violin numbers, accompanied by Mr. Schill on the new Steinway grand piano. The Girls Glee Club and the Welsh Glee Club also provided entertainment. School Superintendent Slawson addressed the audience. Former Super-

intendent Stockton and some school board directors offered some remarks. School board members were Mr. Rutledge, Mr. McFeaters, and
Mr. Krebs. The formal opening of the auditorium occurred later with
the presentation of an opera. The Dedication Ceremony at Cochran
Junior High School took place on Monday, November 24, 1924. Later,
the water system for the school was upgraded. On August 27, 1928, the
school board voted to abandon the Cochran well pumps and cap the
deep well.

The Cochran auditorium has remained a favored concert hall for
the residents of Johnstown. It is known throughout the Greater
Johnstown Area for its magnificent structure and its extraordinary acous-
tic qualities. Musical people have marveled over the building's acoustics,
which cannot be matched in the area. International orchestras and tour
groups including the Boston Pops, have performed in the auditorium.

Many students did not continue their high school education. Therefore, Cochran's Junior High School held graduation promotion exercises
similar to high school graduation ceremonies.

Promotion Exercises June 3, 1937

Cochran Junior High School

Dale McMaster	Superintendent
Walter C. Davis	Principal
J.D. Rutledge	School Board President

Class Officers

Wayne Wolfe	President
Richard Waters	Vice President
Rose Sanson	Secretary
Jack Nicholson	Treasurer

Honors

Highest Honor	Amelia Bondy
American Legion Award	Wayne Wolfe
A. Legion Auxiliary Medal	Lois McGeary
Class Colors	Blue and White

Number of Graduates	*309*

In 1971, Cochran had a student body of 1,383. In 2002, Cochran is now the senior high school, with ninth through twelfth grades.

Cochran High School, *Courtesy of Judy Browne Photography*

New Greater Johnstown High School (Cochran)

On August 31, 2001, the board of directors, community leaders, and students broke ground for a $38 million Greater Johnstown High School. The major part of the old structure will be razed. The Hiller Group from Princeton is the architectural designer. The existing lobby areas of Cochran Auditorium are being restored and refurbished. The cost of the restoration of Cochran Auditorium will be an estimated $4 million. A new emergency lighting system was designed in accordance with the Pennsylvania new emergency lighting. An exit sign system will be installed using a new natural gas-fired emergency generator. The electrical system has futuristic capacity, designed to utilize fusible main distribution switchboard.

The air distribution system is designed to incorporate low velocity supply air delivery. Diffuser installation and coordination will match the existing structural conditions in the loft space. The equipment will fit in between existing ceiling wood joist support structure, thereby, eliminating the requirements for costly structural modifications.

An address system will be installed with audible and visual devices and an automatic fire detection and sprinkler system will comply. The sound-absorbing ductwork is designed to provide low system sound pressure levels. Theater-style linear ceiling diffusers will be installed. Diffusers with adjustable throw pattern arrangements will be utilized for proper terminal air velocity over two sloping balconies. Public restrooms will be designed to comply with ADA standards. Dynamic System Design Engineering, Inc., is responsible for upgrading the restored auditorium and new construction.

Casino Vocational School

Location: Main and Jackson Streets

The Casino Vocational School building, located on Somerset and Napoleon Streets, was purchased for $800, with one thousand chairs included. According to the *Tribune-Democrat,* plans for a complete revision of the Casino were made at a school board meeting on June 25, 1917. On August 20, 1917, contracts were awarded for the renovation of the Casino Building.

Casino Building Contracts

Johnstown Heating Company Heating	$2,218
E. T. Cooper–Repair roof–arcote it	$325
Moxham Lumber–Lumber for flooring and frames	$1,200
W. J. Rose Lumber–Lumber for interior finish	$187
Furnishing and equipment	$136,000
Thomas Kinzey Lumber Co.–16,800 sq. feet	
Cornell wood boards @ $24.50 per square foot	
Penn Traffic Glass–	$155

The entire interior of the Casino Building was dismantled except for a few rooms that were used for storage. After extensive renovations the building housed a metal work shop, electric workshop, auto repair shop, a concrete and brick laying shop, a house painting and finishing shop, classrooms, and offices. The Building was remodeled and opened as the vocational school. The school served as an annex to Johnstown Central High School (Joseph Johns). Mr. H. J. Stockton was the high school principal, and the first director of vocational education was Mr. Arthur F. Payne. The Casino Building was used as a vocational school until the 1922–1923 school year and demolished for the building of a new Johnstown Central Senior High School.

The Casio Auditorium had served Johnstown as the entertainment center. The center had a capacity of five thousand spectators.

Greater Johnstown High School

Location: Somerset and Napoleon Streets

The site for the Greater Johnstown High School was purchased in three parcels. The first purchase of 1.91 acres was made in 1917 from the Cambria Iron Company for the amount of $1. During the same year, the board of directors purchased two-tenths of an acre from the Jacob Fend Estate for the amount of $3,000. The third purchase of land, in 1920, was for $1 from Mr. Francis J. O'Connor. The third purchase was the composite of these three sites that totaled two and one-half acres to build the high school.

In the first graduating class, 1926 ½, the principal, Mr. James Killius, led 54 high school teachers and 120 students in the graduation march to the Cambria County War Memorial Arena. Priscella Rhodekamel was the valedictorian and Kathryn Huges was Salutatorian. Sara Rhodes was the vice president and John Egan was the class president. This marked the beginning of the annual graduation march with the peak of the graduating class occurring in 1940 with 864 graduating seniors, the largest Johnstown High School graduating class. Even after the building was closed, graduates assembled in the massive Napoleon Street entrance for their graduation march to the nearby War Memorial.

Cambria County War Memorial Arena, *Courtesy of Recci Patrick*

The high school served for educational purposes from 1926–1980. The *Johnstown Tribune* reported, June 17, 1923, that after the board announced the plan to build a school, Mr. E. L. Tilton arrived immediately in Johnstown with preliminary plans for the building. The Chairperson of the Grounds and Building Committee, Mr. George Fockler, called a special meeting to discuss the draft. After several meetings, the board authorized the construction of the new building, with work to begin on October 23, 1924. The supervising architect was Mr. J. E. Adams; the consulting and designing architect was Mr. E. L. Tilton. The board awarded twenty-three contracts to renovate the building for educational purposes. The general contractor was Berkebile Brothers.

Bids for Greater Johnstown High School–1924

Adams and Tilton Architects	$48,855.18
Berkebile Brothers–General contractors	$928,479
Barns and Clark–Plumbing	$54.45
Reese and Bernard–Electrical	$53,788.09
Stanton and Barnhart–Ventilating	$107,228.50

The first floor had six shops that included the machine shop with updated equipment, a print shop, a pressroom, and a composing, binding, press, and cutting areas. Additional rooms on the first floor were two drawing rooms, a wood finishing room, two classrooms, two storerooms, two toilets, washrooms, and two football rooms. The second floor included a room for the administration and/or a separate room for school directors. Rooms were formed by temporary partitions. When necessary, the rooms were converted into classrooms. The third floor had seventeen classrooms, three lavatories, two toilet rooms, two gymnasiums, the director's office, one girls' restroom, and the assistant principal's office. The fourth floor had sixteen classrooms, one drawing room, two applied art rooms, one girls' restroom, and the assistant principal's office. The fifth floor had one music recreation room, one assembly hall, and one dramatic recitation room. There were forty-five classrooms exclusive of laboratories, shops, and all special rooms. All rooms provided ample entrances and exits that met existing federal, state, and local laws, pertaining to public buildings.

The architectural style was Jacobean, a popular style of the seventeenth century. The building was considered a community monument.

The Gothic interior features had the extensive use of natural products such as oak and marble, accented with brass. The cost of the 112-room high school building was $1,328,805. The Greater Johnstown High School, opened in 1926, withstood the two major floods of 1936 and 1977 and was demolished in 1985. In 1971, the high school had a student body of 1,700.

According to G. Fattman, the vocational courses failed to attract many students. In the *Tribune*, July 23, 1963, he stated that the enrollment in city schools had dropped sharply over the last ten years. However, Johnstown High School offered the widest selection of vocational studies of any school in the country. Mr. Albert Rubis, principal of the high school said that most students went right into the job market. However, pressure for students to seek higher education was increasing and the newly built Vocational Technical School in Richland Township was attracting vocational students and some academic students. The Johnstown Schools discontinued evening classes when the Vocational Technical School opened.

Greater Johnstown Vocational Technical School, *Courtesy of Recci Patrick*

Bicentennial Class 1976

Class Officers

Michael Zupan	President
Carl Basoi	Vice President
Francine Ward	Secretary
Valeria Simon	Treasurer

Student Council Officers

Bob Long	President
Nick Klym	Vice President
Mike Allen	Treasurer
Dawn Hewitt	Secretary

Some Organizations

Art Club	Interact Club
Junior Achievement	National Honor Society
Para-Medical Career	Ushers Club
Centralizer Staff	Chess Club
Y-Teens	Library Assistants
Archery Club	Spanish Club
Enrichment Self-Help	French Club
Varsity Cheerleaders	German Club
Boys Pep Club	Trojan Forensic League
Girls Pep Club	Trojan Band
Trojanettes	Ski Club
JHS Orchestra	JHS Mixed Chorus
Student Council	JHS Mixed Chorus
Senior Activities	Jazz Rock Ensemble
Black Senior Club	Stage Band
Science Club	Concert Band
FHA-FBLA	Yearbook Staff
Color Guard	

Bicentennial Sports

According to the *Spectator*, "Artrell Hawkins ended his senior year with 1,499 yards rushing in 209 carries. As the running back, he had a three-season record of 3,552 yards and 234 points. In 1975, he broke a Johnstown High School scoring mark of 106 points, against Altoona. In 1924, Louis Von Lunen had scored 106 points, but Artrell scored 108 points in 18 touchdowns. 'The Hawk' was named a first team all-star in the Foothills Conference as a senior and to the first-team of the WPIAL's class AAA." As a junior and a senior, he was also named to the Associated Press second team (p. 159). The bicentennial year is the first year that the Trojans played in the Foothills Conference of the WPIAL.

In Golf Chuck Lamberson, Chris Cascino, and Greg Adams qualified for district finals. Greg Adams unfortunately missed state qualifications by one stroke.

The boys varsity basketball team played in the district play-offs and were runner-ups to Altoona. Dan Crawley placed third at regional and was voted into the inter-county all-star team.

The girls varsity basketball team captured league title.

Girls Championship Team

Cheryl White	Rosalyn Brandon
Brenda Tate	Heidi Wild
Kathy Andrews	Judy Varchol
Jay Rozich	Kathy Weidlein
Connie Leventry	Cindy Cuppett

1976 Athletic Contests

	Won	Lost
Trojan Football Varsity	6	4
Trojan Football Junior Varsity	4	3
Girls Softball	7	3
Cross Country	9	4
Golf Team	9	3
Jr. Girls Basketball	3	7
Girls Varsity Basketball	15	1
Boys Varsity Basketball	15	10
Girls High School Swim Team	3	11
Wrestlers	6	6

The Trojan Band won six trophies in the Niagara Falls Parade. The girls won the first pom-pom girls, second for rifles, third for color guard, and fourth place for majorettes. In the Miss USA Pageant, the marching block took first place and the color guard took second. The Trojan Band also played for the championship game between Charlestown and Syracuse.

Athletic Awards

Mike Zupan	John Kamnikar Award
	Football, Basketball, Ninth in Class
Artrell Hawkins	New JHS Scoring Record—Football
Missy Hedglin	Girls Track

Other Bicentennial events included the first female, Mary Russo, to complete a course of study in Graphic Arts. Since the print shop opened in 1915, that was a sixty-year accomplishment.

The Quiz Team made semi-finals rounds. Windber High School defeated Johnstown High School at the semi-finals round. The University of Pittsburgh at Johnstown awarded $1,800 in scholarships to Tim Oaks, Jodi Ruke, and Jack Fourst.

Closing of Greater Johnstown High School

The board of directors closed Greater Johnstown High School at the end of the 1979–1980 school term. The philosophy and the promise that echoes from the halls of Greater Johnstown High School live in the more than 32,000 graduates. The Johnstown Marching Band played the Alma Mater, as the majestic building came tumbling down with much difficulty.

With the declining city population after the 1977 flood, the public high school enrollment was affected. The building was demolished for a price higher than the building price. Lee Hospital MRI building occupies the site in 2002. Consequently, Cochran Junior High School became the senior high school.

The 1980 *Spectator* gave tribute to graduates by dedicating the yearbook to all graduates who called Johnstown High School their alma mater.

Excerpts from the 1980 Spectator

All good things must pass, no matter how permanent we once felt they were. And so it's with our high school…this landmark along the Stonycreek River. But although the building will no longer serve as Johnstown High School, we graduates will still have memories and education this school has provided. No one ever can take that away from us.

As the class of 1980 joins with the fifty-four classes proceeding, it is leaving Johnstown High, we must all pledge together to keep alive the spirit we shared in being part of the "Trojan tradition."

1980 Class Officers

President   Dennis McCullough
Vice President   Sandy Vitalie

Secretary   Elaine Jackson
Treasurer   Mike Filia

1980 Student Council Officers
President   Ken Rozich
Vice President   Charles Gutilla
Secretary   Lee Ann Keiper
Treasurer   Cindy Orrie

1979–1980 Sports

The 1979–1980 Trojan Football Team has on record one win and nine losses. The football season's theme was "mud" with the weekly monsoon striking every Friday. The team was known to play "blood and mud" football. The Trojan football teamed scored only 32 points for the season. However, the 1979–1980 boys basketball team achieved a better record for Johnstown High School. They recorded fifteen wins and five losses.

1979–1980 Basketball Team Members
Rich Kris   Jeff Figura
Fred Myers   Ed Hessler
Stacy Hall   Nick Molchan
Dave Pisarchik   Neal Andrews
Mike Jones

The Trojan Sports Events 1979–1980

Event	Wins	Losses
Baseball	4	5
Basketball	15	5
Basketball (Girls)	5	9
Cross Country (Boys)	8	4
Cross Country (Girls)	0	4
Football	1	9
Golf	2	6
Softball (Girls)	11	4
Swimming (Boys)	0	9
Swimming (Girls)	0	8
Tennis (Boys)	4	3
Tennis (Girls)	6	6

Wrestling (Canceled)		
Volleyball	10	3
Track (Boys)	8	3

The boys track team placed favorably in invitation meets in the AAA Division.

1979–1980 Invitational Meets

Meets	Place	Number of Teams
East Allegheny	9	30
Shippensburg	15	35
State College	3	24
West Central Coaches	2	6
District VI Champs	3	10

Outstanding team athletes were Ralph Davis, Harry Shaffer, Mark McCann, and Jeff Dick. They were also members of the State qualifying 3200m relay. Herbert King qualified for the 100m and triple jumps. Ed Dana qualified for the 300m hurdles. Rich Kanuch won the district's pole vault. Kanuch broke the school record in the pole vault.

Trojanettes-Majorettes won first place recognition at the Altoona Majorette Spectacular at the War Memorial Majorette Contest. The John Kamnikar Award was presented to Michele Troutman. Troutman was the Senior Varsity Letter Winner with the highest class standing. She was also the first African-American in the history of the Johnstown Schools to graduate as class valedictorian.

Closing Excerpts—1980 Edition of the Spectator
The Spectator preserves the memories
Of all our high school friends,
And the many times we shared;
Times we wished would never end.
So when we've turned old and gray.
And silently rock away old age,
We'll still have these precious memories,
Preserved on each yearbook page.

—Lynn Johnson

Memorial Hospital

Location: Franklin Street

Memorial Hospital, located on Franklin Street, provided space to the Johnstown Schools to educate crippled children in 1927. Many students spent much volunteer time at the hospital.

Conemaugh Memorial Hospital, *Courtesy of Recci Patrick*

Twentieth Ward Vocational School

Location: Decker Street

Twentieth Ward Vocational School was built on Decker Avenue in 1919. The name was changed to Garfield Vocational School for the 1924–1925 and 1929–1930 school years.

Garfield Junior High School

Location: Garfield Street

Garfield Junior High School new building was built on Garfield Street in 1914. The old Garfield School Building was sold to Mr. H. F. Robertson for $500 at an auction, February 10, 1915. A coal shed located on the property was sold separately to Mr. W. D. Wire for $4. At the school board meeting, July 16, 1917, the director of vocational education advised the board that more room was needed at the Garfield

Junior High School. Subsequently, on December 1, 1917, the Grounds and Building Committee was instructed to lease the Robertson Store Room located at 194 Fairfield Avenue for three years, with an option of leasing it for two more years. The annual rent was $500 per year, with water and heat provided by the landlord. This arrangement was honored until 1920. On February 16, 1926, construction began on the new building on Decker Avenue and was completed on November 15, 1927. Dedication of the building took place on November 28, 1927.

Contractors for Garfield Junior High School

General Contractor: R. R. Kitchen, Inc.	$642,871.69
Heating and Ventilating: Stanton Barnhart	87,545
Electrical: Reese and Bernard	33,782.86
Plumbing: Cambria Plumbing and Heating Company	39,037.90
Architect: J. E. Adams	31,946.30

Furnishings and equipment for the school amounted to a total of $45,856.62. The building was 404 feet long and 116 feet deep. The first floor, east side, contained the boys' gym with shower and locker rooms, athletic field rooms, and a director's office. The annex had two shops, a lumber storeroom and a heating room. The main building had a principal's office, six shops, two mechanical drawing rooms, a cafeteria, a balcony over the boys' gym and an auditorium with a seating capacity of 1,200. The second floor had twelve classrooms, matron's room, library, girls' gym, a domestic science room, and a balcony over the auditorium. The annex of the second floor had a conservatory. The third floor had twelve classrooms, a supply room, sewing rooms, home economics apartments, a balcony over the girls' gym, and a balcony over the auditorium. The fourth floor had twelve classrooms. Each floor had restrooms for boys and girls.

At Garfield Junior High School, female students worked in the cafeteria. They cooked the food and served it. Under the supervision of a teacher, the female students served about 600 persons a month. On one occasion it was reported that students prepared a meal for workers of Cambria Wire. On the afternoon of special cooking lessons, the girls were excused to go home and prepare the family meal from their in-class lesson. The following morning, the girls would bring in a loaf of bread or other specimens to display their skills.

Garfield Students–1934, *Courtesy of Hoss's Family Steak and Sea House*

At a special meeting, June 29, 1972, the board took action to renovate Garfield Junior High School. Contracts were awarded to firms within fifty miles of the city.

Contracts for the Renovation of Garfield Junior High School

General Contractor: Gamble and Gamble Construction Company	$1,757,500
Heating Contractor: John Hall–Ligonier	$662,000
Plumbing Contractor: Inland Company	$236,404
Electrical Contractor: Church and Murdock	$511,200

Garfield Junior High School, *Courtesy of Judy Browne Photography*

The general contract included water blasting of all existing exterior masonry and wood flooring in the gym. When renovations were completed, the school contained a new cafeteria, two locker rooms, a weight room on the first floor, and a new gym. A newly renovated library and five additional classrooms were on the first floor. On the third floor there were nine additional classrooms. Some rooms in the older section of the building were also remodeled. After the renovations were completed, board action renamed the school Garfield Middle School. In 2002, the school houses sixth through eighth graders and three preschool classrooms.

Secondary High Schools

School	Location	Building	Abandon/Closed
First High School	Franklin & Canal (Washington Street)	1868	1875
Johnstown High (Joseph Johns)	Market Street	1899 1926	1970
Cochran Jr. (Greater Johnstown)	Central Avenue	1917 1980	
Johnstown Central Sr. High	Somerset Street	1924	1980
Garfield Jr.	Garfield Street	1914	1992

Special Education

Chapter VII

Mentally Challenged

School districts began to establish their first special education classes for mentally challenged children at the end of the nineteenth century. In 1846, the first known class for mentally challenged children in the public schools was started in Providence, Rhode Island. In 1898, the same type of school was started in Springfield, Massachusetts. In the fall of 1900, a public school class for fifteen students for the mentally retarded was organized in Chicago, Illinois. The interest in developing classes for the mentally challenged grew rapidly. In 1911, 222 cities reported the development of special classes for mentally challenged children. By 1914, the number of students had increased to three hundred classes.

Opportunity Rooms

In 1913, the Johnstown School District was third in the commonwealth to establish special education classes, classified as Opportunity Rooms. In 1917, the school district had eight Opportunity Rooms for extending special teaching to mentally slow or unduly retarded students. The class size was limited to eighteen students. (See Learning Disability.) The rationale was to remove these students from regular classrooms, so extra time could be spent with them to provide a better education. Superintendent Adee thought that the mentally challenged students could make faster progress in the Opportunity Rooms. Some Opportunity Room teachers thought that part of the academic problem was hunger; learning was impeded because their students were not eating properly. Consequently, some teachers bought food for their students and were able to influence administrators that a food program was needed because some students needed extra nutrition. It was estimated that $500 would cover the cost of food for 186 students for nine months.

In a school report of 1922–1925, administrators made a distinction between backward children and subnormal children. The report stated that backward children were considered retarded and needed application of a different education process. Backward students in any class should be handled by individual teaching. Subnormal children were considered eligible for the Opportunity Rooms. For Opportunity Room placement, students were administered the Simon-Binet or another intelligence test. With psychological testing, all regular classrooms were freed of backward students. Students in the Opportunity Room were then challenged to their highest academic level. The administration established special opportunity centers for subnormal students.

Opportunity Schools 1922–1925

Moxham District	Park Avenue Building
Horner District	Meadowvale Building
Central District	Hudson Street Building
Cambria District	Benshoff Building
Morrell District	Bheam Building

The board later established an Opportunity School for the Cambria District in the Chestnut Street School. The Benshoff School was also used for backward students. The board of directors and Superintendent Slawson recognized and accommodated a small group of students who needed special attention, who were unable to function in the average classroom due to low mental ability. Teachers assigned to these centers provided opportunity work for children placed in Opportunity Rooms. In 1922, five teachers were assigned to Opportunity Rooms. Twelve students per class were placed in these Opportunity Rooms by virtue of work in their classes and their age. The curriculum was designed to meet individual student needs in academic and handwork areas. The reported results were that opportunity students were gainfully employed after their schooling. Some students worked in steel mills or became streetcar conductors, clerks in stores, or truck drivers. Most of these students developed consciousness of their peers, with a better social attitude and more self-respect.

Providing food for students in school began in the Opportunity Program. A teacher discovered that students worked better if they were fed during the day. Some children reported that they had a cup of coffee and bread for breakfast. Nurses indicated that they often went out and bought a loaf of bread and milk after a visit to homes. Six Opportunity Rooms with eighteen students per room were served. Five hundred dollars were allocated for nine months to cover the cost. The per capita cost was two and one-half cents a day per student.

In 1955, the Pennsylvania Department of Education mandated programs and classes in special education. The legislature made provision to give special financial aid to special classes for the education of the physically or mentally challenged children of the commonwealth. The commonwealth paid three-fourths of the salary of all approved special education teachers for all special education classes. The Johnstown School Board did not rate supervisors and special teachers on any established salary schedule.

Student Mental Ability, 1966–1967

I. Q. Range	11th Grade	12th Grade	Number	Percent
121–140	93	94	187	12.2
111–120	163	200	363	23.7
91–110	413	421	834	54.5
81–90	80	59	139	9.1
71–80	4	3	7	.5
Total	753	777	1530	100

The Mental ability chart is an indication of students who might be identified for special programs. Although secondary gifted classes were not established in the Johnstown Schools until 1979, data of this nature were perused to have a base for establishing classes for Special Education students. Greater Johnstown High School housed eleventh- and twelfth-grade students.

Special Education (1973–1978)

Secondary Educable Mentally Retarded Classes

Year	Garfield	Cochran	JHS	Totals
1973–74	38	44	92	174
1974–75	35	41	91	167
1975–76	30	35	90	155
1976–77	30	30	71	131
1977–78	30	30	65	125

In the 1970s, enrollment in special education classes declined in secondary schools. The number of 174 students in 1973, dropped to 125 in 1977. However, in 2002, the special education student enrollment has more than doubled. The increase in the number of special education students identified may have accelerated with the commonwealth's increased allocation. The Pennsylvania public schools serve more than 1.8 million students. More than 220,000 students ranging from the ages of three to twenty-one have some disabilities. Mentally challenged students, with 80,000 additional students classified as gifted, comprise the special education population. Special education students are almost one-third of the students enrolled in the public schools in the commonwealth. For the 1992–1993 budget, Governor Robert P. Casey proposed an increase of $35.6 million or 7% to $544 million (Pennsylvania Education, 1992, Vol. 23).

At one time, school staff attempted to make decisions and to plan a student's academic program. However, special education programs began to include parents in the decision making. A team of educators selects special education students, with parental approval for eligibility in special classes. The team makes a two-part decision. One criterion is that the student has one or more of the eleven disabilities defined by the commonwealth. The other criterion states that the student must test mentally gifted. Therefore, criteria are based on both ends of the academic spectrum. After the test for special education, the team must also determine that a particular student needs special education. Special education for students with disabilities was designed with frequent and intense strategies, adaptation to the classroom environment, and reasonable accommodations. Special education for gifted students included some of the same criteria, but also acceleration and enrichment programs.

Special Education Eligibility

Mentally Retarded	Speech Impaired
Deaf and Hearing Impaired	Blind and Visually Impaired
Severely Emotionally Disturbed	Physically Disabled
Other Health Impaired	Specific Learning Disability
Traumatic Brain Injured	Developmentally Delayed
Autism and Pervasive Development	Gifted

Dr. Levi Hollis introduced secondary gifted programs in the schools in 1979. In a memorandum, May 9, 1979, to district personnel, he said, "It is the district's tentative plan to have the Secondary Gifted Program instituted at Cochran, Garfield, and Johnstown High, in the fall of 1979." According to his files, state guidelines were reviewed in September 1978 and IU-08 support service was set up in November.

Gifted Program Model

Student Identification

1. Students recommended for individual testing based on group I.Q. scores
2. To qualify, students need to attain an I.Q. of 130 or above
3. Due process must be followed; i.e., parental permission needed

Class Program

1. Subjects: English, Math, Science, and Social Studies (Depending on the needs and number of students identified)
2. Classes may be nongraded
3. Inclusion of grades six through ten
4. Instruction to be horizontal, open-ended, academic and creative
5. Program curricula to be designed by teachers assigned to gifted education

Staff In-Service Content

1. I.E.P. writing
2. Characteristics of the gifted
3. Special learning needs of the gifted
4. Other data germane to teaching the gifted

Special Education Services are the responsibility of the Pennsylvania Department of Education (PDE). PDE ensured all students with disabilities, residing in the commonwealth, including students attending private schools, regardless of the severity of their disabilities, special education, and related services. The federal law called the Individuals with Disabilities Education Act Amendments of 1997 (IDEA) covered this responsibility.

Secondary Special Education Enrollment Data, March 2000

	Regular	Special Education	Students
High School	747	156	903
Middle School	660	154	814
Homebound	25	2	27
Home Education	15	1	16
Total Secondary	1379	312	1691
Elementary			
East Side	650	86	736
West Side	900	180	1080
Homebound	1	6	7
Home Education	8	1	9
Total Elementary	1604	272	1876
Grand Total (Does not include Home Education)			*3567*

Parents have the opportunity to voice an evaluation of their own child. If they think that their child should be considered for exceptional programs, they may request a multidisciplinary evaluation of their child's skills at any time. The Individualized Education (IEP) Program team makes the determination of whether a student is exceptional. The IEP team includes one regular education teacher, one special education teacher and a representative of the school district. The evaluation is based on the multidisciplinary evaluation.

Rosedale Borough School District 1901–1948

Chapter VIII ❖

An Ethnic Community

Rosedale Borough was located near the northern boundary of Johnstown, in West Taylor Township. The Borough was named after Allen Rose. The July 14, 1886, edition of the *Tribune* stated that lots in Rosedale were laid out and sold by Cambria Iron Company and Benjamin Benshoff. This borough was removed from West Taylor and became a township, by a court decree on December 17, 1894. Rosedale was classified in the 1911–1912 Johnstown Directory as a suburb of Johnstown. Many of the African-Americans who migrated from the South to labor for the Cambria Iron Company settled in Rosedale Borough. The custom was to settle in ethnic communities, most likely an extended family area, close to work. Mr. John "Jack" Johnson recruited African-American laborers from the South for Cambria Iron. The Com-

Cambria Iron Company, *Courtesy Johnstown Area Heritage Association*

123

pany provided housing for incoming African-Americans in Rosedale and Conemaugh (Johnson and duPont, 1985, p. 547).

Mine Number 72 handled the coking operation of the company in Rosedale. In 1919, the Rosedale Coke Plant was erected. With additional batteries operable by 1922, the annual production of coke totaled 1.6 million tons. The coal in the region was high in ash and sulphur content; therefore, some impurities were removed. The process for removal included crushing the coal and transporting it to washeries for cleansing. The Rosedale site was one of the two washery plants. Rosedale had 24 tables with a combined capacity of washing 350 net tons per hour. Coal washed at Rosedale was used at that coke plant or shipped outside of the borough to other Bethlehem plants (Cooper, 1985, pp. 342–344). In 1923, Bethlehem Steel Corporation purchased the Cambria Iron and Steel Company (Burkert, 2000, p.17).

According to Ms. Claudia Jones, an African-American historian, the first residents of Rosedale were European immigrants, who migrated to Johnstown for the opportunity to work in the steel mills. As they became Americanized and other opportunities became available, the Europeans moved from Rosedale to other sections of Johnstown. They could not tolerate the tremendous heat and dangerous working environmental conditions of the coke plant. The available housing was company improvised buildings. To supply a labor force for the mills, Cambria administrators thought it would be prudent to recruit African-Americans from the South, because they thought that African-Americans would be habituated to the heat. Their rationale was that the South had extremely hot climatic temperatures, conducive to the environment of the coke plant. However, African-Americans did not have the same mobility to acquire some wealth and a better house as their white counterparts. Until fair housing laws, African-Americans were not mobile, regardless of income or education.

The first significant migration of African-Americans came before World War I, and most settled in the ethnic community of Rosedale. Ironically, World War I was the war to make the world safe for democracy (Riggenback, 1984, p. 344). As a suburb of Johnstown, Rosedale and Johnstown Boroughs were different school districts with separate administrations. Records from Rosedale Borough do not indicate the date of construction of the Rosedale School building, located on Hinckston Road. However, the Rosedale School Board minutes of June

29, 1901, documented the appointment of Mr. B. W. Gambing as teacher for the upper room and Miss Flora Gibson as teacher for the lower room. The same minutes reported that the school should open on the first Monday in September. A committee was also appointed at that time to provide a coalhouse and kindling apartment building. The board directed the closing of the cellars and for the necessary repairs to be made on the building. Appointed to the building committee were Mr. T. J. Benshoff, Mr. B. F. Burkhart, and Mr. J. M. Peer. The grounds committee was composed of Mr. Edward Mackell, Mr. Ephraim Shaffer, and Mr. Hirem Kocher. The committees were to oversee the recommended renovations so that the schoolyard and schoolhouse would be ready for students. At the August 31, 1901, meeting, textbooks were adopted for the 1901–1902 school term.

At the October 12, 1901, meeting, the board received a report from Cambria Steel Company listing children less than sixteen years of age, whom they had employed. If the children passed an examination in reading and writing, they were permitted to continue to work for the company. However, if they did not successfully pass the examination administered by the Steel Company, they were provided another opportunity. On the second testing, parents or children had an option to have the test administered by the school's board of directors.

Learning Disability

At the same meeting, on October 12, 1901, a mother of one of the students, asked for her son to be exonerated from attending school. (See Special Education.) She argued that her son had attended school since he became six years old and had not been able to retain what he had been taught. She had supplemented the teachers' classroom instructions with additional instructions at home. The mother appealed to the board to exonerate her son from school because he was mentally challenged. The board honored the request. This is the first documentation of learning disability in the Johnstown schools.

Other Excused Absentees

The board also excused other students of age sixteen or over from attendance based on their home situation. Other parental concerns honored were the child was needed at home because of illness of a parent, the mother was a widow, or the father was a widower. Of course, schools were quarantined and closed with any scare of a contagious disease.

The board, on October 8, 1902, directed the secretary to write to teachers to inform them that they were expected to resume duties as teachers by Monday, October 13, 1902, because no new cases of small-pox had been reported in the district. The board also ordered School Number One to be closed from September 26 to October 13. The board later ordered School Number Two to be closed from October 21 to October 28, 1902.

At a special meeting on January 24, 1903, the school board directors, again, ordered the closing of schools because of a smallpox epidemic. They voted to close the schools for two weeks or longer, as necessary.

On April 3, 1905, the Rosedale School Board was informed that one Rosedale school building was not safe; therefore, students could not attend classes in that building. The school board solicitor advised the board to retain a building inspector to inspect the building. The board retained Mr. Emmet Lucas, a "most competent" building inspec-tor. On April 19, 1905, Mr. Lucas condemned the building as not safe to be used as a school. At the same meeting, the board voted to adver-tise for bids to erect a new building. The plans called for a two-room schoolhouse to be heated by hot water heat.

1905 Bids for Rosedale Schoolhouse

A. L. Lape	$2,152.75
Lincoln Overdorff	$2,460
Thomas Keenan	$2,327

After consideration of the difficulties and expense of hot water heat, the Rosedale School Board of Directors rejected all bids and decided that the building should be heated by hot air. On May 24, 1905, the board awarded a contract to Mr. Thomas Keenan to construct a two-room schoolhouse, to be heated by hot air, at a cost of $2,110. On May 29, 1905, the Rosedale Board approved the signing of the contract and the school was to be completed before August 15, 1905. The board, June 1, 1905, authorized Mr. Ben Benshoff, a member of the board, to store the furniture and fixtures in the Grist Mill Building for $10.

On August 19, 1905, the board adopted the calendar for the 1905–1906 school year, commencing on September 11, 1905, and continuing for seven months. They voted on August 21, 1905, to borrow $1,800 from the National Bank of Johnstown, for construction of the new school building. On June 3, 1907, the Rosedale School Board approved the auditors' report.

Auditors' Report for Rosedale

Balance in treasurer from last settlement	$310.32
Balance on Duplicate	$72.92
State appropriation	$326.63
School Furniture sold	$3.50
Face value of duplicate (1907)	$873.15
Total	$1,586.52

Expenditures

Teacher Salaries	$636
Janitor	70
Supplies	151.37
Note interest	285
Miscellaneous	11.25
Exoneration	23.94
Coal and kindling	30
Secretary fees	25
Collectors' fees	31.98
Treasurer	24.29
Auditors	6
Total	$1294.83
Balance on duplicate	$291.60
	$73.36
Cash balance in treasury	$218.33

On October 15, 1908, the board voted to direct the teacher of Room Number One to resign her position, because she was unable to control the behavior of students in her class. The teacher refused to resign; the school board "ejected" her from the classroom.

Rosedale Segregated School

Data indicated that students in the borough, both white and black attended the Rosedale School until 1917. According to the Rosedale School Board minutes, the Rosedale School became segregated on August 13, 1917. The Rosedale School Board authorized Mr. Bentz, the county superintendent, to retain two "colored" teachers, a male and a female. At the same meeting, the Rosedale Board directed the secretary to contact the Johnstown School Board to make provisions for white students of the Rosedale School District. On December 17, 1917, the Rosedale School Board signed a contract with Mr. T. W. Thomas to transport, daily, ten white children to and from the Johnstown City Schools for the remainder of the term. Mr. Thomas' salary was $40 a month. The joint action of the Rosedale School Board and the Johnstown School Board is the first record of students in Johnstown being transported out of their neighborhoods to public schools. Since the Johnstown Traction Company provided public transportation in the early 1900s, the authors assumed that Mr. Thomas transported the white students by horse and buggy (Coleman, 1985, pp. 439–440).

The president of the Rosedale School District called a special meeting on February 8, 1918, to review a letter from the Cambria Steel Company. Relative to the aforementioned correspondence, the school board accepted an offer of $3,500 from the Steel Company for property located on Hinckston Avenue. On March 13, 1918, the school board received a report from the health commissioners about the unsanitary conditions of the property at the rear of the school. The school board referred the matter to the new owners, the Cambria Steel Company. Later in 1918, Rosedale Schools became a part of the Johnstown School District.

The 1918–1919 Johnstown Public School Directory listed for the first time Rosedale School (Colored). Mr. W. E. Cephas was listed as the principal. Mr. Cephas taught 5B with two students, grade 4A with nine students, and 4B with sixteen students. Miss Retta V. Norman was listed as the teacher for grade 2B with two students, grade 1A with six students, and grade 1B with sixteen students. On September 15, 1919, the Johnstown School Board authorized the superintendent of schools and the secretary of the board to arrange for an ungraded school for Rosedale. With the small number of students, a graded school system was a mockery. The Rosedale School Board's minutes of October 20,

1919, stated that the Cambria Steel Company offered the Mexican Hall in Rosedale as a school for white students. The 1919–1920 Johnstown School Directory lists Ralph Duwell as teacher of classes 1A, 1B, 2B, 2A, 3B, 3A, 4B, 4A, and 5A, for white students. Mr. Ernest E. Swanston and Ms. Retta V. Norman taught the 4A, 5A, 6B, and 6A colored students.

Rosedale School, *Courtesy of Reverend James Jarvis*

The 1919–1920 Johnstown Public Schools' Directory listed two schools at Rosedale, one for "colored." The board of directors appointed Mr. Ernest E. Swanston, a graduate of Howard University, as the principal of the "Colored" school (Johnson and duPont, 1985, p. 553). At first, Mr. Swanston commuted to Johnstown from Carlisle, Pennsylvania. According to Cora Jarvis-Redden, Mr. Swanston, became a boarder in her grandparents' home, Richard and Cora Jones, who lived in Rosedale. Mr. Jack Johnson had recruited Mr. Jones from Eufala, Alabama. Mr. Jones, a Tuskegee Institute graduate, had moved north to work in Rosedale's coke plant.

Mr. Swanston married the granddaughter of the pastor of Shiloh Baptist Church, Roberta Calloway, and moved to nearby Tanneryville. Mr. and Mrs. Swanston opened their home and yard to accommodate many social, academic, and religious events. Many public recreational places were not opened to African-Americans in the 1920s. Mr. Swanston was a skilled pianist. He gave piano lessons to his public school students in the church. The Rosedale School and the two African-American churches worked closely together to educate children in Rosedale.

The other "Colored" teacher, Miss Norman was listed as the grade 6A teacher. She traveled from Washington, D.C. The Report of the Teachers' Committee, September 21, 1921, item number eleven, states "[t]hat Miss Virginia Riley, teacher of the Rosedale "white" School, receive [sic] $10 additional to her regular salary, for the time taught each month at this school." Therefore, the teacher of white students, Miss Riley, in the Rosedale Schools received a salary of $10 more per month and $90 more per year than Miss Norman, teacher for the black students. The separate but unequal education was not challenged. Equal Opportunity in education was established in 1954 by the decision of Brown versus the Board of Education of Topeka, Kansas, based on the Fourteenth Amendment that guarantees equal protection under the law (L. P. Hollis, 1998, pp. 2–3).

In 1937, Mrs. Blanche Johnson was unable to secure a teaching position, because "Johnstown already had one colored teacher." She worked, unofficially, as a substitute teacher at Rosedale School. The board of directors did not pay her, but Mr. Swanston paid her wages (Redden, 1988, p. 312). The congregation of Shiloh Baptist Church that was located in Rosedale appointed her husband, Reverend Leroy Johnson, as the pastor. Mrs. Johnson used her skills within her church to move her culture forward.

Field Trials

Field Trials were a popular sport in Rosedale. The Fourteenth Ward Hunting Club held their Second Annual Field Trials in 1938. Men and boys of the area gathered on the Rosedale schoolyard for the event. The chief master filled large burlap sacks with "something." This "something" could be a cat, a chicken, or a wild animal. He would dip the filled sacks into the nearby creek. Men and boys, dressed in business suits, hats, and ties, would line up with their dogs to sniff one of the sacks. People also came as spectators. The Chief Master would have dragged another filled wet sack with the same contents around the schoolyard, through the woods, and up and down the nearby hills. Dogs were released to trace the scent and to retrieve the other sack (Crawley-Grigsby, 31 January 2002). Rosedale students were assigned a creative writing class assignment of the spectacular event.

Fourteen Ward Hunting Club, *Courtesy of Jessie Crawley-Grigsby*

Shiloh Baptist Church

The Rosedale section of Johnstown became comprised mostly of African-American residents; gerrymandering in ethnic, cultural communities was an established practice. In June 1917, the large population of African-Americans from Alabama organized Shiloh Baptist Church in a storefront in the lower part of Rosedale. The organizers were Mrs. Minnie Chambers, Mrs. James Livingston, and Mr. and Mrs. Ed Shipman. The congregation was moved to Chestnut Street in 1946. In 1966, the congregation broke ground for its present day church on Menoher Boulevard (*Tribune*, 15 February 1997). Note that Shiloh Church's organization and development in Rosedale Borough paralleled the segregated school system from 1917 to 1947. Consequently, the church provided African-American students with the opportunity to express themselves on the church's junior boards, in the choir, and special events. The church also provided leadership and musical opportunities for African-American students that was lacking in a segregated school system.

Bethel A.M.E. Church

Bethel A.M.E. Church also had its beginning in Rosedale Borough, under the pastoral of Reverend Joseph H. Flagg, in 1917 (Church History, 1998, King). The first meeting of the congregation was held in Reverend Flagg's home located in Rosedale Borough. For a year, the members of the church met in the Cambria Iron and Steel Building, Mine Number 72, in Rosedale. In the 1940s, Reverend James Jarvis was instrumental in moving the congregation forward. He was a good friend of the principal of Rosedale School, Mr. Swanston, and was very active working with students to break racial barriers. When Reverend Jarvis was assigned to Bethel A.M.E. Church in Tarentum, Pennsylvania, he continued his crusade for racial equality. He befriended and later performed the wedding ceremony for the late Dr. Levi B. Hollis, Jr., who lived in the area.

Rosedale Incident

The separate school structure of the 1920s supported other incidents of disparaged treatment. In 2002, African-Americans are still talking with contempt about their parents and grandparents who suffered public humility in 1923. According to the *Survey of The Negro Population of Metropolitan Johnstown Pennsylvania* (1941), published by the *Johnstown Tribune-Democrat* in the fall of 1923, a Negro (African-American) wanted by the police shot and killed two detectives. Oral history reveals that the shooting was caused by a domestic dispute. Notwithstanding the details, a white man was killed in the subsequent action of a riot. After the incident, Mayor Joseph Cauffiel of Johnstown issued two directives. His first directive was addressed to African-Americans to leave the city if they had not been residents for five or more years. The second directive was addressed to police officers to search the homes of every African-American in Johnstown for weapons and anything that could be used as such. The police seized guns, kitchen knives, and hammers from African-Americans' homes. Lacking money and being frightened, some African-American families left Johnstown without destinations. The NAACP and leading citizens asked Pennsylvania's Governor Pinchot to settle the dispute. According to Johnson and duPont, the Ku Klux Klan had been active in the area against blacks, Catholics, and Jews. Nonetheless, James Weldom Johnson, executive secretary of the NAACP (National Association for the Advancement of Colored People) appealed to Governor Pinchot to conduct an investigation. From the findings of a full investigation, the Governor censured Mayor Cauffiel and directed him to "observe the law" (Johnson & duPont, 1985, pp. 555–556). As this incident is retold through generations, the NAACP has remained a watchdog over the city government, the police department, and the school district.

Prejudiced treatment from elected city officials and the police department, coupled with the segregated Rosedale Schools, left untold, lingering misery and suffering in the African-American community. Many African-Americans remained withdrawn and sensitive to the needs of their own group and their own communities. Some were also suspicious of newcomers and the greater community. Needless to say, after the community's publicized racial incident, African-Americans continued to attend separate schools in Rosedale.

Unemployed Relief Class

The superintendent of the Johnstown Schools reported to the school board on January 8, 1934, that he had started another unemployed relief class in the Rosedale School District under a "fine young lady," Miss Ruth Walton, a "colored" girl. Superintendent McMaster said that certain funds of the Emergency Educational Relief Program could be used for teaching supplies in the classroom for emergency education. Another unemployed relief class placed in the segregated Rosedale school indicated that deprivation of students and neighborhoods was based on ethnicity. Nonetheless, the Rosedale School remained the smallest of the Johnstown Schools. During the 1939 school term, only twenty-seven "colored" students were enrolled.

Rosedale Incorporated

The 1947–1948 Johnstown Public School Directory listed Mr. E. E. Swanston as Principal of the Rosedale School. However, the 1948–1949 directory listed Mr. Swanston as a teacher at Chestnut Street School. According to one of his former students, Ms. Joyce Johnson ('59), he was also assigned to home-bound instruction. Mr. Swanston's name does not appear in the 1954–1955 directory. Prior to 1948, the Johnstown Public School Directory listed two school districts, one for "colored"; however, the "colored" school is not listed in the 1948 directory. Since the principal of Rosedale School is listed as a teacher in the 1948 school directory, the authors assumed that Mr. Swanston was the first black or African-American teacher in the Greater Johnstown School District. He taught first through sixth grades. All schools and classrooms were relatively small in the early 1900s. Combining the "colored" school and the white school was an economical move toward providing a better education for all students.

Mrs. Blanche Anderson Johnson, an African-American, pursued a teaching position in the Johnstown School for eighteen years. About 1955, she became the first teacher for the trainable mentally retarded children in Pennsylvania (Johnson, 1988, p.312).

The village of Rosedale simply disappeared. The village was developed with row houses, just rental shacks constructed for the laborers in the coke plant. The 1936 flood did not cause significant damage to the settlement, with the Hinkston Run Dam. However, when the steel mill needed the land for other enterprises such as coal stockpiles, the people were asked to relocate. Since the village had not really developed with substantial houses surrounding the area and places of business, it was returned to a valley of nature among the hills. Unlike the borough of Westmont, where the Cambria Steel Company built substantial homes for top and middle management, laborers, and supervisors, Rosedale did not have a foundation to continue as a community.

Late 1800s Census

The census of the black population or any other minority group was not tabulated until 1860. In the 1860s with a population of 4,155, the African-American population was 54, which totals 1.3 % of the total population. However, in the 1900s, the head count was 314 African-Americans (colored), which tabulates to .9 % of the Johnstown population of 35,963. Although the population grew to 55,000 white in 1910, with 442 African-Americans, the percentage dropped to .8. In 1920, the population grew to 67,327 with 1,671 African-Americans, for an increase of 2.5 %.

When local people retell an event for seventy-five plus years, the event becomes legendary folklore. However, newspaper reports document the facts of the incident. Consequently, the 1923 legendary event of "blacks run out of town," and the sting of separate public schools may have some impact on the lack of influx of African-Americans to the city of Johnstown. Underrepresented groups remained small, even when the various coal mines and steel mills in the area were at high production. During World War I, Cambria Steel had 18,000 employees (Burkert, 2000, p. 17). Notwithstanding the city's folklore, the largest minority group in Johnstown has continued to be African-American. The census from 1850 to 1890 supports the aforementioned analogy.

Johnstown Population from 1850–1890

Year	Total	White	Black
1840	1269	1244	26
1860	4185	4131	54
1870	6028	5991	37
1880	8380	8269	111
1890	21805	21538	259

The population distribution, before the Rosedale incident, shows that the black community was a compressed and suppressed growing population. The community climate may have triggered the incident.

The 1922 school directory listed Rosedale as a Johnstown School.

Principals in the Johnstown Public Schools, 1922
(According to the 1922 Johnstown City Directory)

School	Principal
Johnstown High School	J. D. Ripple
Adams School	Katherine Baumer
Andrew Jackson	Sara McGough
Benshoff	Mary Carmiddy
Bheam	H.C. Bohn
Chestnut Street	Anna McGlade
Cochran Junior High	Dale McMaster
Cooperdale	Elizabeth Crocker
Cover Hill	Clyde M. Reynolds
Cypress Avenue	A. C. Ober
Dibert	Nellie S. Jennings
Garfield Junior High	G. B. Murdoch
Horner	Martha Hoffman
Hudson	E. A. Korb

School	Principal
Johnstown Vocational	James Killius (Director)
Meadowvale	L. G. Shaffer
Morrell	W. F. Grumizer
Oakhurst	R. M. Palmer
Osborne	Martha M. Graham
Park Avenue	Edith Ferner
Peelor	B. J. Bowers
Rosedale	Ernest E. Swanston
Roxbury	W. W. Heck
Somerset Street	Clara S. Menges
Union Street	H. W. Weller
Village Street	I. G. Lambert
Walnut Grove	J. E. Long
Washington	B. J. Bowers
Woodvale	Kathryn Carthew

In 1922, Johnstown School District operated 29 public schools.

Johnstown's Three Schools Systems of the 1920s

In 1890, the population of the city of Johnstown was 21,805, with the Greater Johnstown's population totaling 30,307. The city continued to grow with a population of 66,993 in 1930, and a greater Johnstown population of 94,223. Migration for the bountiful industries and consolidation of the smaller boroughs with Johnstown can be credited for the population explosion. During this period of time, immigration from Russia, Austria, and Hungary increased to 22% of the population, reaching approximately 12,000. Industry also attracted families from the South.

Johnstown became a stable community late in the 1920s, with the population remaining in the 60,000 range. The children of the community were educated in three school systems in the city of Johnstown, that is, the Johnstown City Schools; subscription or parochial schools; and Rosedale, the "colored" school. Johnstown separate school districts were justified with statements that African-Americans wanted their separate schools. The authors argued that a group of people in their infant stage of development was not in a position to make decisions about what they needed or wanted. The newly arrived Southern residents to Rosedale experienced different types of jobs, new people within and without their culture, and severe climatic changes. They probably trusted the establishment to provide proper education. Data show that schools throughout the county were neighborhood schools, with all students attending. Before fair housing laws, housing was not a matter of choice; it was a matter of restriction. Some ethnic groups could not live or own property outside of their designated areas.

In Rosedale, white students were transported to schools in Johnstown from 1917 through 1947. When white students attended the Rosedale School, school board minutes show that the teacher who taught white students was paid more. The larger salary was an indicator that more work was demanded and expected of the teacher and the students. Although, the teacher may not have been more qualified, it is also an indicator that the school board valued her credentials more than those of the teacher of the African-American students. The community recruited African-American workers for their needs and exploited their children by providing inadequate education, with separate and unequal schools, for thirty years, almost two generations. The Americanization paradigm was forsaken.

Superintendents Propelling the School District

Chapter IX ❖

The board of directors appointed superintendents as the chief executive officers (CEOs) to propel the schools to conform to the regulations of the commonwealth and federal laws pertaining to education. Superintendents are trained, academic leaders who lead the school district and the community to upward mobility through education. A community is only as good as its schools, and the superintendents appointed by the board.

Superintendents of the Greater Johnstown School District, 1890–2001

1.	T. B. Johnson	1890–1896
2.	J. M. Berkey	1896–1906
3.	J. N. Muir	1906–1911
4.	J. N. Adee	1911–1918
5.	H. J. Stockton	1918 ½–1922
6.	J. W. Slawson	1922 ½–1929
7.	J. Killius	1929 ½–1933 ½
8.	D. D. McMaster	1934–1940
9.	J. E. Wagner	1940–1946
10.	R. W. Wiley	1946–1953
11.	W. C. Davis	1954–1955
12.	F. M. Miller	1956–1967
13.	M. W. Vonarx	1967–1974

14.	D. B. Zucco	1974–1984
15.	L. B. Hollis	1984–1989
16.	W. M. Grove (Interim)	1989–1990
17.	R. S. DeLuca	1990–1993
18.	J. D. Merryman	1993–1997
19.	G. L. Zahorchak	1997–2002

From 1890 to 2002, the slate of superintendents reveals that the fifteenth superintendent, Dr. Levi B. Hollis, Jr., was the only superintendent from the underrepresented group as defined by EEOC Guidelines. Dr. Hollis, an African-American male, died in 1989, as superintendent of the Greater Johnstown School District. Noteworthy, also, is number eighteen on the slate, Dr. June Merryman, the only female superintendent. In the two-hundred-year history of the Johnstown Schools, only one minority and only one female have been appointed by the board of directors to head the Johnstown Public Schools.

However, each superintendent has advanced the academic culture, as he or she considered the Americanization paradigm to change environmental and cultural climates of the schools and the city. Under Superintendent Berkey's administration, the first class for manual training was taught in the district in 1902.

Under Superintendent Adee's administration, the high school Girls Bible Class was very progressive. In September 1914, the attendance was more than 100. The class made $17 from the sale of White Cross Cards and dressed dolls. The book used for study was *Christina Citizenship for Girls* by Helen Toburn. Mr. Adee is also accredited with publishing the names of students who raised their grades in every subject. In May 1917, thirty-three students for seven terms were honored. The tradition of posting names of students with academic achievement has continued. It motivates students, and parents are especially proud.

The city of Johnstown fell on hard times during the thirties. According to the author of *For Bread With Butter*, 5,000 people left the city for better employment. These were the pre-depression days and income decreased per household. Most families struggled to survive on a $1000 annual income (Morawska, 1985, pp. 209-210). With impoverished daily living, education was not a top priority for the common person. Many incomes were needed within the home for survival. Although the area was weighty with poverty, elected school board directors considered it their duty to accommodate the superintendent of the school district. According to the board minutes of March 12, 1934, Superintendent McMaster was accommodated with a Chevrolet Master 6 Coupe at a cost of $645 with the trade-in of a Chevrolet 4 Roadster.

In Johnstown, as in most cities, there were pockets of affluent people. Consequently, some community leaders felt the need to encourage higher education. According to the school board minutes of November 14, 1930, Mr. Max Schwartz, in his last will and testament, bequeathed $15,000 to Johnstown Central High School to further the education of high school graduates. Extending the educational ladder on both ends became popular, with people investing in higher education and the commonwealth encouraging kindergartens.

Kindergarten

Kindergartens were established in the commonwealth before 1876 as private schools. Interest in early child education caused formulation of public kindergarten associations. In 1897, shortly after the Compulsory School Attendance Law in 1895, the commonwealth permitted the establishment of kindergartens. In 1917, Superintendent Adee announced that kindergarten was an accepted institution and should be provided where facilities prevailed. His rationale was that students were leaving school after the sixth grade and it would be wise for them to gain two additional years of schooling at the kindergarten level. In 1918, Kindergarten Centers were established in Oakhurst and Cambria City. In 1926 the State Department of Public Instruction organized a division of Kindergarten and Elementary Education. In the same year, Superintendent Slawson propelled the establishment of a kindergarten in the Johnstown School District at Cypress School.

In 1931, the Commonwealth of Pennsylvania State Department of Education extinguished previous kindergarten laws. The new law stated: "The Board of School Directors of each school district of the first, second, third, and fourth class may establish and maintain kindergartens for children between the age of four and six years. When established, the kindergarten shall be an integral part of the elementary school system of the district." Once the kindergarten system was established in Johnstown, by law, it became an extension and an integral component of the elementary schools. Therefore, educational aid from the state for public education was extended to kindergarten students and programs in the district. The growth in kindergartens reflected the growing value of the importance of early education.

Vocational Education

According to Superintendent Adee, in a monthly report to the board of directors, he started Vocational Evening School classes in November 1917, with one hundred registered students for nine classes.

1917 Vocational Classes

Miners' Class	Mining Class for Examination
Telegraphy	Elementary Mechanical Drawing
Blueprint Reading	Estimating
Practical Carpentry	Dressmaking
Advanced Sewing	

The Federal Board of Vocational Education in Washington requested an evening class in Radio and Buzzer Operations. The course was conscripted to men to meet the Signal Corps of the United States Army's demand. The Signal Corps wanted 15,000 skilled men trained and able to use radio instruments.

Red Cross Courses

Superintendent Stockton approved the first class in Home Nursing in December 1919. The course was authorized by the Red Cross and furnished by the Red Cross Chapter of Johnstown in the high school building. After the 1889 Flood, home nursing was a course that attracted much interest. Clara Barton had arrived in Johnstown during the disaster and stayed for five months. The elderly, petite woman had given much vitality to interest in the nursing course curriculum. In 2002, the Red Cross does not make a difference between male and female employees. However, the nursing profession continues to attract females. With the September 11, 2001, terrorist attack on the United States, the demands for the services of the Red Cross have increased.

The Red Cross' interest in the Johnstown Schools has been constant. To help meet the demands of the need for blood, the Red Cross partnered with the NAACP to identify students to train in phlebotomy.

The Red Cross provided two annual scholarships for graduates of Johnstown High School to study phlebotomy at the Cambria County Community College. The Education Committee, under the chairperson of Ms. Claudia Jones, screened the applications.

In the fall of 2001, the Red Cross and the NAACP announced their partnership. Ms. Tara Johnson was the first recipient of the scholarship. She successfully completed the course and accepted full-time employment as a phlebotomist with Red Cross.

Red Cross and NAACP Partnership for the Johnstown High School Students

Tom Angle, Red Cross' CEO and Clea Hollis, President of the Johnstown Branch of the NAACP have announced their partnership to establish a Diversity Scholarship Program. The Program will encourage community interest in a career in Phlebotomy and will also increase the number of skilled blood collection technicians.

Tom Angle said, "We want to find a way to satisfy the growing need for skilled phlebotomists, while increasing the participation of members of the diverse community, served by our region. We believe that helping individuals to move from 'Learning-to-Earning' fulfills that goal."

The Scholarship in the amount of $2000 will cover tuition for the Cambria County Area Community College Phlebotomy I Course. Scholarship funds will also cover fees, books and limited miscellaneous expenses, such as transportation, childcare, uniforms and insurance. The Greater Alleghenies Region will offer full-time employment to successful graduates of the program, after pre-employment screening.

Angle stated that partnering with the NAACP for the Phlebotomy Scholarship, demonstrates their continued appreciation for the NAACP's Organization Freedom Award, in 1998. The Red Cross will continue its efforts to assist citizens of the Johnstown Community in those areas to which the NAACP is committed.

Interested persons must complete an application and submit a high school transcript and three references to be considered for the scholarship. The Education Committee of the NAACP will choose the scholarship recipients.

Building partnerships with the community to invest in students was a strategic procedure to improve the community.

Sports

Superintendent Berkey propelled the Greater Johnstown School District athletic program that started in 1897. According to the *Johnstown Tribune* on September 29, 1897, the Johnstown High School Athletic Association was organized at a meeting of local high school students. The school's athletic teams were called the "Black and Blue." In October, the Black and Blue Football team lost its opening game of the season. The contest was played with the South Side Monarchs on the Eleventh Ward field. In 1903, the Johnstown football team played Kiskiminetas High School with a losing score of 0 to 11. The match with Philipsburg High School ended with a winning score of 11 to 0. In a repeat match against Philipsburg, Johnstown won with a score of 18 to 6. Johnstown High School had a victory over Apollo High School with a score of 39 to 0. However, Quaker High School defeated Johnstown High School with a score of 0 to 3. Sports were just beginning in the commonwealth and the Trojans were the fourth team to accept an invitation to become a member of the WPIAL (Western Pennsylvania Interscholastic Athletic League) in 1904. The other schools that preceded Johnstown High School in WPIAL were Pittsburgh High School, Shadyside Academy, and Allegheny Prep.

Greater Johnstown–1904 Football Team, *Courtesy of Hoss's Family Steak and Sea House*

During the 1899–1900 school year, a new high school opened on Market Street. The athletic association rented the Armory Hall to play basketball. The team record for that year was one win and five losses.

Under the coaching of Victor (Vic) Schmidt in 1917, the Black and Blue defeated Pittsburgh South High School with a score of 140 to 0. However, after ten straight victories, the Black and Blue settled for a scoreless tie with Washington High School. The title game was played in the snow at Point Stadium, which the Johnstown Schools used for high school athletic events. Chad Reese, quarterback for the historically undefeated Johnstown Black and Blue, scored 360 points that season, giving up one touchdown to Harrisburg Central High School. Reese continued his football fame at Washington and Jefferson College and later became an assistant football coach at Johnstown High School.

1917 Football Squad

Powell Stackhouse, III, manager

Howard (Bish) Roberts, end

John Buchovecky, guard, captain

George Bellack, end

Dean Joy, halfback

Clarence (Buckie) Buchanan, end

Joseph Connell, halfback

Dr. Charles R. Colbert, assistant coach

(Red) Harrigan, fullback

Paul (Gumboat) Smith, guard

Cellestine (Cellie) Harrigan, halfback

Michael Hartnett, center

John C. (Jack) Ogden, tackle

James Griffith, guard

The 1917 ½ champion game, between Johnstown High School and Washington High School, was played on December 8, 1917, to decide the football champion of Western Pennsylvania. A major snowstorm hit before the game and thirty male students shoveled the snow from Point Stadium. Although, the largest crowd in history came to watch the game, both teams failed to score. From 1912 to 1917, Johnstown High School dominated the Western Pennsylvania Conference as football champions. In 1921, the Johnstown Black and Blue smothered Mt. Union High School with a score of 115 to 0.

Class of 1921–Football Graduates College Selection

Bernie Kristoff	Carnegie Tech
"Zack" Wissinger	University of Pittsburgh
Whitie Fyock	University of Pittsburgh
Bill Baker	Penn State
Gene Baker	Penn State
Bill Logue	St. Bonaventure
Charley Reed	St. Bonaventure
Bill Hickey	St. Bonaventure
"Cad" Reese	Washington and Jefferson (Quarterback)

1922–1923 Football Team

Under the coaching of Paul R. Beeler, Johnstown High School football team won 9 games and lost 2. The team scored 481 points to their opponent's 48 combined points. However, Johnstown High School did not compete in the championship games because Greensburg-Scott High School had defeated them.

Johnstown High School vs. Windber High School—1936 Contest

At a special meeting, on November 2, 1936, at 11:00 A.M., the board of directors canceled the Johnstown–Windber Football game, scheduled for Thanksgiving Day. The board decided that they would take a great risk of serious disturbance if the contest between the schools took place. The students and community tensions in both Johnstown and Windber School districts were at a high level. The board did not want to assume the responsibility for the safety of many innocent persons being seriously hurt. The board took action and Superintendent McMaster released the following statement: "The Board of Directors has decided to cancel the Thanksgiving Day Game with Windber. The action is not in the nature of a reprisal or a 'run out' on Windber."

Three years later, about 1939, Johnstown High School adopted the Trojan as their mascot, thus naming their team. The mascot was used for all sports, football and basketball. Many of the same students on the football squad played on the high school basketball team. Early in the 1900s, Johnstown, also known for basketball, had many professional basketball teams providing sports entertainment for the residents.

Basketball

According to the *Spectator*, December 1909, Mr. J. E. Smedley introduced basketball to the city schools. In 1901, a city league that competed against the high school was organized. The game was played in the library hall with the high school winning the contest. They were awarded a golden vase. Apparently the library hall was not appropriate, because basketball contests were abandoned for a year for lack of a court. For the 1903–1904 season, the captain of the team, Donald Lindsey, and the manager, Harry Hager, procured the Armory Hall for the basketball contests.

1904–1905 Greater Johnstown High School Basketball Scores

JHS	5	Windber	18
JHS	10	KISKI	35
JHS	14	Johnstown YMCA	24
JHS	12	Johnstown YMCA	9
JHS	9	KISKI	33
JHS	13	Windber	18

The high school basketball team came into its own during the 1904–1905 season. They were able to successfully place for the Western Pennsylvania Championship games. However, they lost to Butler by a score of 13 to 12. In the following year, Johnstown High School lost to Butler in the third deciding contest. In 1907, Superintendent Muir negotiated for an auditorium and the team received championship honors from the commonwealth. The 1908–1909 team won the championship of Western Pennsylvania, Interscholastic Athletic League.

During the 1914–1915 season, the Johnstown High School basketball games were played at the Casino School Auditorium. (See Casino School.) Altoona beat Johnstown with a score of 30 to 24. This was the first Altoona victory in the history of the rivalry. That year, the Johnstown High School team won eight games and lost four games. Johnstown was leading in the DuBois Game 25–16, when a dispute between the teams occurred. After the dispute was settled in the DuBois basketball contest, the game was forfeited to DuBois. The DuBois team left the court.

The 1915 Johnstown basketball cheerleaders chanted JEST-NUTS. (*Spectator* April–1915)

JEST-NUTS

F = is for FOOLISH, many on earth; it is required after birth.

U = is for UNIT meaning just one.

L = is for LONGITUDE, LATITUDE positions, wherein

L = foreseeing positions, some see very dim.

D = is for DIGNITY, appearing the best.

R = is for ROBURST, stick out the chest. Stick it out further to show a white vest

E = is for ELEGANT in appearance, you see. Sealing some elegance, homespun for me.

S = is for SYMPATHY, felt by us all.

S = we will close by SINGING. "Oh you Beautiful Doll."

The 1921–1922 high school basketball team won ten out of fifteen contests. The team scored 524 points to the opponents' 469 points. The highest point victory was against Pittsburgh Academy, with a favorable score of 32–9. The 1922–1923 high school basketball team won 24 games and lost 3 games. The team scored 927 points to their opponents 740 points. Coach Simmons' team included, Weigel, O'Connor, Shaffer, Lambert, and Harris.

The 1924–1925 season found Johnstown High School short of one game to win the title. Westmont High School won the champion game. Johnstown was eliminated in District 6 for the state championship when the Ferndale team defeated them by one point in Altoona.

Lettermen–1924–1925

Doc Krise	Basketball Captain, Star Center
Sam Bowman	Football and Basketball
William Bowman	Two-Year Varsity
Karl Harris	Football and basketball
James Carney	Football
Howard Picking	Basketball Manager

In 1924, entering high school freshmen were excluded from playing a varsity sport, because Term I freshmen remained in the Ward Building. The renovation project eliminated the room for additional students. More than half of the first floor of the high school building was renovated to accommodate the vocational education department. Crowded conditions became problematic for students, teachers, the board of school directors, and Superintendent Slawson.

During the 1925–1926 school term, Johnstown High School won the championship game of Cambria County at the YMCA defeating Gallitzin. They defeated 15 teams that season.

Lettermen–1926

John Fitzpatrick	Three letters
	Football, basketball and Track
	Track team manager
Roger Brown	Track
	High jumper; Record of 5 feet, 3 inches
James Colley	Football
Joseph Murray	Basketball Manager

Track—1921–1922

Johnstown High School Track Team competed in the Penn Relay Carnival. The team won the mile relay race from the field of nine con-

testants. The time of the rail was 3:38 minutes. The relay team consisted of Young, O'Connor, Reed, and Tremellen. The team took fifth
place in the annual Penn State Relay, University Park, Pennsylvania,
and fourth place in the interscholastic meet at Carnegie Tech, Pittsburgh, Pennsylvania. The track team took fifth place in the annual Penn
State Track Meet.

Johnstown Point Stadium Award

The Point Stadium Award was established in 1938 and presented as
an annual award to an outstanding athlete in Johnstown who had played
at the stadium. Since 1995, the Helsel family sponsored the awards and
scholarship. Awards were not presented in 1977, 1993, and 1994.

Point Stadium, *Courtesy of Johnstown Area Heritage Association*

The Point Stadium Awards Recipients

1938	Joe Wisor	Football
1939	Bob Longacre	Football
1942	Spiro Pappas	Football
1950	Ray Gmuca	Football
1952	Joe Burgo	Football
1953	Bob Felton	Baseball
1954	Bernie Grunza	Football

1955	Bill Spanko	Football
1957	Bill Faust	Football
1958	George Azar	Football
1959	John King	Football
1961	Havert "Tojo" King	Football
1964	Rick Brett	Football
1965	Joe McMillan	Football
1965	Tony Renzi	Baseball
1966	Joe McMillan	Football
1966	Fred Katawzik	Baseball
1967	Barry Shellhammer	Baseball
1968	James Gruca	Baseball
1968	Ed Seaman, Jr.	Football
1969	Jim Burton	Baseball
1969	Dennis Baltzer	Football
1973	Jack Buchan	Football
1974	Artrell Hawkins	Football
1974	Michael Peel	Baseball
1986	John Rok	Football
1991	Brian Mangiafico	Football

The *Spectator*

The *Spectator* was first published in 1899. In 1903, the subscription price was 40 cents per year; the cost was 5 cents per copy.

The Spectator Editors 1899–1910

Harry F. Confer	1899
J. J. Dramer	1900
A. P. S. Turner	1901
Edward F. Entwisct	1902
Francis P. Horn	1903
J. Earl Ogle	1903
Ernest J. Cohoe	1904
Fred G. Smith	1905
Robert G. Gipe	1906
Todd D. Cochran	1907
Maurice M. Rothstein	1908
Frank McMillan Breniser	1909
Earl E. Glock	1910

Editors of the *Spectator* addressed school issues, community issues and the economy.

Excerpts from the Spectator, *October 1903*

Wolf and Reynolds Store advertised that "Just Men's and Boys' Wear. Boys' suits" were $1.48 and up. New hats were $1.50 to $5. Topcoats were $10 to $18. It is interesting to note that suits were priced lower than hats. With the economy and the culture of 1903, clothing was pricey for most families. Also interesting is that students were aware and interested to advertise clothing of the day. Women in the home made most of the clothing for the family. Since education was the primary focus of the *Spectator*, students were educated about the cost of clothing. In 1922, physical education became a focal subject. The *Spectator* also wrote about physical development.

Education in Our Public Schools

Excerpts from the Spectator, December 1922

Physical development should be given greater prominence in public school education. The experience with the selected men in World War I should have convinced the nation to its necessity. An astounding proportion of the five million men called were found physically unfit for military service. If a man is unfit for war service he is certainly handicapped in time of peace for business duties and the upbringing of family.

Our democracy takes great pride in its public school system for universal intellectual training. Physical training, however, has not received sufficient concern. A dozen years ago, Johnstown high school had no compulsory provision at all for the bodybuilding of the students. The football, basketball and track teams furnished opportunity for those of naturally splendid physique and super abundant energy, but the majority of the students, lacking the talent or the urge to qualify for athletic teams, were entirely neglected. The High School had no equipped gymnasium, no swimming pool, no athletic field of its own, no course of instruction in hygiene, and no classes in physical training. A modern school should have all of these.... Healthy bodies help healthy minds.

Carl E. Glock—Grade 10

This freshman class that entered Johnstown High School on January 29, 1923 was the largest class to enroll at midterm.

Excerpts from the *Spectator* (1925)
School News

The Student's Code of Courtesy

The Student Council recently adopted the following code, which should be of interest to every boy and girl in Johnstown High School:

I hereby pledge myself to do my best to uphold the standard of my school and to make my conduct on the school grounds, about the building, in the halls and classrooms fitting to my position as a pupil of the Johnstown Senior High School.

About the Building
• I will endeavor to be polite by my conduct to outsiders.
• I will not throw snowballs in front of or about the building.
• I will not deface the building by writing or painting anything upon the walls, and will refrain from smoking while near the building.
• I will not drop waste paper on the grounds or about the building.
• I will be sportsman like and considerate of visitors at all games.

In the Halls
• I will remove my hat upon entering the building.
• I will assist whenever possible by opening doors for teachers and pupils.
• I will be orderly in the halls and respect the rights of others by not hurrying, and will refrain from boisterous talking and laughing.
• I will refrain from unladylike and ungentlemanlike conduct in the halls.
• I will be considerate when in lunch-line and take my turn.
• I will not eat in any part of the building except such places set aside for that purpose.
• I will not carelessly drop bits of paper in the halls but will deposit all papers in receptacles.

In the Classroom
• I will enter classroom promptly and orderly.
• I will show my respect for teachers by speaking politely and by complying with their requests.
• I will assume an attentive attitude during the class and will rise to recite.
• I will not make annoying noises or indulge in conversation with my neighbors.
• I will not make my toilet in public.

In the Auditorium
• I will be quiet and attentive during chapel exercises even if I am not interested and cannot hear.
• I will not cause the speaker discomfort by laughing at slips he may make during a mass meeting or class meeting.
• I will not push or hurry when entering or leaving the auditorium.
• I will aim at all times to give outsiders the right impression of the Johnstown Senior High School by being courteous and by being a good loser as well as a good winner.

The Bond Issue
Martha Jane Goughnour
Garfield Jr. High School

Our Board of Education tries to give every girl and boy in the city of Johnstown the best education possible, but to do this they must provide more and better educational equipment to accommodate the rapidly increasing population. The building, for educational purposes, is not sufficient to meet the pressing demands in many sections of the city. The board needs more funds to finish the School Building Program they have begun and will ask the voters to approve a Bond Issue at the coming election on Nov. 3, 1925.

No one section of the city will be beneficial particularly by this program, but it will cover the following:
• The Completion of Garfield Junior High School in the Twentieth Ward.
• Erection of a grade school in the Eighth Ward.
• Erection of a grade school in the Seventeenth Ward.
• Erection of other school buildings as may be required.
• Furnishing and equipping of the buildings.
• Purchase of additional real estate for school purposes.
• The schools in many sections of the city are crowded.

Woodvale is filled beyond its capacity. Moxham must have a new school at Cypress Avenue. Two schools from Moxham are now going to Meadowvale. There is also a new school needed in Roxbury. When a child reaches the fifth grade in the Osborne School he must pass the Osborne School and climb up the hill through the rain, snow and slush to Roxbury, which is filled with its own pupils. But in the Morrellville district the most crowded conditions exist. In that section thirty-five groups of teachers and pupils have to carry on their work in rented storerooms, basement rooms and portables, making a total of more than a thousand pupils and teachers without a permanent building. In Garfield alone there are sixteen portable and basement rooms, which cannot be heated or lighted properly. The basements are damp and must be constantly lighted by electricity, the portables are too warm near the furnace and too cold in other parts of the room, and, besides they are easily inflammable.... Moreover, if the Junior High School pupils were removed from the Garfield building there would come from the immediate vicinity enough grade school pupils who are housed in rented rooms, portables and basements to fill the Garfield building above the basement rooms.

The West End of the city is very much in need of an auditorium. On a number of occasions we were permitted through the kindness of the Calvary Methodist Church to use their church, but if the school wants to get together to sing, or if a speaker comes to Garfield the pupils are compelled to stand in the halls, which is not only unsatisfactory and tiresome, but often injurious.

Garfield also needs a gymnasium. The girls have to carry on their work during the warm weather at Fichtner field and in the winter months in an old church on Decker Ave., which cannot be heated because the windows are broken. On a number of occasions pupils have been compelled to go over to the Coopersdale School to practice for athletic meets.

We have a right to admire many things about our school. We have several good up-to-date buildings, and the best of teachers had instruction to be had anywhere. If parents would take the time to visit our schools they would be surprised to know what their boy or girl is receiving. The fact of the matter is we have outgrown our present equipment; we need more room, we must have it, and we trust the voters will make it possible by placing their mark in the proper place on Nov. 3, 1925.

Reorganization of the Johnstown Education System

Superintendent Killius presented a proposal to reorganize the Johnstown Public Schools of Cambria County, Pennsylvania, to the board of directors. The reorganization proposal was submitted at a meeting on June 12, 1939. The first article submitted was the Teachers' Tenure Act Section 1205 (b).

Teachers' Tenure Act

Whenever it shall become necessary to decrease the number of professional employees by reason of substantial decrease of pupil population within the school district, the Board of School Directors (or Board of Public Education) may suspend the necessary number of professional employees, but only in the inverse order of the appointment of such employees. No employee suspended as aforesaid [sic] shall be prevented from engaging in other occupations during the period such suspension. Such professional employees shall be reinstated in the inverse order of their suspension. No new appointments shall be made while there are suspended professional employees available.

The act simply said that professional employees may seek and obtain other employment, but they will remain on the priority list for district hiring. Before new professionals are considered, persons on the suspension list must be given an opportunity to return. With reorganization, teachers were classified as elementary teachers or secondary teachers. The district adopted the six-six academic plan; that is, six secondary grades and six elementary grades. They developed a seniority list of all teachers. The board also adopted a "Waiting List" of applicants. The applicants were placed on the list if they met the selective criteria.

Criteria for Elementary Teachers

1. Pennsylvania teacher's certificate
2. Resident of the city or suburban Johnstown
3. Graduate of Johnstown High School
4. Examination on the theory of Education administered by an out-of-town educator
5. Rating on the teacher's training institute
6. Personal interview with superintendent and board members

In addition to the elementary teachers' requirements, the secondary teachers also had test requirements in the subject that appeared on his or her training certificate.

Early Johnstown Band, *Courtesy of Hoss's Family Steak and Sea House Historical Collection*

High School Band

The 100-member Johnstown High School Band shared honors with the United States Navy Band at the Ninth Annual National School Safety Patrol Parade held in Washington, D.C., on May 1, 1940. The board of school directors and Superintendent McMaster were most pleased when the Johnstown High School Band had the distinct honor of leading the entire Pennsylvania delegation of young patrolmen. The evening before this fantastic celebration, the Johnstown Band presented their talents at the Sylvan Theater, an outdoor theater located at the Washington Monument. They presented the Swiss flag-twirling demonstration. Mr. Charles L. Aikey directed the band. The band arrived in Washington, D.C., adorned in new uniforms for the occasion. The uniforms cost $20.50 each. The uniforms were blue, trimmed in black,

1988 Drum Major—Alvin McCray, *Courtesy of Burns Photography*

the school colors, with black and white citation cords. The hat had a plumage of feathers.

In *Memories of Johnstown,* (2001) Nancy Miller talked about her band days at Garfield when she had an opportunity to participate with the Johnstown High School Band.

"Twinkle Toes" Memory

When I was a 10th grader at Garfield in 1958, the band director selected a few of us to go to play with the Johnstown High School Marching Band, then directed by Charles Aikey. We were very excited until we discovered that we had to wear our Garfield uniforms, which were prison garb, glow-in-the dark, brilliant orange. We were never sure who had picked these hideous garments, but were convinced it had to be someone either obsessed with Halloween or totally colorblind. Among the blue and black clad high school band members, we vibrated. But Mr. Aikey needed us, and I'm sure he thought that the color of the uniforms was irrelevant, as we would be performing our major routine of the year in a darkened stadium with only our feet and hats lighted. Enter "Twinkle Toes," performed to American Patrol. We practiced so hard that even after 40 years, my feet start to prance whenever I hear it strains! It was a worrisome experience: aggravation at the trolley ride to the Point Stadium after school for practice, embarrassment about my uniform, concern about whether my lights would stay put and lighted, and fear that my feet

1988 Marching High School Band, *Courtesy of Burns Photography*

would stray and take my points of light along to further illuminate my mistakes. One friend remembers a night when someone (not me) did take a wrong turn in the darkness, and wandered the football field doing a solitary performance. We performed "Winkle Toes" more than once during the season and each time was an exercise of frustration. That year Johnstown went to the W.P.I.A.L. football Championship at Pitt stadium. Luckily for the band, the game was played during the day, so performing "Twinkle Toes" was not an option. It's funny, though, that every fellow band member I've talked to can't remember what program we performed at that most important game of the year, but EVERYONE remembers " Twinkle Toes!"

Nancy Scrudders Miller

War Days

In the early 1940s, the school district became concerned with students going to War. Superintendent J. Earnest Wagner, in the 1943 *Spectator*, referred to John McCrae's poem, "Flanders Fields," as he watched young men and women departing from Johnstown High Schools.

Dr. J. Earnest Wagner
Spectator—1943

It is not only during the time of war that keeping faith is of utmost importance, but at all times. If the road to victory lies through education, then it must be an education which has trained our young Americans not to break faith with those people who have placed their belief in them. If there is ever a time for graduates to instil [sic] ideals into their hearts and maintain them, it is now.

June 1943 will mark a memorable year in the history of the United States. A high percentage of the boys and girls of the present graduating class will be entering war work of various kinds. We are proud that they will become a part of that "forward America" campaign which will ultimately mean victory. Their years of preparation in the high school serve as their background for the future. When they take their place in life, this preparation should rank them with all those who can hold their own. We know they can, and we congratulate them on the successful completion of the high school course. We also congratulate the parents, who helped make this Commencement Day possible through their cooperation with teachers and administrative authorities.

As they travel the road to victory for themselves, as well as to victory for our country, we offer to these fine young Americans the torch of hope and trust. Let it be theirs to hold it high!

Mr. W.C. Davis, the acting superintendent, addressed the class of 1943 as a class of uncertainty, but yet a class to hold on to an ideal. He recognized that students had had a difficult time focusing on high school work. He thought that those who graduated could use their high school training to enable them to render service wherever they were called upon to serve. He mentioned that some members of the class had already left for the armed forces and would be on the battlefield on commencement day. Mr. Davis also praised those who had elected to enter college to become better prepared to serve their country. He encouraged the members of the class of 1943 to hold to the ideal that behind all preparation is service. With this ideal, the Girls Reserve Club organized.

As a subsidiary of the Young Women's Christian Association, the Girls Reserve Club organized to uphold the high standards of Christian character. The 1943 theme was "Growing UP." Club membership totaled 310 girls, divided into eight committees. Members attended the Tri-State Mid-Winter Conference in New Castle, Pennsylvania.

YWCA, *Courtesy of Recci Patrick*

1943 Girls Reserve Officers

Natalie Keller, President   Dorothy Stober, Vice President
Charlotte Bantley, Secretary   Kathryn Buchanan, Treasurer
Morjorie Myers, Inter-Club Council Representative

With families separated for war, the Johnstown School faced troubled times. Paradoxically, as the student body spoke out for better schools and more teachers, the war caused a slight decline in teachers in the district from 1942 to 1947. The war was real in the Johnstown community. A prisoner of war (POW) camp was located on Goucher Street and housed captured German soldiers during World War II. The first Upper Yoder Fire Hall was part of the camp. The Garnell Associates building was the dining hall of one of the camps. The POW camp became low-rent G.I. homes after the war (Beuke, 1998, p. 214).

Teachers in the Johnstown Schools (1942–1947)

Position	1942–1943	1943–1944	1944–1945	1945–1946
Supervisors	7	7	7	8
Special	2	2	2	2
High School	58	55	54	56
Cochran	52	51	52	52
Garfield	52	52	51	52
Joseph Johns	50	48	48	48
Bheam	9	10	10	10
Chandler	13	11	11	11
Chestnut	14	13	13	11
Coopersdale	6	5	5	5
Cypress	11	9	9	10
Dibert	6	6	6	7
Horner	8	8	8	8
Hudson	14	14	13	12
Maple Park	10	9	9	9
Meadowvale	12	12	12	12
Morrell	4	4	4	4
Oakhurst	7	8	9	9
Osborne	7	7	8	8
Park	4	4	4	4
Rosedale	1	1	1	1
Roxbury	10	9	9	9
Somerset	10	9	9	9
Union	7	7	7	7
Village	7	7	7	7
Washington	10	12	13	13
Woodvale	10	9	8	9
	401	389	389	393

On August 4, 1955, there were 290 elementary and 246 secondary classrooms in the Johnstown Public Schools. The elementary and secondary classrooms totaled 536 public classrooms in 28 school buildings in the Johnstown City School System.

Johnstown Public School Classrooms (1955–1956)

Central High	76
Cochran Junior High	67
Garfield Junior High	53
Joseph Johns Junior High	50
Bheam	12
Chandler	18 (plus 6 basement rooms)
Chestnut	18
Coopersdale	12
Cypress	23
Dibert	8
Horner	6
Hudson	20
Maple Park	16
Meadowvale	20
Morrell	11
Oakhurst	15
Osborne	8
Park	12
Rosedale	3
Roxbury	14
Somerset	13
Union	11 (plus 3 portables)
Village	13
Washington	22
Woodvale	18 (plus 4 portables)
Highland Park	2
Oakland	10
Riverside	6

In 1956, the *Tribune Democrat* and Pennsylvania State University awarded a "Good Teacher's Award." Superintendent Miller proudly announced Miss Ellen A. Curran, an English and Latin Instructor at Joseph Johns Junior High as the recipient of the award. This annual scholarship was given to a teacher for summer study at Pennsylvania State University. According to Mr. Miller, Miss Curran received the scholarship award for her special teaching style, which raised her students' interest in becoming emotionally involved with the classics. She felt a discussion of good literature could influence the students' ideals. Miss Curran shared the teaching profession in the Johnstown City

Schools with siblings in her family. One of her sister's, Rose Alice Curran, taught at Roxbury Grade School, and another, Sara Curran, taught at Maple Park School. Her brother, Eugene Curran, taught at the Junior High School. In many cases, working at the Johnstown Schools was a family affair.

Greater Johnstown Vocational-Technical School

On January 12, 1966, the two top school administrators of the Greater Johnstown School District resigned. Dr. Frank M. Miller, superintendent of schools, submitted his resignation, to be active at the end of the term, on June 30. He had held the superintendent's position since 1955. According to the *Tribune Democrat* on January 12, 1966, Dr. Miller was a key figure in the establishment of the area's vocational-technical school. He is credited with the preparation of the articles of agreement and preliminary planning for that school. His salary was $20,000 per year.

Since opening, Vo-Tech has remained a much-discussed controversial school system. The student body is generated from various school districts that decreased the enrollment of the home school. Ironically, the school forms its own teams of various high school sports. Students compete, in football, basketball, and other sports, against their friends and family members still attending the district high school. The district school also offers vocational-technical courses, so it appears in many cases a duplication of educational services.

Mr. Charles E. Boyer, administrative assistant, also tendered his resignation. Mr. Boyer was a native of Johnstown and a graduate of Johnstown High School. He had worked in the Greater Johnstown School System since 1936. His salary was $16,500 per year.

Some Greater Johnstown High School Graduating Classes

In the class of 1962, Superintendent Miller led six hundred students in the graduation ceremony at the Cambria County War Memorial Arena. Representative H. G. Andrews of Johnstown was the keynote speaker. Jean Marie Allison was the class valedictorian. The officers of the class were David Homer, student council president; Robert McCleary, senior class president and salutatorian; Patricia Antonazzo, secretary; and Jeanette Sikirica, treasurer.

In the class of 1977, Superintendent Zucco led 413 students in a graduation ceremony from Greater Johnstown High School. The student speakers were Gene Cadierux, valedictorian; Tracie Wearer, salutatorian; and James Kist, class president. In the class of 1978, 388 students graduated from the Greater Johnstown High School. The graduation speakers were Robert Grasso, valedictorian; E. Christopher Curkel, salutatorian; and Craig Bachik, class president.

In the class of 1980, 372 students graduated from Greater Johnstown High School. The graduation speakers were Michele Troutman, valedictorian; Joyce Xanak, salutatorian; and Dennis McCullough, class president.

In the class of 1981, 327 students graduated from Greater Johnstown High School. The graduation speakers were Sharyn D. Siehl, valedictorian; Requetta M. Audrey, salutatorian; and Marco Romane, class president.

In the class of 1983, 320 students graduated from Greater Johnstown High School. The graduation speakers were Karyn Siehl, valedictorian, and Melissa Lengyel, salutatorian.

In the class of 1985, Superintendent Hollis led 266 students who graduated from Greater Johnstown High School. The graduation speakers were Dana Lynn Singer, valedictorian; Michael Slenska, salutatorian; and Marlo Fontana, class president.

In the class of 1987, 306 students graduated from Johnstown High School. One hundred five or 34.31 % of the seniors went on to college. The leading college for Johnstown graduates was Indiana University of Pennsylvania, followed and tied by the University of Pittsburgh at Johnstown and Penn State University. The *Trojan Centralizer* stated that the graduates would attend colleges in eight states including Boston University, Massachusetts, and Notre Dame, Indiana.

These classes were randomly selected to illustrate the constant decline in the senior class enrollment, and the class of 1987 illustrated the number of students who pursued higher education. From the class of 1962 to the class of 1985, the senior class lost more than half of its class enrollment. These numbers do not suggest that students dropped out of school. In most cases, families relocated. Relocation is reflected in the graduating class of 1978 with a logical reason being the 1977

Johnstown Flood. The Greater Johnstown Vocational Technical School, located in Richland Township, also attracted many of the Johnstown high school students.

Evening School

In 1939, Superintendent McMaster initiated Johnstown free evening school courses for students who lived within the district. One hundred thirty-seven students who resided beyond the boundaries of the school district registered for the Johnstown Schools' evening classes. Of course, these students paid tuition. By 1945, 1,047 students attended these classes. However, only 82 % of attendance for the year was reported. The youngest student was sixteen years old in contrast to the oldest student at fifty-nine years old. The age range supports the theory that learning is a lifelong occupation.

Evening School Classes

Accounting	Commercial law
Physical Education	Air Meteorology
Dictation and Translation	Salesmanship
Air Navigation	Elementary subjects
Shop Engineering	Algebra
English	Show Card Lettering
Auto Mechanics	Metallurgy
Shorthand	Mechanics
Mechanical Drawing	Algebra
Blue Print Reading	Mining
Bookkeeping	Mechanical drawing
Business English	Nursing
Business Economics	Office Practice

The 1945–1946 school year marked thirty-eight years of evening classes in the Johnstown School District. Due to World War II and scarcity of males, classes became smaller but none were eliminated. The school year was divided into quarters of fifteen evenings each. The evening sessions were held for two hours beginning at 7:30 and ending at 9:30 P.M. Classes were held on Monday, Wednesday, and Friday evenings. The minimum class size was fifteen students. The evening school centers were the high school for academics, commercial, trade, and related subjects. Rosedale evening classes were held for elementary education. Cochran Junior High School was used for auto mechanics shop training. The registration fee of $3 was required and returned if students attended 75 % of the session. Out-of-district students paid $5 tuition per semester.

In 1946, 474 students attended evening school. The youngest student was fourteen and the oldest student was fifty-seven. Several classes were established for veterans in conformity with P.L. 356, the GI Bill. Under the GI Bill, veterans employed as apprentices were required to attend evening school to obtain related instruction.

When Congress declared World War II, ration stamps and surplus commodities became the order of the day. Essentials such as gasoline, sugar, and shoes were on the ration list. However, young men fortunate enough to return had the opportunity to finish their education.

Veterans High and Trade School

The Veterans Program commenced on February 18, 1946, and was terminated on June 30, 1957. Superintendent Wagner said that the school was primarily organized for war veterans from Indiana, Somerset, and Cambria Counties. However, the Veterans Program did accept veterans from other areas. The Pennsylvania Department of Education and the Veteran's Testing Service of Chicago, Illinois, approved the school. The school offered courses for discharged veterans who had not completed their high school education. Veterans were provided the opportunity to continue their high school education to complete courses that would meet graduation requirements. They were also able to take refresher courses as a foundation for college studies. The school was established to meet the needs of returning veterans who were not able to attend high school during the regular semester; they needed an accelerated program to complete their schooling as soon as possible. Therefore, older

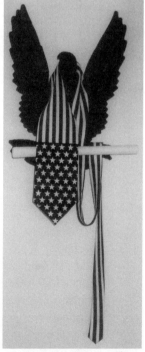

Veterans School, Soar like an Eagle with a diploma, *Courtesy of Recci Patrick*

veteran students were taught in separate classes from regular high school.

Daytime classes for veterans were offered during the entire year. A veteran could complete a maximum of two credits in eight weeks or a full year of high school studies in sixteen weeks. At first classes were offered in a few select courses.

Daytime Classes for Veterans

English	Civics
American History	Other history courses
Latin	Modern Language
Typewriting	Problems of Democracy
Algebra I	Algebra II
Plane Geometry	Solid Geometry
Trigonometry	Biology
Physics	Chemistry
Trade Machine Shop	Mechanical Drawing

If ten or more veterans requested a course, Superintendent Wiley stated that the additional course would be offered. All academic classes were taught on the third floor of Johnstown Central Senior High School. Vocational courses were held on the two lower floors of the high school at Cochran Junior High School or the Garfield Junior High School Vocational Shops.

1946–1947 Veterans School Vocational Courses

Total Length of Course (Months)

Courses Offered	Original Requirements 1946	Revised Requirements 1951
Auto Body Repairman–Metal	18	15
Automobile Mechanics	30	25
Bricklaying	24	20
Industrial Carpeting	30	25
Commercial Artist Illustration	24	20
Draftsman Mechanical	24	20
Electrician	30	25
Radio Repairman	24	20
Sheet-Metal Worker II	24	20
Television-Technician	9	7 ½
Refrigeration	24	20

Evening classes were held from 7:00 P.M. to 10:00 P.M., Monday through Friday, for a period of eight weeks. Veterans had the restriction of enrolling in one class per term. Tuition of $35 per credit, per veteran, was paid by the Veterans Administration. The tuition was reduced from the veteran's allocation for college education. After 1951, the credit time requirement increased to 30 hours of class time and the tuition increased to $43.20. The Veterans Administration also took the financial responsibility for the increased tuition. From 1946 through May 1951, approximately 2,300 veterans attended the various academic programs and 1,209 attended classes at the vocational shops. From May 25, 1951, until the school closed on June 30, 1957, an additional 3,010 veteran students attended classes. Both the Korean War veterans and the World War II veterans attended the Veterans School. With the veteran student enrollment and the changing culture to adjust to postwar times, within ten years significant changes had been made in the evening school program.

By 1968, some gradual changes had been made to the Evening School Program. Instead of quarters, the school year was now divided into two semesters of ten weeks each, with class starting at 7:00 P.M. However, the curriculum remained the same for the senior high school. Courses added were drafting, blueprint reading, and sewing classes. These new courses were taught at Joseph Johns Junior High School. The tuition for out-of-town students was paid by their school district. The youngest student was seventeen and the oldest student was listed as sixty-eight. Five hundred twenty-three students attended night school in 1968.

1968–1969 Night School Courses

Algebra and Geometry	Sewing
Americanization	Shorthand I and II
Blueprint Reading	Typing I
Candy Making	Typing I and Bookkeeping
Ferrous Metallurgy	Typing II and Business English
Machine Shop	Upholstering
Office Machines	Wood Shop

The shift of course offerings indicated a shift in societal needs. Females were beginning to enter the workforce in greater numbers. Skilled trades that had often been taught in the homes were now being taught in vocational education courses in evening school. A sewing machine had been standard equipment in most homes. Mothers and grandmothers had taught females the art of housekeeping that included sewing, candy making, and cooking. However, three courses in sewing were taught in evening school. Curriculum for secretarial preparation for the business courses was also offered.

Curricula were organized for three divisions. The commercial curriculum prepared students for clerical work in the business world. The academic curriculum prepared students who were going on to higher education institutions. A component of the academic curriculum was titled Special Education. In a course titled Americanization, teachers taught beginning English for immigrants and preparation for citizenship. The vocational and home economics components prepared students for life and to do handiwork at their homes or as a profession. Curriculum was used as a vehicle for social change to meet the socioeconomic and psychosocial needs of students (C. Hollis, 2000, p. 60). Wars have had a great influence on education through national cultural change; on the other hand, floods have been Johnstown's environmental devastations that have caused regrouping. The city and the schools have had to make adjustments for three great floods, within a century.

The Great Flood of 1889 is an historical event that gave Johnstown the identity of Flood City. The great wave sent a forty-foot wall of water through the Conemaugh Valley, took 2,235 lives, and deposited twelve feet of earth in the city, destroying most of the city and its industry. On St. Patrick's Day in 1936, a less serious flood reinforced the Flood City identity. Engineers developed and completed a Flood Free Project on the rivers in 1943. Nonetheless, the heavy rains of July 20, 1977, devastated the city, again. Torrential rains cascaded down the steep mountainous slopes surrounding the city to raise creeks in downtown Johnstown. The amount of water that hit the city of Johnstown that day exceeded normal runoff channels and absorption capacity of the Flood Free Project. Many stores and plants did not rebuild. After this flood, families and individuals have continued to leave the area to find employment. Accordingly, the school population continued to decline.

Population Trends 1940–1980

Location	1940	1950	1960	1970	1980
City of Johnstown	66,668	63,232	53,949	42,476	35,496
Lower Yoder	3,447	3,440	4,828	4,099	4,026
Stonycreek	2,120	2,735	4,650	4,543	4,430
West Taylor	1,664	1,712	1,580	1,193	1,050
Total Districts	73,899	71,119	65,007	52,311	43,002

The Greater Johnstown School Board took action with a five-to-three vote to not grant salary increases to administrators in 1977. The raises proposed before the July 20, 1977, flood for six administrators totaled $11,800.

The school district also responded to the decline of the student population by closing schools. Maple Park School was closed in 1977. In 1980, Johnstown High School was closed and Cochran Junior High School Building was converted to the senior high school. Garfield became the only junior high school in the district. In 1981, Coopersdale Elementary School was closed. In 1983, the Cypress Annex, Meadowvale Annex, and Chestnut Street Offices were eliminated. The district's administrative offices were placed in the second floor of the Meadowvale Elementary School. As administrators and the school board made modifications for another flood and a declining student population, the teachers' morale festered into organized labor.

Surveys, Unions, Federal and Civil Influence

Chapter X ❖

Student Revolt

In 1969, the Johnstown School Board of Directors relaxed the adopted school dress code that required students to dress conservatively and neatly. Blue jeans were not permitted as school attire and girls were not permitted to wear slacks. Restrictions included no conspicuous hair-dos and no facial hair such as beards and mustaches (Reabuck, *Tribune*, 17 March 1970). Allen Andrews ('69) said that the code was relaxed to give consideration to white style such as long sideburns. However, a mustache, considered as a "black" style, was not permitted. Black students also requested that black ethnic food be added to the cafeteria menu. Daniel Perkins ('69) spearheaded a movement for blacks to leave class at a certain hour to meet in the gymnasium to convince faculty they were serious about wanting "Soul Food," some culture identity on the school menu. In this attempt to gain some racial identity, Mr. Perkins said that all black students did not show up.

Ethnic clothes, such as dashikis were also prohibited. Bright colors such as lime green and hot pinks from head to toe were also prohibited. Allen Andrews ('69), Alan Cashaw ('69), and Daniel Perkins ('69) made several attempts to talk with administrators about considering African-American culture. The principal referred to African-American male students as wearing their sisters' blouses and did not recognize dashikis as male attire.

The controversy came on the heels of Dr. Martin Luther King's assassination, a wake-up call to Johnstown's black youth. Although, Johnstown was not known as a Muslim community, the Black Panther Party and Black Muslin groups frequented the area after Dr. King's assassination. Although they had a different point of view, feelings toward the establishment reflected the same disparaged treatment that African-American students were experiencing. With racial tension generated by the media, Dr. King's dream became the same for underrepresented students in Johnstown. In 1960, a group of black college students conducted a sit-in at a segregated Woolworth's lunch counter in Greensboro, North Carolina, with widespread media coverage. In the late sixties, many recreation areas and amusement parks were still closed to African-Americans for entertainment and enjoyment in Johnstown. African-American students viewed the dress code as more differential treatment. Consequently, they staged a walkout of the Greater Johnstown High School.

The African-American community displayed solidarity; many households made dashikis for the high school students to wear. As one native said, every sewing machine in every black home was stitching dashikis around the clock. "The African heritage, with its emphasis on extended families and fictive kin, probably laid a foundation for this adaptable family unit and certainly helped...to work with the personal resources they had" (Thompson and MacAustin, 1999, p. 2). The African-American students had planned to wear the dashikis on the same day and they had planned to walk out of school if one student was asked to leave.

Administrators, who knew of the plot, threatened students that if they walked out, they would be suspended, expelled, and would not graduate. Some students were college bound and had received scholarships to major universities. Consequently, only twenty-three African-American students walked out of Greater Johnstown High School, for fear of reprisal. The twenty-three students walked to nearby Joseph Johns Junior High School and whistled and called to the students to get their attention inside the opened classroom windows. The high school students were successful in attracting about 200 junior high school students to walk out of class. Dee Fisher, a seventh-grade student at Joseph Johns Junior High School, said that in a matter of minutes the school went wild. Black students lighted their brown lunch bags and tossed them out of the school windows. The African-American students were, conversely, organized and the plan called for them to march across the bridge to Cambria A.M.E. Zion Church.

School administrators appeared at the door of the church, but were turned away. Mr. Bruce Haselrig, was called in as a counselor and mediator. Mr. Haselrig had been the black student president of the 1962 Class. From 1961, black students held their own post-prom activities. Black families raised funds all year to financially sponsor the post prom. Fish fries were held in Cambria A.M.E. Zion Church. The Post Prom was supervised by adults. In 1962, the post prom was held at the Elks Club on Bedford Street.

Reverend W. M. Cunningham, pastor of the church, and members of the NAACP talked with students about developing a realistic list of demands. Since the curriculum was void of black history, the students adopted a history text, *Before the Mayflower,* and wanted it added to the curriculum. They held black history classes at Cambria Church and had more meetings to discuss an inclusive curriculum. They wanted racially biased books, like *Little Black Sambo,* removed from elementary classrooms, and the singing of "Ole Black Joe" discontinued in music classes. According to Mr. Andrews, African-American students carried bitterness due to humiliation in the classroom from their early school days. Their parents had had the same crushing experience; therefore, students had empathy in their homes. African-American students simply wanted identity with their ethnic hairstyles, acceptance of their attire, and to be able to wear sneakers to class. Spouting facial hair is symbolic of maturation and masculinity. For a suppressed group of students, this expression was deemed significant, after reticent years of not speaking to the ills of inequality.

Ms. Claudia Jones, the only African-American teacher on the secondary level, taught tenth-grade biology at Joseph Johns Junior High School. The Johnstown School District used the six-four-two grade plan: that is, elementary schools had first through sixth grades; junior high schools had four grades, from seventh through tenth; and Johnstown High School had two grades, eleventh and twelfth. According to Ms. Jones, the echoes from the halls were raged with students running out of the building. A student would open the door to a classroom and beckon to other students and the classes were emptied of African-American students. She said that only one student left her class and she did so in an orderly manner. Ms. Jones continued to teach with turmoil in the halls and below her. She looked out of her fourth floor window to see a police cruiser arriving. Joseph Johns Junior High School students turned the police car over. They dismantled fire hydrants en route to their meeting place at Cambria A.M.E. Zion Church. Students knew that it was not safe for them to be on the streets. Ms. Jones went to the church after school dismissed and was permitted in the building.

First Cambria A. M. E. Zion Church, Corner of Menoher Boulevard and Haynes Street

Reverend Cunningham kept actions on the premises of the church under control. With a compromise, Mr. Haselrig persuaded African-American students to return to class. Mr. Andrews stated that they were out of class for two days. However, senior graduation was not problematic for those who were scheduled to graduate. The dress code was changed to consider ethnic differences. In 1975, the Greater Johnstown Board of School Directors appointed Dr. Levi B. Hollis, with a moustache, to an administrative position. However, the facial hair restriction was aimed at students, not administrators. In 2002, the moustache is a hair style of personal choice.

Reflecting on the African-American student revolt, in 2002, the incident could have been avoided with sensitivity training that is very popular today. In a community built around preserving one's own identity, educators needed to step out of their box, to promote the Americanization paradigm. The schools should be the vehicle to preserve and promote all cultures. With the dress code, the first step would have been to research African attire to understand the significance of the dashiki, the significance of African-American students, and the African-American community's need to show solidarity. The intensity and expense of the movement are indicators that frustration had prevailed for a group of people for some time. Educators were in denial, yet empathy could have eased students' mental pain and created an arena for healthy discussions and solutions. The dress code was the straw that broke the camel's back. For generations African-American students had been exposed to negative, demeaning literature, music, and art.

Joseph Johns Junior High School was closed the following year and students were sent to Cochran and Garfield Junior High Schools.

2001 Community Harmony

On December 26, 2000, Aaron Coyle, a white student from Greater Johnstown High School, was shot in a Moxham parking lot. Two African-American males apparently attempted to rob him. Aaron fought back. The town was shocked. Portia Witten, an African-American student and president of the student council, organized a unity march on January 11, 2001. The marchers assembled at Greater Johnstown High School, where candles were distributed. Dr. Donato Zucco, the mayor, Dr. Gerald Zahorchak, the school district superintendent, and Dr. Clea Hollis, president of the NAACP, marched with two thousand students and organizations for an organized movement against this hideous crime. Some other organizations including the executive board of the NAACP and members, administrators, and teachers from the Greater Johnstown School District, Unity Coalition of the Southern Alleghenies, and City Council Members. Mr. Allen Andrews, who led the 1969 student revolt, marched with the group as vice president of the NAACP.

Unity Coalition of the Southern Alleghenies,
Courtesy of Dorothy Thomas

The march started at the school and took a significant path past the Moxham parking lot where Mr. Coyle was slain. A wreath hung on the door of the Moxham Pool Hall, at Coleman Avenue and Village Street, Aaron's destination on that fatal night. The march continued to St. Patrick Roman Catholic Church. A service was held on the grounds of the church with lighted candles. The day after the march, Dr. C. P. Hollis spoke to the student body at Garfield Junior High School about the significance of the nonviolent march for peace.

After thirty years, there appears to be some understanding of different cultural groups and the good and bad in all-ethnic communities. The march was symbolic of solidarity of the community against crime and hatred and a call for peace among all cultures. Whites and African-Americans stepped beyond the legal process to burn candles together to help heal the community.

With the Greater Johnstown Schools, organizations have partnered to work for harmony and understanding in the community, with an emphasis on the positive. In 2001, shortly after the incident, community organizations partnered for the sponsorship of the MLK Weekend of Service, for January 19, 20, and 21, 2002. Dr. Jonathan Darling, Associate Professor of the University of Pittsburgh at Johnstown and Mary Beth King of AmeriCorp spearheaded the weekend of activities.

The 2002 MLK Unity Partners

AmeriCorp Pennsylvania Mountain Service Corps
Bedford-Cambria County Retired Senior Volunteer Program
Cambria County Community Action Council, Inc.
Cambria County Foster Grandparent Program
Chamber of Commerce Leadership Imitative
Johnstown Branch of the National Association for the
    Advancement of Colored People (NAACP)
Johnstown Housing Authority
Johnstown Senior Community Center
Partners for Neighborhood Revitalization, Inc.
Planned Parenthood of Cambria-Somerset
Sociology Department of the University of Pittsburgh at
    Johnstown (UPJ)
The Family Resource Center
University of Pittsburgh Lee Regional (UPMC)

The Education Committee of the NAACP launched the first annual poster and essay contests for students in the Johnstown Schools. Ms. Claudia Jones supervised the essay component for the high school students. Mr. Recci Patrick supervised the poster component for the middle school. The grand prize was presented to Ms. LaShae Jeffers, a junior at Johnstown High School. Laquita Easter from Garfield Junior High School won first place in the poster contest.

The Johnstown School District advanced from segregation in 1946 to a 1969 student revolt. A generation later, a 2001 March for Peace was supported by many ethnic groups to dismiss hatred and bigotry, with some of the same participants of the revolt. The 2002 MLK Weekend celebration was a culminating event to transcend the misery and discomfort of past generations and move forward as a community for the students of Johnstown with unity in the community.

Black History Month

Following the MLK Celebration, the NAACP received many inquiries about "Why do we celebrate Black History Month?" Other questions included: "Do African-Americans have their own history?" and "Is black history different from regular history?" "Why is Black History Month celebrated in February, the shortest month?" As an attempt to answer these questions, the president of the Johnstown Branch of the NAACP submitted an editorial to the *Tribune Democrat* that was published on February 17, 2002.

Righting a Wrong
Omissions From Books Prompted Black History Month

Dr. Carter G. Woodson called attention to the nation's void of African-American contributions in history books, in the early 1900s. Although Dr. C. G. Woodson's parents were disenthralled from slavery, he earned a Ph.D. from Harvard University. During his studies, he was disturbed to find that American history books were really white history books. Textbooks and literature were void of the black American population, except as inferior, societal, stereotypical characters.

Dr. Woodson's first major effort was to bring forth awareness of omitted black contributions. Consequently, Dr. Woodson took on the major task of integrating black contributions into the nation's history books. He founded the Association for *the Study of Negro Life and History*. The Association is now titled the *Study of Afro-American Life and History*. In 1916, he founded the *Journal of Negro History*. As another challenge, in February, 1926, Dr. Woodson launched Negro History Week as an initiative to call attention to the contributions of black people throughout American History. With overwhelming black

American contributions, suddenly recognized, Negro History Week became Black History Month, celebrated in the month of February.

Dr. Woodson selected the second week in February as Negro History week, because it marked the birthdays of Frederick Douglas and Abraham Lincoln, two men who greatly impacted the black population. When the week was extended to Black History Month, other celebrated significant African-American milestones were included. William Edward Burghardt DuBois's birthday was February 23, 1868. DuBois was the cofounder of the NAACP. On February 3, 1870, the right for African-Americans to vote, was granted in the 15th amendment. Societal power is in the vote of each individual. On February 25, 1890, the first black U.S. Senator, Hiram R. Revels took his oath of office. The month could also be called, NAACP month, because the NAACP was founded on February 12, 1909. On February 1, 1960, the first civil-rights' milestone occurred when a group of college students in Greensboro, North Carolina, began a sit-in at a segregated Woolworth Department Store's lunch counter.

The NAACP's mission is to end racial discrimination and segregation, that is, remove all barriers for equality of jobs, education, housing, and human dignity. The organization was formed as a direct result of the lynching of 1908. As a reaction Mary W. Ovington, a white woman, called for a meeting of leaders of all races to discuss ways to combat political and racial injustice. From that conference, the NAACP emerged with a board of directors of eight prominent members, seven white and one African-American, W.E. B. DuBois. The organization grew rapidly and successfully boycotted the motion picture, *The Birth of a Nation*, which portrayed blacks of the Reconstruction Era as distinct stereotypes.

The longevity of the NAACP can be attributed to dedicated leadership and members, who have strongly endorsed the Civil Rights Movement. In 1995, Kweisi Mfume of Maryland, head of the Congressional Black Caucus was appointed President and CEO of the NAACP. The 1995 membership was more than 400,000, distributed in 1,802 local branches. Thus, the NAACP is the biggest and the most influential civil-rights organization in the United States...[and by nature of our mission supports Black History Month].

Clea P. Hollis
President of the Johnstown
Branch—NAACP

School Finance

An integral part of providing education for eligible children was an understanding of school finances. In 1957, the board of school directors of the Johnstown Schools was composed of nine members of the city of Johnstown and five from Stonycreek Township. A joint school committee managed the joint operations and had the power delegated by the Commonwealth of Pennsylvania, except for the adoption of the budget. Adoption of the budget was the responsibility of each school board meeting in a session. However, the adoption of the joint budget required a favorable vote of both boards. The school boards operated with several committees that included finance and purchasing. Financial and fiscal affairs included preparation of the annual budget, operation and maintenance of the school cafeteria, all personnel matters, and acquisition of goods or services. According to the report, if the jointure is interested in maximizing home rule, greater local effort must be made. The partnership program was started with Dr. Levi Hollis as superintendent. The project was designed to interest local businesses to invest in education. With the partnership program, Crown American Corporation became a very active partner with the Greater Johnstown Schools.

In 1957, the Office of Field Services, School of Education at the University of Pittsburgh, Pittsburgh, Pennsylvania, conducted a year-long study. The study in discussion showed property tax receipts for ten years. The 1956–1957 taxes reflected increase from 20 mils to 22 mils. From 1949 to 1950 to 1955–1956, there had only been a token increase of approximately $70,000 in receipts for property taxes. However, the wage tax increase doubled since 1949–1950. Surprisingly, Johnstown as a healthy community had a substantial quadrupled increase from 1947–1948 to 1955–1956.

The committee stated that the school district's boundaries serve as barriers to logical school planning. The problem of schools in the Johnstown community cannot be solved satisfactorily within the boundaries of the present municipalities; the industrial and business enterprises of the city cannot survive within the city limits of Johnstown. For people twenty-five years or older, the medium years of school completed were eight years, eight months. The educational program must soon contribute in greater measure to the leadership vigor and civic competence necessary for the improvement of Johnstown. The committee structure of the board violates certain basic principles. The work of each committee should become the work of the entire board as a whole. In the 1966–1967 survey, Johnstown ranked first with real wealth in the area, and number three for dollars spent for students. The shift in wealth may have indicated the shift of industry leaving the city after the 1977 flood.

Districts' Financial Ability to Educate Students 1966–1967

District	*Real Wealth*	*Rank*	*Pupil*	*Rank*	*Per pupil*	*Rank*
Blacklick Valley	10,203,600	12	1,666	10	6,124.60	12
Cambria Heights	19,764,200	8	2,198	8	8,987.35	9
Central Cambria	37,297,700	5	2,797	5	13,334.89	5
Conemaugh Valley	37,893,600	4	2,339	6	16,200.70	2
Ferndale	18,932,100	9	1,611	12	11,751.76	6
Forest Hills	23,014,300	7	3,601	2	6,391.08	11
Greater Johnstown	165,957,400	1	10,866	1	15,273	3
Northern Cambria	17,099,400	10	1,845	9	9,267.96	8
Penn Cambria	23,644,800	6	2,304	7	10,262.50	7
Portage	11,966,700	11	1,614	11	7,414.31	10
Richland	44,547,100	3	3,227	3	13,804.49	4
Westmont Hilltop	69,510,500	2	3,024	4	22,986.27	1

(*Real Wealth* heading over District/Real Wealth columns; *Pupils to Educate* over Rank/Pupil/Rank; *Wealth Per Student* over Per pupil/Rank)

The wealth of a district determines the amount of funds and grants received for federal programs.

Federal Programs

By 1968, federal programs named Title I and Title II consisted of Adult Basic Education, School Aides, E.S.E.A Reading Programs, Head Start follow-up, and lunch programs. A policy for the free lunch program was revised in May 8, 1969. The directors voted not to distribute surplus meat commodities from the government, but would continue to receive other types of surplus food. The development of federal programs suggested an economic crisis in the city. Dr. Deremer surveyed the schools to ascertain the community's awareness of the schools' functions.

1969 Comprehensive School Survey

Dr. Richard W. Deremer from the University of Pittsburgh conducted a Comprehensive School Survey of the Greater Johnstown School District. The study was to ascertain the community's attitude about the functions and services that the school district provided for residents in the district. The surveyed population consisted of parents and sixth graders in the Greater Johnstown School District, during the second semester of the 1967–1968 school year. Every Greater Johnstown sixth-grade student took a twenty-eight-question instrument to his or her parents and a neighbor, to be completed and returned. The student distribution of the questionnaires enhanced the study, by generating a broader representation of the community. Questionnaires distributed totaled 1,520, with a return of 1,290 computable questionnaires. The adjusted sample of 1,250 was 85% of the sample population, which gave a strong indication that the community was interested in the schools.

The survey sought general information about the respondents that included school-community relations and general attitudes toward the school district. Attitudes toward specific aspects of the educational program and attitudes toward support of the schools were also surveyed. For analytical purposes, the returned questionnaires were placed in one of four categories based upon gross family income.

Gross Family Income Groups

Gross Family Income	Percent	Classified Group
Less than $5,000	19	Low Income
$5,000. To 7,999	44	Medium Low Income
$8,000. To $10.999	27	Medium High Income
More than $11,000	10	High Income

More males in the higher income groups responded to the questionnaire. A significant gap in responses existed between the low-income group and other groups. Dr. Deremer's hypothesis appeared to be that specific attention should be given to "the power of the individual vote" in the educational program of children of lower income families, to impact on individual progress. The district appeared to have a stable population; however, findings in the "Community" section of the survey show that "static or "declining" would be more appropriate modifiers.

The "Community" section respondents indicated that the 1966 unemployment in the Johnstown area was 3.9%. The low percentage on responses to property ownership invalidated the findings. Owning property had been considered a middle and upper middle class value; therefore, the response was interpreted as negative. Approximately 75% of respondents had at least part of their education in the schools now called the Greater Johnstown School District. However, 24 % of the respondents indicated that they attended another school district in the commonwealth. The low-income and high-income groups had a greater percentage of children both "below school age" and "out of school." Students attending parochial schools totaled 25%. However, parents in the low-income group reported that their child had dropped out of school at a rate that was more than the combined dropout rate for the other groups. Nevertheless, the comments about dropout rates indicated that parents are concerned about the physical, ethical, and educational welfare of their children in all groups. Respondents acknowledged that individual differences existed among teachers regarding concern for students.

The percentage of school contact per respondent indicated that high-income groups contacted the schools at a higher ratio. Consequently, the high-income group appeared to be more informed about the schools. The newspaper supplied the most information about the schools. The higher income groups probably subscribed to the daily newspaper that reported school news. The school used this indicator to maximize instruction in newspaper reading and reporting.

Emphasis on reading the newspaper may carry over to the home. Many respondents lacked knowledge of the accomplishments of the school district. Therefore, they had difficulty judging the district for adequate educational programs. The findings indicated that the community needed to be educated about educational programs. Parental comments indicated that all school systems need improvement. The mention of innovations indicated that the educational system is not dormant. As the findings revealed, respondents had varied reactions to the teaching of various courses. Respondents ranging from 30 to 50 % indicated that "labor relations" and "politics" should begin subsequent to ninth grade. However, 60 to 80 % of the same respondents indicated, "Race Relations and "Sex Education" should begin prior to ninth grade. These results paralleled similar studies in other districts. Other studies have found that children need and are ready to study race relations and sex education at an early age. On the other hand, they lack the maturity to study politics and labor-management relations before high school. The findings indicated that the amount of homework assigned was "about right."

Parents seemed satisfied with the type of report card issued. However, some parents indicated a need to have a written explanation that would help with identifying levels of skills. The percentage that selected "no option" to the response to this question indicated that parents might think these activities do not relate to the objectives of the educational program. Findings indicated that respondents favor expansion of special programs such as vocational and occupational training, technical studies, and special classes for the slow and handicapped. Findings also indicated that more respondents thought that average was inadequate in regard to religion, moral, and ethical training. The findings also indicated that respondents are relatively satisfied with discipline rendered at the elementary level. However, there appeared to be dissatisfaction at the high school level.

The findings indicated that a sizable percentage of the respondents were against additional taxes. Nonetheless, they indicated that teachers were worthy of a salary increase on a merit system. In money matters, findings indicated too much inefficiency existed relative to supplies and textbooks. Findings further indicated that more respondents think changes should be made in the curriculum and that the physical properties of the buildings should also be upgraded.

School information was made public by the media, school board minutes, brochures, and inquiries. The survey was based on household knowledge about the schools. Consequently, parents may not have been fully knowledgeable about all of the items on the questionnaire. Some of the information is listed below.

Distribution of Supervisory and Administrative Staff
1967–1968 Greater Johnstown Secondary Schools

	High	School	Cochran	Garfield	Joseph Johns	Total
Principals	1	1	1		1	4
Ass. Principals	2	2	2		1	7
Art Teachers	1	2	2		2	7
Librarians	2	1	1		1	5

	High	School	Cochran	Garfield	Joseph Johns	Total
Music Teachers	2	2	2		2	8
Special Edu. Teach	2	2	2		5	11
Guidance Teachers	2	2	2		2	8
Physical Edu. Teach	4	2	4		3	13
Vocational Teachers	9 ½	–	–		–	9 ½
Others	56 ½	49	47		31	183 ½
Totals	82	63	63		48	256
Total Students	1696	1346	1249		770	5058

Greater Johnstown School District Salary Schedule. 1967-1986

Mandated State (1965)		Standard	Bachelor	Master's	Doctorate
1.	4500	4800	5000	5300	5700
2.	4800	5100	5300	5600	6000
3.	5100	5400	5600	5900	6300
4.	5400	5700	5900	6200	6600
5.	5700	6000	6200	6500	6900
6.	6000	6300	6500	6800	7200
7.	6300	6600	6800	7100	7500
8. S*	6600	6900	7100	7400	7800
9. B*	6900	7200	7400	7700	8100
10.	7200	7500	7700	8000	8400
11. M*	7500		7800	8300	8700
12.				8400	8800

1968–1969

1.	5400	5400	5600	5900	6200
2.	5700	5750	5950	6250	6550
3.	6000	6100	6300	6600	6900
4.	6300	6450	6650	6950	7250
5.	6600	6800	7000	7300	7600
6.	6900	7150	7350	7650	7950
7.	7200	7500	7700	8000	8300
8.	7500	7850	8050	8400	8700
9. S*	7800	8200	8400	8800	9100
10. B*	8100	8600	8800	9200	9500
11.	8400		9200	9600	9900

Mandated State (1965)	Standard	Bachelor	Master's	Doctorate
12. M* 8700			10000	10300
13.			10400	10700
14.				11100
15.				11500

* State Maximums

Starting Salaries for Teachers

1950	2000
1951	2400
1952	2400
1953	2400
1954	2400
1955	2550
1956	3500
1957	3700
1958	3900
1959	4100
1960	4100
1961	4100
1962	4100
1963	4100
1964	4800
1965	4800
1966	4800
1967	5000
1968	5600

(Employees at maximum increased $600. Others $700.)

1969	6300
1970	6600
1971	6900
1972	7200
1973	7200
1974	7500
1975	7800
1976	8700
1977	8700
1978	8700
1979	8900
1980	9100
1981	9400

1982	11,300
1983	12,700
1984	14,100
1985	15,550
1986	16,975
1987	18,525
1988	19,725
1989	20,484
1990	21,743
1991	23,723
1992	25,710
1993	26,570
1994	27,770
1995	29,070
1996	30,430
1997	30,430
1998	27,500
1999	30,000
2000	32,000
2001	34,000

Recognition of Johnstown High School Community Leaders

Many Johnstown High School graduates are community leaders and were awarded the Johnstown Achievement Award. When graduates of Greater Johnstown High School receive recognition, they validate their excellent education in the schools to promote American values.

Johnstown Achievement Recipients

Year	Name	Class
1975	John P. Sheehan	1947
1983	Rear Admiral—Joseph R. Rizzo	1940
1985	Frank J. Pasquerilla	1944
1986	Frank J. Jordan	1944
1990	Major General Joseph S. Laposato	1956
1993	Edward J. Sheehan, Sr.	1953
1995	Frank Kush	1964
1996	Most Reverend Father, Midila Bonaventure Midila, T. O. R.	1944

Pennsylvania Football Hall of Fame
Johnstown High School Coach Inductee
1986   Harold J. "Duke" Weigle
1987   Tom Vargo–(Class of 1937)
1988   John Kawchek–(Class of 1932)
1989   Steve Trebus–(Class of 19320
1991   Clark Shaffer
1997   Dave Hart

Astin Study

As a follow-up to the Deremer Study, the data was compared with the Astin Study of the American Freshman National Norms, from 1985 through 1990, in the "Weighted National Norm for All Men" sections. The Astin Study concurred with the Deremer Study that males in the higher income bracket were more knowledgeable and more selective. However, the study also showed that if the father graduated from college, the percentage of their children going on to college doubled. Therefore, the assumption is that education and not money is the most significant factor in students' going on to higher education. There was also a difference whether students elected to go to a public college or private college.

Family Income

Income	1985 Public	Private	1988 Public	Private	1990 Public	Private
$29,999	6.9	5.3	6.0	4.2	5.7	3.7
34,999	10.4	8.0	7.9	6.0	7.7	5.0
39,999	10.2	7.8	8.5	6.3	7.8	5.3
49,999	13.9	11.3	12.7	9.5	12.5	8.9
59,999	12.7	12.0	12.6	11.1	13.2	10.0
74,999	10.4	11.7	13.5	13.1	13.9	13.1
99,999	6.4	9.4	9.2	12.1	10.4	13.2
149,999	4.0	8.8	6.5	11.6	6.9	13.0
150,000	3.3	9.8	5.3	14.0	5.5	17.3

Engineering surfaced as the profession with the greatest number of children attending college, about 20 %. Engineers also favored public universities.

Engineers	1985		1988		1990	
	Public	Private	Public	Private	Public	Private
	10.8	9.8	9.9	8.8	9.6	8.6

One significant finding of this study is that fathers as head of the household, with a graduate degree, had more children attending college than the percentage of parents in the higher income bracket, that is, over $100,000. The father's level of education is more significant than his income in placing him in the social stratum. Although some highly educated people may fall into the high-income group, in comparison, there is a significant difference in the college freshman enrollment to support this conclusion.

As an underrepresented group, African-Americans have been put in a position that, although they may have earned graduate degrees, their income does not reflect their skills or academic levels. Therefore, the National Association for the Advancement of Colored People (NAACP) is constantly monitoring and looking out for inequalities.

NAACP and the Board of Education

According to the school board minutes of March 6, 1969, Mr. Charles Collins, president of Johnstown Branch of the NAACP, and two other members met with Superintendent Vonarx and five members of the administrative staff. The purpose of the meeting was to discuss NAACP recommendations about negative practices in the schools, submitted to the board on February 10, 1969. The only partial agreement that occurred from the meeting was to bus fifty to sixty black African-American students from Joseph Johns High School to each of the other high schools. The board recommended moving school boundaries to shift the population of the Cochran and Joseph Johns buildings. After discussion of the tentative plans with the NAACP, the three representatives reported that all of the plans had "elements of discrimination which to them were distasteful." The board objected to the request of a written response to the letter. An African-American Student Revolt occurred in May. (See Student Revolt).

As follow-up to the NAACP inquiry, the Pennsylvania Human Relations Commission (PHRC) made an on-site visit to the Johnstown Schools. The Commission presented eight findings and recommendations.

PHRC Commission Findings and Recommendations

1. Finding

In its school desegregation plan titled," Proposed Plan Number 2 to Correct Racial Imbalance and Timetable of Implication" page 3, approved by the Pennsylvania Human Relations Commission, the Greater Johnstown Board of School Directors committed itself as follows:

(a) The school district will follow this procedure to establish an effective recruitment program to establish an integrated staff for all levels by September 1973. We will contact the various colleges and universities within the State of Pennsylvania, predominately black and white to secure applicants who may wish to come to Johnstown.

(1) We will arrange to visit and interview applicants from those school whose director or placement indicates there are at least six (6) applicants who are interested in our school district.

(2) Specific contact will be made with the following universities and conferences will be held at the university for the purpose of recruiting applicants for professional staff members in the Greater Johnstown School District.

Cheyney University	University of Pittsburgh
Lincoln University	Penn State University
Wilkes College	Indiana University of Pennsylvania

Blacks are under-represented to a statistically significant degree among classroom teachers as a whole and among elementary and secondary teachers (1 % black in each category), compared to Blacks employed by Pennsylvania school districts being 6 % of all classroom teachers, 8 % of all elementary, and 4 % of all secondary teachers. In practice, the school board gives preference to residents of the Greater Johnstown area in filling vacancies for professionals. This area has almost no black educator residents. Such a preference has the effect of limiting the hiring to predominantly white applicants, which is a violation of the following provisions of the Pennsylvania Human Relations Act. "Section 5, Unlawful Discriminatory Practices. It shall be an unlawful discrimination practice...(b) For any employer...to (4) Subsequently confine or limit...hiring of individuals,...to...any other employee- [sic] referring source...predominately of the same race,..."

Recommendation

a. For professional employee vacancies, cease and desist from the practice of giving preference to applicants who reside in the Greater Johnstown area.

b. Consider the amount and kind of experience with the Black community and its families as a relevant asset in evaluating applicants for both professional and nonprofessional positions.

Response

The Greater Johnstown School District has been and currently continues to experience the decline of student enrollment at the rate of three hundred pupils per year. This significant decrease in annual enrollment and reduced federal finding has placed the district in the position of not filling vacant positions whenever possible, and the furloughing of professional and nonprofessional employees in areas of over staffing.

When substitute for temporary vacancies and permanent vacancies occur, priority is given to furloughed employees as per stated in the "Professional and Non-Professional Contracts" between the Greater Johnstown School District and the employee union.

2. Finding

In filling vacancies for permanent professional employees, preference is shown to those on the district's substitute list. There is a negligible number of Blacks on the substitute list because of the scarcity of Black educators who live in the Johnstown area.

Recommendation

a. For as long as the substitute list is not as bi-racial as the residential population of the school district (% Black by 1980 U. S. Census), cease giving such preference to substitute teachers to filling vacancies for permanent employees.

Response

The increased posting and advertising notices for temporary and permanent vacancies as recommended in "Finding #3" will provide the district with a cross-section of applicants from which the school district may select quality educators.

3. Finding

Of 24 colleges notified of educator vacancies, 23 are in Pennsylvania but do not include either of the Commonwealth's predominantly Black colleges; i.e., Cheyney State College or Lincoln University.

Recommendation

a. List professional vacancies with predominantly Black colleges in Pennsylvania and adjoining states that grant the degree relevant to the vacancy.

b. Limit recruitment sources to colleges with the largest number or percent of Black enrollment in the relevant degree programs. These colleges in Pennsylvania are indicated in the PHRC's publication "Pennsylvania Affirmative Action Recruitment Sources for School District Professional Personnel."

Response

The District shall include Cheyney State College and Lincoln University on the list of colleges and universities to apprise of vacancies. The District request that the PHRC send several copies of it's publication "Pennsylvania Affirmative Action Recruitment Sources for School District Professional Personnel," to facilitate the district's list of colleges and universities to apprise of vacancies.

4. Finding

Although the application forms for professional and noninstructional positions say "An Equal Opportunity Employer," newspaper and magazine advertising of school district vacancies has not included this wording.

Recommendation

a. In all advertising of vacancies, include the phrase "An Equal Opportunity Employer."

Response

The District has implemented the inclusion of "An Equal Opportunity Employer" in the advertising of school district vacancies.

5. Finding

For the past five years, with the exception of a vacancy for a vocational education teacher, newspaper ads about vacancies have been placed in local newspapers only.

Recommendation

a. List all vacancies for professional positions in at least one Pittsburgh newspaper.

b. Prepare a brochure about the school district that will encourage minority applicants.

Response

The Greater Johnstown School District will expand advertising to include the Pittsburgh Press. A brochure regarding the school district will be developed to encourage applicants.

6. Finding

To serve the needs of some 768 Black Students, the school district has no Black counselors. There is need for better relations between school personnel and Black students and their families.

Recommendation

a. Affirmatively recruit a qualified Black to have some responsibilities regarding discipline and counseling. Such a position might be classified as a home and school visitor or coordinator, rather guidance counselor or social worker.

Response

At the present time the Greater Johnstown School District provides counseling and home and school visitors in excess of the Pennsylvania minimum requirements. As available positions develop in these areas the district will seek qualified minority applicants.

7. Finding

Blacks are under-represented to a statistically significant degree among Secretarial/Clerical personnel (2% Black), compared to the 12% Black enrollment majoring in the high school's Business Education Curriculum. Although called for in the school board policy of July 19, 1976, the Business Manager has not been actively recruiting or recommending applicants for vacancies in noninstructional positions.

Recommendation

a. Have the Business Manager resume the school board mandated role actively recruiting and recommending to the full board applicants for noninstructional positions.

b. Have the Business Manager meet with representative of the Johnstown Advisory Council to the PHRC, the local branch of the NAACP, The Greater Johnstown Affirmative Action Council, Community Action Council, and the Pennsylvania Bureau or Employment Security to work out a procedure of adequate notification about noninstructional vacancies to make possible referral of applicants.

Response

When the high school building was closed at the end of the 79–80-school term, 5 clerical employees and 9 maintenance employees were laid off and 5 maintenance employees were bumped down to lower...classifications. Since that time, the district has been calling laid off and lower classified employees (as per union contract) to nonprofessional vacancies. There have only been 2 instances when an "outsider" was hired to fill vacancies. On January 7, 1981, a handicapped white female was hired to fill the vacant tax collector position and on March 16, 1981, a black male clerk was hired to fill a vacant payroll clerk position.

As displayed by the attached letter, the Business Manager has sent announcements of job vacancies for non professional positions to the local NAACP and will continue to send postings to the local agencies as listed in the PHRC recommendation.

8. Finding

An I. Q. score of 130 is required for a student to be selected for the gifted Program. Black students are under-represented to a statistically significant degree among the participants in the Gifted Program (3% Black), compared to their 14% of the school district enrollment.

Recommendation

Replace the 130 IQ score requirement with other educational criteria that indicate gifted potential or ability. Consult the Chester Area School District for such possibilities.

Response

The Greater Johnstown School District's gifted program follows procedure of identification as outlined in 22 PA. CODE CH 341, Standards for Special Education. The District has written to the West Chester School District for a description of its Gifted Program.

Running concurrently with the PHRC and NAACP investigation, a committee was named to review the interaction of public employees and employers.

Act 195—Public Employer/Employee Relations Act

On May 14, 1968, the governor appointed a committee that became known as the Hickman Commission to review the entire area of interaction between public employees and employers. The Commission's responsibility was twofold. First, the Commission was to make recommendations for the establishment of orderly, fair, and workable procedures. Second, the Commission was directed to recommend appropriate legislation. After ten meetings in May and June, the Commission presented a summary of the recommendations to the governor on June 25, 1968. The Commission proposed that the Public Employee Act of 1947 be repealed for three major weaknesses in the basic structure.

1947 Act Weaknesses

1. The Act did not require public employees to bargain collectively with their employer.
2. The Act forbids any and all strikes of public employees. Twenty years of experience illustrates that the policy is unreasonable and unenforceable when compared to ineffective collective bargaining.
3. The Act has mandatory penalties that are self-defeating. The forbidding of a public employer to get normal pay increases for three years, compared to an employee who has gone out on strike and has been re-employed. This procedure reduces the value of the position to that employee and drives this employee to seek other employment.

The Commission recommended new legislation to govern public employer and employee relations through mandatory utilization of collective bargaining, with a limited right to strike. The right to strike is curtailed when public health, safety, or welfare of individuals are endangered or when an impasse occurs after collective bargaining procedures had been exhausted.

The Commission submitted to the Governor, proposed legislation to shape the expansion of the duties of the State Labor Relations Board and the State Mediation Service. This proposed legislation promoted the legal framework for Senate Bill 1333 and became known as Act 195. In March 17, 1970, the bill was brought before the Senate with amendments for second consideration on July 13, 1970. After concurrence of the House, the bill was signed into law on July 23, 1970, and became effective on October 21, 1970.

The Greater Johnstown Education Association went on strike during the 1969–1970 school year. Act 195 became effective on October 21, 1970. Teachers from the school district challenged the Public Employee Act of 1947, forbidding all strikes by public employees. Records in the Cambria County office show that legal papers were served on the Greater Johnstown School Administration. However, records were not located to support that a hearing was held regarding the complaint.

According to the *Tribune* of May 14, 1970, school officials announced that split sessions would be held at Greater Johnstown High School and the three junior high schools during the duration of the strike. Elementary schools were to operate on a normal schedule. Teachers, who were not members of the Greater Johnstown Education Association, reported to their classrooms daily. Problems occurred at Joseph Johns Junior High School with a shortage of teachers. During the strike, 40 % of the teachers in the school district did not report for duty.

After the school directors of Greater Johnstown School District and Superintendent Vonarx met with the Negotiating Committee of the Greater Johnstown Education Association, on Sunday, May 17, 1970, an agreement was reached. Noteworthily, the meeting leading up to the agreement was lengthy, with numerous caucus sessions. The salary agreement for the 1970–1971 school year was as following:

Salary: All professional and temporary professional employees would receive an adjusted salary increase of $600 above the state mandated minimum. Professionals at maximum in the 1970–1971 school year were granted a salary increase of $100 above the allocated $300 increment.

School term: The school term, for teachers was 187 days, included 181 student instructional days and 6 noninstructional teacher days.

Health Benefits: The Board would pay the full individual Blue Cross-Blue Shield and Major Medical premiums for individual for the amount of $11.49 per person.

Life Insurance: The Board would pay life insurance premiums for professional employees in the amount of $3,000 per person. The employee had the option of purchasing additional insurance of $10,000 at 33 cents per thousand with a payroll deduction.

Severance pay: With the 1970–1971 School District, each individual leaving the district would be granted a severance pay of $100 for each 10 year period of service, not to exceed $300, with a one time payment.

Fringe Benefits:

a. Professional development: The Board will provide a fund of $2,346 for professional development for teachers.

b. Professional dues: The Board shall collect by payroll deduction, professional dues, upon the request of the employee.

c. Preparation Time: The Board shall grant 125 minutes of preparation time to all elementary teachers.

d. Personal Leave Days: Two days of personal leave days, with pay, were granted for professional employees

e. Tax Sheltered Annuity Plan: The Board shall give professional employees the option of payroll deduction to participate in an annuity plan of their choice.

f. Free Lunch Period: The Board shall enforce the law, relative to a duty-free lunch period for processional employees.

Committee for merit program: A committee of administrative staff, professional employees and the Board, and members of the Greater Johnstown Education Association will be designated to develop a voluntary merit program for professional staff. The decision to participate in the merit program would be at the discretion of the individual employee.

Teachers' work day: Teachers will agree to arrive at a minimum 15 minutes before the start of the school day and depart no sooner than 15 minutes after the students.

Amnesty: The seven members of the Board in attendance and the Negotiating committee extended amnesty to the nonworking employees with a salary deduction for not working during the two-day strike. Amnesty hinged on the court decision.

By the 1970s, unions had become prevalent among educators. According to the *Tribune Democrat* of March 17, 1972, the Greater Johnstown Education Association asked the school board to dismiss fifty-nine teachers, because they had not renewed their membership as outlined in the teacher's contract. The grievance was based on Public Relations Act 195 that stated: "Maintenance of membership means that all employees who have joined an employee organization must remain members during the duration of a collective bargaining agreement." The teachers resigned from the organization after the September teachers' strike. The penalty under Act 195 was dismissal. However, the Greater Johnstown School District's Board of Directors and Superintendent Vonarx took a stand not to dismiss the striking teachers.

Civil Action

The Greater Johnstown Education Association filed the suit based on the Public Relations Act 195 in Cambria County Court, after the school board refused to submit the grievance to binding arbitration. The board stated that the school law did not permit it to dismiss teachers for reasons outlined in the grievance. The June 8, 1972, suit asked the court to direct the school board to submit the dispute to binding arbitration as prescribed in the teacher contract (Equity Docket Vol. 10, p. 52.) However, at a regular school board meeting, the board approved a two-year contract that included twenty-eight supervisors and principals. The contract included an increased salary range for supervisors and principals of $175 to $900.

Items of the Contract Agreement

Full family medical insurance

Life Insurance Policy (Starting at $3,000 and going to $5,000)

Severance Pay ($200–10 years, $400–20 years, $600 30 years)

A $1,500 salary increase for a doctorate

Increase in salary of $1,000 for certified supervisors and
   Principals with 30 credits in administration beyond the
   masters

Uncertified administrators would receive teacher's salary

Length of school day (one-half hour before student arrival and
   one-half hour after students depart).

Funding for the new contract was factored into the new budget. According to Sandra K. Reabuck of the *Tribune Democrat,* the board voted unanimously to give final approval to a $12.7 million dollar budget for the 1975–1976 school year, which showed a deficit of nearly $840,000. At the same meeting the board took action to appoint Dr. Levi Hollis of Warren, Ohio, as Director of Secondary Education. When Dr. L. B. Hollis vacillated about relocating, he received numerous calls from Dr. B. K. Johnson, a local dentist and former president of the Johnstown Branch of the NAACP. Dr. Johnson stated that he was calling on behalf of the Johnstown School Board members, who had asked him to intervene. Dr. Hollis also received many calls from the 1975 president of the NAACP, Mrs. Hope Johnson, stating that the school district and the community needed his expertise. The new position was created on the recommendation of the superintendent, Dr. Donato Zucco, in an effort to upgrade the district's curriculum.

The board also took action to request a recommendation from Mr. William Grove, the high school principal, to name Miss Olive Katter, a high school English teacher as chairperson of the English Department. Miss Katter had filed a complaint with the federal Equal Employment Opportunity Commission (EEOC), charging discrimination in the district. Dr. Zucco stated that EEOC had found reasonable cause and he proposed that Miss Katter be reinstated. Robert Green, the solicitor, said this process was in accordance with the approved policy to authorize principals to name chairpersons on the advice, consent, or approval of the board.

American Federation of Teachers vs. Greater Johnstown Education Association

On July 1, 1981, the American Federation of Teachers granted a charter to thirty-eight teachers of the Greater Johnstown School District. This group of teachers became known as the Greater Johnstown Federation of Teachers, AFT Local 4180, and AFL-CIO. The Federation petitioned the Pennsylvania Labor Relations Board to conduct an election by secret ballot, to ascertain the bargaining agent for teachers of the Greater Johnstown School District.

The Pennsylvania Labor Relations Board conducted the election on June 7, 1982. Three hundred fifty-five ballots were cast. Eighty-nine ballots favored representation by the Greater Johnstown Federation of Teachers, AFT Local 4180, AFL-CIO. Greater Johnstown Education Association, PDE-NEA cast 263 ballots in favor of representation. One ballot was cast for no representation and one ballot was void because it was blank. The Pennsylvania Labor Relations Board ruled according to the election. The ruling stated that a majority of the votes by employees in the aforementioned election designated Greater Johnstown Education Association, PSEA/NEA as the exclusive representative for the purpose of collective bargaining with the employer.

Greater Johnstown Education Association

The president of the Greater Johnstown Education Association stated that teachers of the Greater Johnstown School District should be walking the picket lines at schools in the district about 8:00 A.M. on Monday, September 13, 1982. On the same day, the *Johnstown Tribune-Democrat* reported that the Johnstown School District teachers had voted by a two-to-one margin to reject the school district's contract offer and go on strike. The Greater Johnstown Education Association had informed the board of directors and the administrative officials of the decision.

Superintendent Zucco responded to the Union that the district would be open for classes on that Monday morning, September 13, except for kindergarten classes. Kindergarten classes were canceled. The board's negative vote for a contract offer on August 30 was an indicator that a strike might be forthcoming. However, teachers agreed to negotiate an agreement from August 30 through September 10. Johnstown's history of strikes included a two-day strike in the 1969–1970 school year and a twenty-day strike in the 1971–1972 school year. The teachers' strikes were gaining in longevity.

On Sunday, October 24, 1982, the *Johnstown Tribune-Democrat* reported that the longest teachers' strike in the history of the schools was beginning to dent the teachers' pocketbooks. The strike polarized the school district and public apathy was swelling. According to the newspaper, the school board terminated medical benefits to the teachers. Teachers had to pay the $525 premium for three months for their health benefits. The six-week strike played havoc with the 180-day state requirement and with the school's fiscal year that ended June 30. When the strike was over, teachers were given credit for 173 working days.

Negotiable Issues in Teacher's Contract

The Board: Offered $5,000 in a three-year contract.

GJEA: Requested $5,700 in a three year contract

The Board: Wanted transfers by the most senior qualified member as determined by administration.

GJEA: Wanted involuntary transfers that were necessitated by reassignments or school closings to be determined by seniority.

The Greater Johnstown School District filed a complaint in Equity, a Petition for Preliminary Injunction in the Civil Division of the Common Pleas Court of Cambria County. After a hearing on November 8, 1982, Judge Creany issued a temporary restraining order.

Johnstown School District Restraining Order

1. The Greater Johnstown School District shall beginning with the opening of the ordinarily schedule for tomorrow, November 9, make all of the classrooms and areas available for functioning as a school for purposes of the education of the children legally in the school district.

2. The association and their respective members shall be enjoined from withholding professional services as teachers and the individuals from withholding their professional services in the instruction of the children legally entitled to attendance at the Greater Johnstown School facilities.

Judge Creany ordered negotiators from both sides to recommend a three-year contract package. The package was to be negotiated in an all-day bargaining session. The judge stated that he was of the opinion that all parties had arrived at a point where further negotiations would be nonproductive. He stated that the issues had been addressed and the contract was an equitable proposal. The judge told representatives of the striking teachers, "You can live with it, preserve the integrity of your Association and be doing a benefit to the community." The president of the Greater Johnstown Association and Superintendent Zucco both stated they would comply with the order of the judge.

The judge followed with ordering both sides to meet in the superintendent's office at 10:30 A.M. on November 9, 1982, to jointly develop a contract. The judge further ordered both sides to hold a meeting at 7:30 P.M. on the same day to vote on the contract. The judge informed the school board that the ordered meetings did not defy the state Sunshine Law and that the order also met the Association's requirement for twenty-four hours of notification before a teachers' meeting.

The Greater Johnstown School District Board rejected the court-authored contract. The board agreed to send the contract back to the Cambria County Judge on November 11, 1982, for clarification. Board members were not clear on the phase "economic reopener." The other item the board wanted clarified was the implementation of the vision and dental plan. The judge thought that since the term had been used in past negotiations, board members understood the terminology. The board agreed to reopen negotiations but disagreed with the prospect of negotiating other economic issues. One economic issue was the dental plan. The board wanted to keep the old dental plan and reimburse teachers for costs that teachers incurred during the strike in October. The other economic issue was the vision plan. The board agreed to provide a less expensive vision plan than the one on the table before the court's written contract. The Greater Johnstown Education Association approved the proposed contract.

The *Johnstown Tribune-Democrat* reported on November 18, 1982, that the Cambria County Court issued a permanent injunction. The injunction filed by the school board directors ordered the district's three hundred teachers to refrain from a work stoppage, to work under terms of the expired contract, and to continue negotiations at least until December 16, 1982. Dental insurance was the outstanding, lasting issue of the proposed three-year agreement. The negotiating teams for teachers and the school board had agreed in principle to provide complete dental coverage. However, school board members became indecisive over this issue.

When the judge imposed the permanent injunction, he requisitioned conditions.

School District's Injunction

1. The defendants (teachers) shall be enjoined from withholding their professional services.
2. The plaintiff (school board) shall return the employees under terms and conditions of the last contract, except the 180-day contract.
3. The new school calendar shall not end prior to June 24.
4. The two parties shall continue negotiations and must file a full report with court on or before December 16, 1982.
5. The newly negotiated contract must provide benefits retroactive to November 9, 1982.

On the controversial dental plan, the board agreed on family dental coverage at seventy to one hundred cost ratios, based on usage, under the expired contract. The association had sought 100 % coverage. They argued that the board could change from a private insurance company to Pennsylvania School Employees benefit at no additional cost, for one year. Some board members maintained that a one-year, no-cost increase guarantee was insufficient in a three-year contract.

Hollis—National Educator

Chapter XI ❖

National Task Force

As the board of directors negotiated a contract with teachers, Dr. Levi B. Hollis, director of curriculum–assistant superintendent, was featured in the Pittsburgh Courier (Pennsylvania) on June 19, 1982, as a National Educator. The U.S. Department of Education named Dr. Hollis as a consultant to the National Task Force on Compensatory Education. The Task Force consisted of educators from all fifty states; however, Dr. Hollis was the only educator selected from Pennsylvania. The Task Force reviewed and evaluated Talent Search Programs and recommended an allocation of $270 million. The article stated, "Dr. Levi B. Hollis is not only a father in his own right but he has been a father-in-education, directly and indirectly to many youth." In a letter dated, May 18, 1982, to Ms. Margaret A. Wingfield, Education Program Specialist for the U.S. Department of Education, Dr. Hollis comments on the excellent leadership provided during the Talent Search 1982 Project.

When Dr. Hollis resigned from the Warren City Schools, in July 15, 1975, he wrote a memorandum to his fellow administrative co-workers. He apprised them that he had been appointed by the Board of Education for the Greater Johnstown Public Schools, as Director of Secondary Education. He informed them that a grant in the amount of $284,407 had been received for Warren and thanked the staff for their support of an unequivocal success of the project. The grant allowed for new programs and provided refinement for other programs. Dr. Hollis stated that the success of students in school hinges on an academic team effort. He mentioned that his future with the Johnstown Schools was bright in the position of Secondary Education and that he was looking forward to the new challenge to help guide a school system.

Interesting to note, Dr. Hollis came to the Johnstown School District with strong credentials, graduating from Duquesne University, in Pennsylvania, and Ohio State University, Ohio. He had earned a Ph.D. from Kent State University, Ohio, and was an administrator in the Warren Schools. When invited for weekday interviews, he turned down the first two requests with the Johnstown School Board of Directors, because of commitments to other programs. When the director of personnel called him for the third time, other candidates had proven unqualified. Therefore, the board changed their policy to interview Dr. Hollis on the weekend. In the spring of 1975, a Johnstown School District administrator met Dr. Hollis and his wife, in front of the Chestnut School building administrative offices. As they waited in their car for the appointment time, a school administrator tapped on the window and said, "Are you Dr. Hollis? I saw the Kent State University sticker." When Dr. Hollis replied, "Yes," the director's response was, "We thought that you might be a black man, with your membership in the NAACP." Superintendent Zucco had said that they wanted the best man for the job and the guy in Ohio had the best credentials. With a background of success with academic initiatives, Dr. Hollis was appointed to the position of director of secondary education by a 5–4 board vote. Notwithstanding his lack of full board support, Dr. Hollis carried the spirit of academic teamwork with him to the Greater Johnstown School District.

Garfield Junior High School In-Service Meeting—August 27, 1975
Welcome Address: Dr. Levi B. Hollis, Jr.

It's time to begin anew! We hope that each of you have had a pleasant and rewarding summer.

It is obvious by now that we have not concluded the renovation of our building. However, that which has to be completed will in no way interfere with our educational program. I am sure you will agree that the maintenance people are to be commended for the excellent condition of our school. We can all be proud to work in such a beautiful environment.

Current literature reflects that the educational pendulum is swinging back to more structure and discipline in our schools. For the past ten years, average scores on the scholastic aptitude tests have fallen. Many urban and large suburban districts have reported a steady decline in students' abilities on math and reading tests. Most of us have been urging the return to teaching basic academic skills. With soaring educational costs, the traditional structured classroom is also the most efficient expenditure of the educational dollar. Of course, the structured setting is not for everyone. For those children who don't "fit," I believe our district should provide an alternative school.

This year we hope to make some significant improvements in the area of curriculum district wide. A number of you have contributed to hopeful changes in the English curriculum and others will be asked to make similar contributions in your specific areas. When asked to help or contribute, I hope that you respond as a professional. We are here to serve our boys and girls and all our efforts should be directed toward helping them grow. It is my desire to make Garfield a Middle School that is second to none. Together, we can achieve such a goal!

We need to get off to a good beginning. We need to reflect a positive attitude toward our job and the individuals with whom we work—both students and fellow employees. Be professional, friendly, cheerful, courteous and enthusiastic. When June 1976 rolls around, I hope we can look back and say that it was a GOOD year.

Several years later, a response to another In-service Committee Meeting was found in the late Dr. Hollis' files. In 1977, he conducted an in-service workshop at the end of the fiscal year for administrators. The superintendent followed with a letter of appreciation.

July 8, 1977
Dr. Levi B. Hollis
Meadowvale Annex
729 Wood Street
Johnstown, PA 15902

Dear Dr. Hollis:

On behalf of the In-Service Steering Committee and the administration of the Greater Johnstown School District, I would like to express our appreciation for your fine assistance at our June 21 Inservice program.

We had our staff respond to an evaluation instrument on June 22. We want you to know that the majority of comments indicated that this In-Service program was the best that our staff has attended to date.

We appreciate your interest and enthusiasm, and your willingness to assist us in developing a worthwhile In-Service program for our staff.

Sincerely,

Donato B. Zucco
Superintendent of Schools

Citizens' Advisory Committee

Dr. Hollis organized the Citizens' Advisory Committee (CAC) of the Greater Johnstown School District, on February 3, 1976. Twenty-three local community people met with administrators monthly, to talk about trends in education. Superintendent Zucco, Director of Elementary Education Louis Bennese and Director of Secondary Education Dr. Levi Hollis attended the meeting. The administrators presented specific problems and programs. The residents had the opportunity to discuss their concerns about particular programs and perceived problems in the school system. Dr. Hollis presented the district's Long Range Plan, the Goals of Quality Education, the Alternative Program, the Secondary Gifted Program, and other initiatives at these meetings. The Citizen Advisory Committee was a very dynamic and ever-changing committee without elected officers.

Class of 1984–Johnstown High School
Administration

Dr. Donato Zucco	Superintendent
Dr. Levi B. Hollis, Jr.	Assistant Superintendent
Donald B. Irwin	Principal

Class Officers

Kerry Dull	President
Kim Martyak	Vice President
Karen Starlzer	Secretary
Janna Audey	Treasurer
College Scholarships	24

Highest Honor

Kimberly Marie Nagrant	Jammy J. Owens
Brian Anthony Grus	Monica Marie Raich
Susan K. Smith	Aileen Terese Petak
Diana M. Kopchik	Kimberly Martha Martyak
Michael G. Rok	Kevin S. Roth
Catherine J. Lugar	Sandra D. Martinek
Theresa M. Legath	Scott Charles Dadey
Cherie Lynn Tennis	Lisa An Mayko

In the fall of 1984, Dr. Hollis was appointed superintendent of the Greater Johnstown School District. In 1986, he was named to the commonwealth's Blue Ribbon Advisory Group to reverse the trend of high school dropouts. Dr. Hollis was one of sixteen educators and corporate and government leaders appointed by Thomas K. Gilhool, State Secretary of Education, to serve on a "Successful Students Partnership Advisory Committee." Dr. Hollis developed the program in 1978, while serving as the Director of Secondary Education. His dropout prevention program led to the district's Alternative Program. In the Greater Johnstown School District, 1983, the Johnstown Schools dropout rate was 8.5 %. In 1983, the state dropout rate was 20.2 %. At the national level 25 % of the seniors failed to graduate from high school. The rate for the 1985–1986 school year was 2.3, among the lowest in the state. Dr. Hollis stated, "Parental involvement and community support are keys to dropout prevention." He continued that it was becoming increasingly clear that the school alone cannot do the job of educating the nation's youth. The Blue Ribbon Advisory Group was organized to maximize learning habits for students in the commonwealth with emphasis on problems that became impediments to learning. Dr. Hollis was also instrumental in starting two community-based educational organizations that included parents.

Community Programs

Dr. L. B. Hollis' first community educational program was started in 1979 with the Greater Johnstown Enrichment Program. Glosser Brothers Department Store initially funded the proposal written by Dr. Clea P. Hollis. The program included above-average kindergarten students and their parents. The program was sponsored by the local branch of the NAACP, with Mr. James Porcher as president. Attorney William L. Glosser, Chairperson of PHRC Advisory Board, was also the Chairperson of the Enrichment Program. Later, the United Way of Greater Johnstown funded the program for more than fifteen years. Kindergarten teachers recommended above-average students to attend classes on Saturday morning at the YMCA. These students were challenged in a small class of fifteen students. Dr. L. B. Hollis often taught these students on Saturday mornings and talked with their parents about their

progress. Dr. L. B. Hollis was president of the Board of Trustees for the YMCA during the construction of the new building on Haynes Street.

YMCA, *Courtesy of Recci Patrick*

The second educational program, the Greater Johnstown Minority Scholars Club for high school college-bound students, commenced in 1984. With the approval of Dr. Frank Blackington, president of the Johnstown Campus of the University of Pittsburgh, Professor Claudia Jones launched a Science Buster's Summer Program for the scholars. Young high school scholars were introduced to the world of science. Noteworthy, Ms. Jones had been a biology teacher at Joseph Johns Junior High School, before accepting a faculty position at the university. From exposure to the sciences, many young scholars were motivated to pursue a science major in college. Dr. Hollis' son, one of the scholars, was motivated to become a software engineer. The Greater Johnstown Minority Scholars Club Advisory Board consisted of educators and parents in Greater Johnstown.

First Greater Johnstown Minority Scholars Advisory Board

Claudia Jones, Coordinator	Mrs. Helen Gunby, Community
Linda Daniels, Secretary	Dr. Levi B. Hollis, Jr., Education
Dr. Clea P. Hollis, Treasurer	Reverend Julius Porcher, Religion
Bruce Haselrig, Scholarship	

Dr. L. B. Hollis provided the initial funds to establish this program and advisory board members have continued to financially support the organization. However, a prominent African-American businesswoman, Ms. Pauline H. L. Gordon, has provided the annual scholarship since the beginning of the program. In 2001, another annual scholarship was begun and first awarded in memory of Mrs. Eleanor Haselrig.

Greater Johnstown Minority Scholars Club
Scholarship Recipients
Seniors of the Year–Greater Johnstown High School

Celeste Myers	1985
Tracy Gaines	1987
Alvin McCray	1988
Agsontina Thomas	1990
DeSundera Williams	1991
Melanie Jones	1993
Simone Williams	1994
Preston K Brandon	1995
Ronette L. Brandon	1996
Nikki L. Gordon	1997
Jamie A. Triplin	1998
Ernest Williams	1998
Takeesha N. Lewis	1998
Dana Redden	2001

Tutorial Program

Dr. L. B. Hollis made arrangements with the Department of Education at the University of Pittsburgh to provide academic tutorial sessions for Johnstown Students. College students met with Johnstown students who needed help, once a week at St. James Missionary Baptist Church. Reverend Dr. Ralph Johnson, pastor of the church, has con-

St James Missionary Baptist Church,
Courtesy of Recci Patrick

tinued the program. College students and volunteers work with students from the Johnstown Schools from first through twelfth grades. Sessions in 2001 were held, once a week, from 4:30 P.M. to 7:30 P.M.

Change Is Inevitable

Not only did Dr. L. B. Hollis promote academic programs, he wrote and presented his own speeches to the student body for special occasions and commencement. On April 1, 1987, as superintendent of schools, he presented this speech to the National Honor Society.

National Honor Society Induction Program
Johnstown High School
It's Worth the Trip

Mr. Irwin, Platform Guests, National Honor Society Participants, Parents, Staff, and friends,

It is a significant pleasure for me to be able to share this very important program with you. There is a national merchandising chain that has as one of its slogans—"It's Worth the Trip." I want to talk to you parents for just a few minutes. You, like me, as a parent, are on a trip through life. As you sit out there, I can just sense the pride you must feel. I have two children, both of whom were fortunate enough to earn membership in the National Honor Society. So I too know the pride you must feel. And at this moment, you parents of the inductees must admit, "It's Worth the Trip." You and the new inductees have made many sacrifices. You have had to make great changes in your schedules. Change is inevitable; however, it is the direction that counts.

For the students who are in the National Honor Society; and those who are inducted this morning; and those who aspire to be in the National Honor Society; I say that you are headed in the right direction. For all of you who make it, I think that you too will find that it is worth the trip. The teacher and the parent in me will not permit me to sit down without giving each student some advice. The advice is this: "Failure is not fatal and success is not final." It is better to do your best than to be the best. When you do your best, you are in control. Don't be afraid to let others decide who is the best. Always do your best and I am sure that you will find that it's worth the trip. Thank you.

Dr. L. B. Hollis always emphasized scholarship and parental involvement. Using the findings of Deremer's Comprehensive School Survey about the Johnstown Schools, he initiated several proactive school programs.

Alternative Program

Dr. Hollis introduced the Alternative Program in 1978. When the program completed its tenth year in 1988, Alternative Program teachers had served more than 1,000 at-risk students. For that calendar year, the program had received $108,567,000 in grants. Students in the Alternative Program were encouraged to focus on their individual goals and to restructure their lives to accomplish their goals. In order to improve attendance, daily contacts were made with each absent student. Efforts were made for tutoring to improve math skills. The Alternative Program was also an alternative for out-of-school suspension.

The Greater Johnstown School District's Alternative Program for Dropout Prevention Phase II was judged to be an exemplary program by the Pennsylvania Department of Education (PDE) and approved by the state Diffusion Panel on February 14, 1980. The Alternative program was an off-campus program housed in the Zion Lutheran Education Building in downtown Johnstown. The program featured diversified basic education, counseling, artisans' program, and a job program. The program had parent and community involvement, with a social adjustment component. Students were selected from grades seven through twelve.

Student Selection Criteria for the Alternative School
1. Poor attendance in regular program
2. Potential dropout tendencies
3. Underachieving
4. Inability to adjust to social requirements of regular program
5. Inability to cope with the time constraints program
6. Inability to cope with authority figures

Job orientation activities are often part of the classroom assignment package. Student contracts determine their basic instruction. Class size was limited to fifteen students.

Curriculum

English	Social Studies
Math	Science
Remedial Math	Reading
Physical Education	Health
Industrial Arts	Vocational Shop

Artisan Classes

Typing	Television Repair
Cosmetology	Macramé
Gem Cutting	Banking
Leather craft	Electronics
Wall papering	Small Engine Repair

Students returned to their home school for industrial arts and vocational shop classes. Classroom teachers attempted to tie artisan and work experience with classroom instruction. The goal was to reduce the student dropout rate. It was believed that students drop out of school when they experience academic failure, expulsion, and suspension. Students' self-esteem was bolstered with success in academics and, of course, their attendance improved. Ultimately, the aim of the program was to help motivate students to be productive citizens. Funding was provided by various state and federal sources.

Funding

	1977–1978	1978–1979	1979–1980
Title IV-C	31,997	32,798	15,699
CETA	00	54,826.95	54,674.69
District	30,000	30,000	30,000

At the end of the 1979–1980 school year, there were 5,850 students. The program staff served seventy students enrolled in the program.

Program Staff

1 Full-time Administrator	1 Full-time Counselor
2 Full-time Teachers	2 Part-time Teachers
2 Part-time Title I Teachers	1 Full-time Clerk

Relative to the funding of the Alternative Program, Dr. Hollis received a letter from the Chairman of the Education Committee of the board.

Letters about the Alternative School

August 26, 1981

Dear Dr. Hollis:

I want to take this opportunity, as Chairperson of the Education Committee, to compliment you on the excellent piece of work, and your efforts in getting the Alternative School funded this year.

I am aware that without this funding, staffing problems would have occurred because additional persons would have been furloughed.

I personally appreciate your efforts; keep up the good work.

> Sincerely,
> Frank Galordi
> Chairperson, Education Committee
> FG/cmk
> Cc: Board Members

Dr. Hollis' Response

Memo

From the desk of...

Levi B. Hollis

September 1, 1981

Dear Mr. Galordi:

I am in receipt of your August 26 letter, regarding my efforts to have CETA restore the funding for our Phase II Alternative Program. Please know that I appreciate your positive remarks and your thoughtfulness.

I shared the letter with my wife. To be sure, we were very pleased to receive it.

> LBH

Vital Issues Project

In 1983, Dr. L. B. Hollis ran a pilot program, entitled Vital Issues Project (V.I.P.). With the responsibility of the Director of Federal Programs, he acquired a grant of $91,000 from the U.S. Department for the Vital Issues Project, in 1984. The project was designed to improve students' self-image in school and also in their day-to-day lives outside of school. The program served 250 students enrolled in grades six through twelve (GJSD Newspaper, December, 1984).

Entitlement Funds

Dr. Hollis was instrumental in acquiring Entitlement Funds for the School District. Entitlement Funds distribution was based on the economic condition of the district and student achievement scores. In 1984, the commonwealth provided $736,000 for Chapter One Reading and mathematic programs. The allocation was for remedial reading and mathematics instruction in both the public and parochial schools in Johnstown. Chapter Two funds consisted of $49,000 to upgrade computer-training facilities in the Johnstown Schools.

Library

In 1987, the library also made history with an innovative project. The school librarian, Miss Connie McClain, described the project, Access Pennsylvania, as a million pieces of information. The computerized system enabled the user to access information beyond library walls, with other schools acting as resources. The board approved the proposal on May 1, 1987. After training librarians, the system was available for high school students in the fall of 1988. For a special reading project, Dr. Frank Blackington, president of the University of Pittsburgh at Johnstown, hosted a luncheon for students who had accomplished their library-reading goal.

TELS

A TELS (Testing for Essential Learning) Improvement Plan directed by the Tri-State Study Council of the University of Pittsburgh was implemented in 1987. The Greater Johnstown Newsletter (Spring 1988) gave the mission statement as "Caring today about your child's tomorrow." An overview of the 1987–1988 accomplishments underscores the mission, because the goal was to improve instruction and learning. Students from the university staffed after-school centers, supervised by two elementary principals. The objective was to increase scores on standardized

California achievement scores. Records illustrated that all grades improved except for the third-grade students' reading level.

HILS

As reported in the Johnstown School District Newsletter (March 1979) a High Intensity Learning System (HILS) was launched at Meadowvale Elementary School in 1980. Random House Publishing Company designed the pilot program to identify deficiencies and strengths of individual students in mathematics by diagnostic testing. It was funded by Title I in the amount of $10,000. The program covered third- through fifth-grade students. Mrs. Marion Slick, with two teacher aides, administered the program. A significant number of the 938 students enrolled at Meadowvale were diagnosed as having some type of academic skills problem. These students received one-half hour individual instruction at least three times a week.

Adelphi Program

The Greater Johnstown School District participated in the Adelphi University National Training Institute at Sayville, New York. In February 1978, a team of twenty-one traveled to New York with Dr. Levi Hollis, director of secondary education. The team included teachers, board members, and administrators. The Johnstown team was caught in a torrential snowstorm en route to New York. The flight was grounded and the Johnstown team spent a night in a hotel waiting for the weather to clear. The desire to learn to develop strategies to prevent student disruption in schools overshadowed the snowstorm. Since the team's primary focus was to develop skills to address truancy, they continued on the flight, when the weather permitted. One of the outstanding interactions of the training was a workshop on "first sight impressions." Each person wrote, on a posterboard hung on the back of each other person in the room, one word of how they personally classified that person on first sight. For Dr. Hollis, this was a lesson in levels of first sight rejection.

Dr. Hollis transferred the experience to students. He thought that if a student did not feel good about him or herself, he or she had perceived rejection in a school environment. Naturally that student would elect not to attend school. Dr. Hollis developed a sensitivity program that he presented at numerous workshops about different phases of rejection. The Law Enforcement Assistance Administration (LEAA) and the Office of Economic Opportunity funded the entire Adelphi Project. In 1979, fifty-six school districts throughout the nation participated.

Summer School–1979

Summer School in the Greater Johnstown School District was started in 1976. Mr. Edward Minium supervised the program. In 1978, 186 students completed summer work in nine classes.

TESA

In 1981, Dr. Hollis introduced TESA, Teacher Expectations and Student Achievement Program, to the Johnstown Schools. Steve Fisher from the Pennsylvania Department of Education acted as facilitator. TESA provided teachers with instructional and management strategies associated with increasing student achievement. A higher level of student achievement would enhance the students' self-esteem. Self-esteem and communication were priority items across the district as indicated by the Faculty and Citizens' Advisory Committees of every building. Teaching strategies were discussed at monthly dinner workshops. Each year, twenty teachers participated in the program. Program evaluation revealed that the Johnstown School program ranked first in four out of ten operational areas when compared with western Pennsylvania school districts that ran the TESA Program.

Superintendent's Awards Dinner

In 1985, Dr. Hollis commenced an annual Superintendent's Awards Banquet. The purpose of the dinner was to offer fellowship and show appreciation to the central office team for their loyalty, cooperation, and outstanding work. Dr. Hollis stated that it should be clear to colleagues, to the board of directors, and to the community that the administration wanted to accentuate the positive and reward excellence.

The third annual Superintendent Awards Banquet was held on May 12, 1988, at the Holiday Inn-Downtown. Rabbi Rav A. Soloff gave the invocation and the benediction. Dr. Hollis reviewed the 1987–1988 accomplishments and Mr. Mark Pasquerilla presented the

Superintendent's Awards. Dr. Charles Gorman, executive secretary of the Tri-State Study Council from the University of Pittsburgh talked about the Tri-State activities in the school district. Dr. Harry Faulk, associate dean at Carnegie Mellon University, gave a presentation. Mr. Gene Artman, administrative services director, provided closing remarks. The theme of the banquet was, "Caring today about your child's tomorrow."

Business-Education Partnership Program

Teachers of the Business-Education Partnership Program established a simulated office environment for students to experience work-related situations. Federal vocational funds were used to purchase state-of-the-art equipment, personal typing systems, wordprocessors, dictaphones, and a telephone system. The program was supported by a $20,000 grant in 1985. Local busi-

nesses, such as Crown American Corporation played a major roll in the partnership program. The district published a brochure entitled "Insights," that was funded by the Business-Education Partnership. According-
ing to a local businessman, with la-

Crown American Headquarters,
Courtesy of Bruce Haselrig

bor unions and changing school board directors, most businesses had difficulty establishing a consistent partnership.

Long Range Plan

On November 30, 1984, the school district submitted a Long Range Plan to the Pennsylvania Department of Education. The Plan was a five-year strategic plan from 1984 to 1989 that developed goals for the board, the staff, and the community. The plan was a guide to enunciate management goals related to the educational mission of the district. The school board adopted Twelve Goals of Quality Education at the

August 31, 1983, board meeting. The goals were related to all programs including special education.

1983 Twelve Goals of Quality Education

Goals	Skills
1. Communication	Acquire understanding of speaking, reading and writing
2. Mathematics	Acquire skills in computation
3. Self-esteem	Develop self-understanding a feeling of self-worth
4. Analytical Thinking	Develop analytical thinking
5. Understanding Others	Acquire knowledge of different cultures
6. Citizenship	Learn the history of the nation
7. Arts and Humanities	Acquire knowledge and appreciation
8. Science and Technology	Acquire knowledge, understanding and appreciation
9. Work	Acquire knowledge and attitudes to become productive
10. Family Living	Acquire knowledge and attitudes for family living
11. Health	Develop practices for physical and emotional well-being
12. Environment	Acquire knowledge and attitudes to maintain the quality of life

The District used nondistrict resources to implement and evaluate the action plan for the twelve goals. The resource evaluation team included the Intermediate Unit 08, the Pennsylvania Department of Education, Tri-State School Study Council, and the districts' Citizens Advisory Committee.

Town Meeting

The Greater Johnstown School District Advisory Council held a Town Meeting on April 30, 1886, at the First Presbyterian Church in downtown Johnstown. Mr. D. C. Nokes was the moderator. Mr. Nokes served on the Board of Johnstown Area Regional Industries (JARI). The meeting was called to address issues of the school board and the departure of Mr. Jerry Davitch, the football coach. According to the April 26, 1986 (B1), *Tribune* the primary issue was that school board members were harassing the administration and teachers. Mr. Nokes said, "We're looking for ideas to achieve academic excellence."

1988–Board of School Directors
Superintendent–Dr. Levi B. Hollis, Jr.

Dr. Bruce Williams, President	John Mulvehill
Theodore Helsel, Vice President	Bernie Oravec
Janeta Aspey	Reverend Julius Porcher
Blaine Gjurich	Gerald Zahorchak
Victoria King	

Kids Clips

Kids' Clips produced by the media department provided students with the opportunity to learn high-tech skills by working with television production equipment. The students' reading and public speaking basic skills were reinforced, while boosting self-esteem. Kid Clips have been feature on WJAC-TV (Johnstown) Cablevision, WTAJ-TV (Altoona), and WPSX-TV (State College). Students wrote, produced, and served as anchors on the popular Kids Clips Television Program. In 1987, students interviewed a United States Senator, the Pennsylvania Secretary of Education, the Pennsylvania Commissioner of Basic Education, and top professional athletes.

Kids Clips, *Courtesy of Wally Leech*

1987 Federal Programs

The Office of Federal Programs operated the school district's diagnostic and clinical educational programs for students in reading and math. Children under the cooperative guidance of classroom and Chapter One teachers gained the greatest level of achievement. A Supreme Court decision forbade teachers to be paid with federal funds for services rendered in religious schools. The parochial schools in Johnstown received Chapter One Reading and Math redemption from public school teachers. To be in compliance, the Greater Johnstown School District placed trailers at the parochial schools, within the city boundaries.

Utilization Plan
Greater Johnstown School District Enrollment

Year	Number of Students
1975	7335
1976	6837
1977	6418
1978	6092
1979	5860
1980	5669
1981	5356
1982	5240
1983	4813
1884	4602
1985	4474
1986	4232
1987	4090
1988	4011

When Dr. Hollis accepted the position as Director of Secondary Education in 1975, the student enrollment was 7,335 students, and in 1985 the enrollment was 4,474 students. The District's student enrollment declined 38 % in ten years. Between 1985 and 1988, the district's enrollment declined 11%. What caused the decline is debatable. Some people think that the 1977 flood caused families to move out of the district, because industries downsized or relocated. Families left to find employment. Regardless of the cause, the district's student enrollment continued to decline. Dr. Hollis had the vigilance to appoint a Building Utilization Committee. The Building Utilization Committee held a Building Utilization Dinner Workshop at the Downtown Johnstown Holiday Inn.

The Building Utilization Committee

Gene Artman	William Grove, Ph.D.
Linda Beard	Levi B. Hollis, Ph.D.
Michael Bichko	Nancy Kline, Ed.D.
Ronald Brougher	Leonard Kucera
Jerry Davitch	Wally Leech
Patrick Ditko	

Invited Guests

J. Anthony Capon, Ph.D.	Demographer
William R. Kory, Ph.D.	Demographer
Thomas Kalinyak, Esquire	Solicitor

The purpose of the workshop was best presented in Dr. Hollis' welcome address to workshop participants.

Welcome

Caring today about your child's tomorrow continues to be the mission statement for the Greater Johnstown School District. Embraced by this statement is our concern for appropriate building utilization for our students. Currently, only one of our seven buildings was constructed after the 1920s. In terms of cost effectiveness, housing a curriculum to meet the needs of our students, as we enter the 1990s, and aesthetics of the learning arena and the work place, our current buildings fall short of the mark.

The purpose of our meeting this evening is to provide our Board with a three-phase plan for building utilization, which would take the district into the twenty-first century. A building Utilization Committee, formed by the superintendent, has been working on the district's building utilization problem. After nearly six months of study, trips, planning, and work, the committee will present its recommendation this evening. Know that the committee has utilized our architect, a national realtor, the Pennsylvania Department of Education, and demographers in preparing its recommendation. The recommendation focuses on student needs and the quality of instruction. Cost effectiveness and declining enrollments were also major considerations.

Upon receiving our report, we hope that each Board Member will fully understand our task and our goal and be in a position to support and encourage us to complete our task. This will not be an easy undertaking, but it is a task which can be done. Its completion will do much to improve education in Greater Johnstown, as well as help build a more positive image for our School District.

Levi B. Hollis, Ph.D.
Superintendent of Schools
June 22, 1988

With approval and consensus of the school board and administrators that the current and projected student population did not support continued operation of the current buildings, Dr. Hollis presented the Building Utilization Plan to the community in the spring of 1989.

The Building Utilization Plan

The Greater Johnstown School Board and the administrative staff developed the Building Utilization Plan, comprehensive restructuring based on several factors. A demographic analysis completed by the state and the University of Pittsburgh at Johnstown revealed a dramatic decrease in student population within the district. This, combined with the fact that many of the existing buildings were old and operated very inefficiently led the board and staff to adopt this strategy.

The Building Utilization Plan involves improving the learning arena for children and the work place for instructional and supportive staff. In order to achieve this, the plan calls for three distinct actions over a ten-year period; i.e. building renovations, building closings and new construction. The idea is to consolidate student housing so that a more efficient, improved education area exists.

When the complete Plan is in effect, some 8 or 10 years hence, students will be educated in four buildings, two elementary and two secondary. With the dividing line at the Stone Bridge, approximately half of the elementary population would be attending the Westwood Elementary and the other half attending the newly constructed East End Elementary School.

The Board and Staff have realized they must reorganize the educational facilities so that our students can be afforded an education, which will permit them to compete with children from other districts as they compete for places in college and jobs in the work force, in the decades to come.

The School District is proud of its students, and to ensure their success in the future, the district is acting now.

The plan will ensure our children's future through quality education!

Dr. Levi Hollis, Superintendent
Spring, 1989

In 2002, the Building Utilization Plan has been modified. However, students in Greater Johnstown School District are enrolled in four schools, East Side Elementary (Meadowvale), West Side Elementary (Westwood), Garfield Middle School, and the Greater Johnstown High School (Cochran).

Sports

The Johnstown Board of Directors voted 7–0 to drop the wrestling team in April 1980 because of lack of interest. However, Milan Svitchan, who was the wrestling coach until 1966, was inducted into the Mat Hall of Fame. He held a record of 128–33–1, the most wins that any District 6 coach had compiled. Under Mr. Svitchan's coaching, the Greater Johnstown High School had state championships in the athletes of John McCray, George Azar, and Jeff Richardson. Jeff maintained two unbeaten seasons and a District 6 title in 1962. Don Hartnett ('48) and Donnie Gallucci ('55) had assisted Mr. Svitchan.

The 1980s were also a trailblazer in sports for Greater Johnstown School District. In wrestling, Carlton Haselrig ('84), a student at Johnstown High School, emerged as the District 6 Champion, Western Regional Champion, and the Pennsylvania State Champion. These were unusual accomplishments, because Carlton was dubbed "a man without a team." Johnstown High School District disbanded their wrestling program in 1980. Before abandonment, Jeff Richardson ('63) had captured the State Championship in 1962. Mr. Curt Davis ('63) of the Johnstown Schools was instrumental with enrolling Carlton in the Westmont program, with special permission to leave school early to work out with the nearby Westmont Hilltop Wrestling Team. His Westmont Wrestling Coach was Mr. Milt Lantz and his manager was Mr. Bob Fleck. Mr. Damian Zamias coached Carlton in his PIAA tournament. Mr. Zamias went beyond the duties of a coach, etching Carlton's strategies for the court and providing funds for financial fees. The coaches worked as a team to prepare Carlton for his success. From 1948 through 2002, Greater Johnstown High School had nine wrestling coaches.

Greater Johnstown High School
Wrestling 1948–2001

Year	Record	Coach
1948	2-7-0	Mike Garbinski
1949	4-7-0	Mike Garbinski
1950	4-5-1	Mike Garbinski

Year	Record	Coach
1951	4-5-1	Mike Garbinski
1952	5-5-0	Mike Garbinski (5 years:19-29-2)
1953	6-4-0	Milan Svitchan
1954	8-2-0	Milan Svitchan
1955	10-2-0	Milan Svitchan
1956	7-2-0	Milan Svitchan
1957	6-3-0	Milan Svitchan
1958	10-1-0	Milan Svitchan
1959	12-0-0	Milan Svitchan
1960	11-1-0	Milan Svitchan
1961	11-2-0	Milan Svitchan
1962	8-3-0	Milan Svitchan
1963	9-1-0	Milan Svitchan
1964	6-4-0	Milan Svitchan
1965	8-2-0	Milan Svitchan
1966	11-0-0	Milan Svitchan
1967	5-6-0	Milan Svitchan (15 years: 128-33-1)
1968	7-3-0	Don Gallucci (1 year: 7-3-0)
1969	6-4-0	Curt Davis
1970	4-7-0	Curt Davis
1971	6-6-0	Curt Davis
1972	4-9-0	Curt Davis (4 years: 20-26-0)
1973	11-2-0	Art Palumbo
1974	7-4-0	Art Palumbo
1975	3-8-0	Art Palumbo (3 years: 21-14-0)
1976	6-6-0	Dave Weber
1977	3-8-0	Dave Weber (2 years: 9-14-0)
1978	1-14-0	Dick Mock
1979	0-3-0	Dick Mock (2 years: 1-17-0)

Mid term 1979 through 1992: No Wrestling Program

Year	Record	Coach
1993	1-11-0	John Mastillo
1994	1-15-1	John Mastillo (2 years: 1-17-0)
1995	4-11-0	Allen Andrews
1996	10-5	Allen Andrews
1997	6-7	Allen Andrews
1998	3-10	Allen Andrews
1999	7-11	Allen Andrews
2001	5-13	Allen Andrews (6 years: 35-57-0)

Wrestling was reinstated as a sport in the Greater Johnstown School in 1992 under Superintendent DeLuca. Johnstown Schools had been void of a wrestling program for twelve years, from 1980 through 1992. During the 40 seasons with an active program, they won twenty District Championships, twelve Regional Championships and four State Championships.

1985 Football Team

In 1984 another Trojan made history. Mike "Tank" Brown ('74) won the regional Golden Gloves Heavyweight title in Hutchinson, Kansas.

According to the *Tribune Democrat* of November 22, 1985, two Greater Johnstown High School Trojans were named to the Keystone Conference all-star team and four others earned honorable mention. From the Trojan football team, Dan Varnish was selected for the offense and Eber Verhovsek was selected for the defense. Gaining honorable mention were Joseph Greenwood, Corey Clites, Brian Fern, and Mickey Miller.

Basketball

Greater Johnstown High School recognized Mr. Paul Litwalk ('62) for his 200th win in 1984 in basketball. Mr. Litwalk was in his fourteenth season at his alma mater. Under his coaching, the team captured two District 6 crowns and the 1974 championship title in the Cambria County War Memorial Invitational Tournament.

1984 Trojanettes Majorettes

The Johnstown High School Trojanettes Majorettes Squad entered two contests in 1984. In Legonier, they placed third out of eleven squads. At the Johnstown War Memorial, they placed fourth out of fourteen squads.

1984 Majorette Squad

Lori Hoover, Captain	Sonya Rose, Co-captain.
Kelly Dunn	Nancy Rupp
Debbie Smith	Jennifer Neautrour
Brenda Voeghty	Marlo Fontana

Alternates

Dena Fila	Barb Smith
Deanne Walters	

1984 Spectator Hall of Fame

Athlete	Sport	Recognition
Joe Greenwood	Football–Track	AP All State
Dave Adams	Golf–Basketball	3-Year Letter-Most Points
Mickey Miller	Football, Basketball, Baseball	Only 3 Letter Winner
Beth Eurkec	Tennis	7-3 Singles–9-1 Doubles
Cindy Duda	Basketball–Softball	Scored over 1000 Points
Dee Reviere	Basketball–Track	Scored over 800 Points
Sharon Wiegard	Softball, Volleyball	All time Batting Average
Larry Wagner	Baseball	4-1 Pitching Record

Other Sports Standouts in 1984

Dereck Lawrence	Football, Track
Pam Gunby	Track
Eric Perry	Basketball, Track

The John Kamnikar Award was established in 1961 by the high school's coaching staff. The award is one of the most prestigious honors at Johnstown high School and is awarded each year in memory of John Kamnikar. John ranked in the top ten of his graduating class and was scheduled to be the starting quarterback on the 1960–1961 football squad. John and his girlfriend, Janet Pentrack, were killed in an automobile accident on June 14, 1960.

The 1984 award was presented to Michael Rok. He was a member of the football, track, and basketball teams. During that year, he also received the *Tribune Democrat* Scholastic Athlete Award for football. He was classified as a scholar athlete, ranking fifth in the senior class, and was a member of the National Honor Society. Upon graduation, he attended the United States Merchant Marine Academy.

Class of 1984–Top Ten

1. Kimberly Nagrant–Valedictorian
2. Brian Grus–Salutatorian
3. Susan Smith
4. Diane Kopchik
5. Michael Rok
6. Catherine Lugar
7. Theresa Legath
8. Cheri Tennis
9. Tammy Owens
10. Monica Raich

The 1988 Football Staff

Jerry Davitch, Head Coach	Mike Dralle, Trainer
Dave Alvares	Tom Fleming
Joe Amsel	Bob Bambino
Don Stanton	

The 1988 Football Squad

Earl Box	Don Daugherty
Ernie Dippo	Doug Goff
B.J. Gibson	John Jones
Lane Peduzzi	Alex Roebuck
Donald Roebuck	Mark Roebuck
William Rok	Scott Spencer
Chris Stewart	Patrick Wagner
Charles Wyatt, Sr.	Tom Yewic*

* Tom Yewic, the former Johnstown High School quarterback played in the NCAA National Championship on the University of Pittsburgh Panther's Football Team.

Dr. Hollis wrote the following letter to Mr. Jerry Davitch, head football coach, for his winning football season.

1988 Winning Football Season

November 5, 1988

Dear Mr. Davitch:

This letter is written in order to avail myself of the opportunity to congratulate you, your staff, and your student athletes on the first perfect regular season since the 1958 squad. I am certain that I speak for the Board of School Directors and the entire Johnstown School District family when I commend you for your 1988, 10–0 season. Going 10–0 is difficult in itself, but when you do it on a schedule, which requires the team to play most of its games on the road, it is simply a wondrous feat.

Know that we all appreciate your long hard hours of work and your "never say die" spirit. I believe that because of your team's success that "pride and tradition" have returned to our football program. You and your team have written a bright chapter in the glorious football history of Johnstown High School. We have benefitted from the perfect 1988 season; I include the general community as well as the school community.

Please express by personal appreciation to your staff and players. On behalf of the School Board, we are very proud to call them "Our Team."

Wishing you, your staff, and "Our Team" continued success, I am

Very truly yours,
Levi B. Hollis, Ph.D.
Superintendent of Schools
Cc: Board of School Directors
Mr. William Farren
Mr. Paul Litwalk

Mr. Davitch's success with the Greater Johnstown High School Football team started as a student. Mr. Walter Jeffers ('59) talked about the Greater Johnstown High School football team of the late 1950s, with Dave Hart as head coach and Jerry Davitch ('59) as a star player. Mr. Jeffers electrified the student, Jerry Davitch, on the football field of the championship games in the late 1950s. Mr. Jeffers was a transfer student in the Johnstown schools. Although he did not play football, the team's activities and student body's comradeship around the games, helped with his academic and social adjustments. Mr. Jeffers has remained in Johnstown as the proprietor of J&O Drapery and Carpet Studio (Jeffers, 2 February, 2002).

1987–1988 Varsity Cheerleaders

Micha Kang	Stephanie Saintz
Beth Harkelroad	Kimberly Roth
Christina Thomas	Vendatta Hilton

Cheerleading Awards

First Place—Elite Cheer Camp
First Place Tri-State Championships
Third Place—Pennsylvania State Championship

1988 Girls Volleyball Team

Laura Bush—Captain	Onjanette Andrews—Assistant Captain	
Damea Haselrig	Kerry Kasper	Claudine Sinoply
Kathee Mussellman	Christine Wesner	Renee Sauro
Sharon Hoffman	Dena Pauhovich	Kim Way
Pam Spisak	Niki Berardi	Peggy Griffith
Laura Devich		

The Greater Johnstown Schools Become Greater 1990–2001

Over the pages of *Saga of the Johnstown City Schools: Echoes From the Halls,* the Johnstown Schools grew from a one-room schoolhouse, Old Blacky (Blackie), to the great comprehensive school system we know today. In retrospect, the December 15, 1898, *Tribune Democrat* provided an editorial about the school newspaper, the *Spectator.*

The *Spectator*—1898

The *Spectator,* which is supposed to publish monthly during the school term in the Johnstown High School has appeared with an editorial staff composed of pupils of the high school. Harry F. Confer is Editor-in-Chief and his assistants are Wesley R. Ellis, J. J. Kramer, Ross D. Baker...[T]he business department is in charge of John Henderson, George O. Suppes, Frank A. Bootert and Robert Judy.

Once the *Spectator,* the monthly Johnstown High School newspaper, was published in 1898, it became a constant for reporting school news and changes in the community that influenced the development of the school district. The *Spectator* wrote about Glosser Brothers Department Store and the steel mills as past icons in the city. These companies employed many families who entrusted their children to the

Johnstown Schools. Therefore, the impact of their existence was signifi-cant to the livelihood of residents and the schools. One hundred years later, the *Spectator* recognized the reverse impact that the losses of these companies have had on the growth of the schools and the community.

Glosser Brothers Department Store at Central Park, *Courtesy of William L. Glosser*

The editor contrasted the one-hundred-year interlude of the *Spectator* by looking at events that occurred and the direction that the schools and the community appear to be headed.

The *Spectator*—1998

One hundred years later, the *Spectator* continues to thrive in Johnstown, Pennsylvania.

Looking back over the past 100 years has brought tremendous change, along with loss for the community of Johnstown. With the closing of the steel mills, families were forced to leave their friends and family on a journey to new destinations. Glossers, Jupiter, Joy Shop, Woolworth's, Franklin Lunch, State Theater, Embassy The-ater, and recently Sani-Dairy closed its doors bringing financial hardship to the economy. Now…the age of technology has invaded the area with satellite dishes, computers for students, DVD's, the internet (information at your finger tips), morning announcements by way of TV, JHS radio station and the list continues. Through all the changes of times and new inventions, the *Spectator* has stood the test of time, along with the Greater Johnstown School District. We possess students that are prepared to meet the twenty-first century being taught by faculty and administration that believe in the students and citizens of Johnstown.

The *Centennial Spectator,* published in 1999, mentioned some academic changes that had taken place over the 100 years. In 1999, the high school enrollment was 975 students. Many honor societies have become part of the academic scene. The honor societies included the National Honor Society, French Honor Society, Spanish Honor Society, and German Honor Society. More than 150 students were inducted into honor societies at Greater Johnstown High School during the 1998–1999 school term. The John Kamnikar Award was given to the senior with highest grade point average and lettered in a varsity sport. David Gallucci was the 1999 winner.

Top Ten Achievers of the 1999 Senior Class

1. Brandi Seese	2. Mark Adams
3. Justin Hanuska	4. Emily Bowser
5. David Gallucci	6. Tony Alberts
7. Melan Pavic	8.Heather Kleitches
9. Chris Facci	10. Ann Schutte

and Breann Sladki

When Governor Robert Casey took office in 1987, he was reported to have had the greatest period of growth with funding in Pennsylvania's school districts. The total was $1.1 billion (Pennsylvania Education, February, 1992). However, the recession derailed anticipated basic education funding in the 1992-1993 academic year.

The music department was one of the programs that was in jeopardy. Members of the Band Booster appeared before the Board of Education with a statement in May, 1995.

Mr. John Kovac ('67) read:

I am here today to make a plea to the Greater Johnstown School Board and Administration to reconsider the budget cut for the Music Department at JHS. Over the past 2 years, the music budget has been cut more than $20,000. The Music Department is the most active group in the school. Our band members and instructors are forced to work with a budget that is equal or less than other bands in the area, in spite of the fact that our band is 2 to 3 times the size of other bands in the area. Last year the band was not able to go to all the away football games for the first time in memory. The band also had to cut down on competition trips, due to cuts in funding. This year we were told there will not be away games and once again to cut down on competition. In spite of the fact that the school district, according to the May 18th-1995 edition of the Tribune Democrat has 1.1 million dollars in reserve. This sends s very bad message to people in our district, as well as other districts. The JHS Marching Band has garnered many awards over the past years. There has always been pride and tradition in the Trojan Marching Band. When will the cutting stop? It is up to us to make sure it stops now. Our current band members should be able to enjoy the memories of football games and competition like those before them did. Our current administrator has voiced her opinion and has left no doubt in our minds about the lack of concern for competition and other functions that the band and guard participate in. Therefore, it is always one of the first departments to be cut. However, the guard members, band members, parents and supporters of the band disagree with her opinion and have been angered over the cuts. In Pittsburgh they say it is a "Burgh" thing. Perhaps the band is a Johnstown thing and one must be born and raised in Johnstown to appreciate and understand the efforts of the band. The JHS band will be celebrating its 75th anniversary this coming school year. It is up to us to make sure it celebrates a 100th!!! The parents and friends or the band members are determined to make sure that the pride and tradition continues. I hope this issue can be resolved without any further action.

> John Kovac
> 1996-1997
> JHS Band Staff

The Band Booster also presented a petition to the Greater Johnstown School Board Directors, with more than three hundred signatures. The petition stated:

The School Board and Administrators of the Greater Johnstown School District have announced plan to cut the music budget. Over the past 2 years the music budget has been cut well over $20,000. The following names are residents, voters, and/or taxpayers in the Greater Johnstown School District strongly opposing any further cuts.

In spite of some financial cuts and programs, some growth can be attributed to alternative programs that enable students to remain in school. One such program was the Elect II- Teen Parenting Program.

Elect II–Teen Parenting Program

Under the superintendency of Dr. June Merryman, the Teen Parenting Program commenced in the fall of 1993. The twelve-month program was funded by the Department of Education and Welfare. The program was designed to assist pregnant students, male and female. The concept was that if a male impregnated a female, he is also responsible for the parenting. Some students enrolled in the program as early as the seventh grade. Jane Matthews, registered nurse, was the program coordinator and handled a caseload of sixty students.

Statistics revealed that about 60 % of students with children drop out of school. Sex education programs with an emphasis on prevention help students to remain in school. Dana Redden of the 2001 graduating class wrote an article entitled "Helping Fathers" in the *Trojan Times* on January 25, 2000.

Helping Fathers
Fatherhood 101 in Effect
Dana Redden

Are you a teen father who would like to brush up on your parenting skills? Are you incarcerated and wondering if there are ways to care for your child? Not to worry, there is a program to help you, a program called Teen Parenting 101.

Whether a teen father, a father to be, incarcerated or just a father needing advice, this program is the one with answers. Funded by a grant, all session are free and confidential for all that would like to learn the basics of being a dad.

The number to call is 533-5538 for Jim Warner, or talk to Jane Matthews in the modular unit. This fundamental introduction to fatherhood is to the convenience of anyone who would like to partake in this beneficial program. Says Lisa Miller, school nurse stated, "Fatherhood 101 is an excellent program because it identifies the influential role that a father has in a child's life." As many that utilize the new Teen Parenting 101 program will see, help is easy, free, and can enrich more than one life.

Jane Matthews, program coordinator, welcomed students to the Teen Parenting Program with a letter, to offer security. She stated that the purpose of the program was to provide information to ensure a healthy pregnancy and delivery. She also included how to care for your child and how to be a good parent. The program offered assistance with graduating from high school and finding employment after graduation. She concluded with stating that the staff recognized that this is a stressful time in the student's life. The staff wanted to provide nonjudgmental help.

The curriculum as well as the school buildings changed over the years. Students enrolled in Johnstown High School for the 1999–2000 school year had a variety of tailor-made activities. A very popular program is the Co-op Program. Students are granted the privilege of experiencing real-life careers. They are enrolled in school for one-half of the day and they spend the other half of the day working with a company in an occupation of their choice. In the Business Program, Ms. Marlene Roberts taught students about the economic world and how to gain insight into business careers and opportunities. Ms. Catherine Lopresti led the Clinical Program. Students were scheduled to observe the medical profession. Students volunteered for four half days a week in various health centers. Some of the centers were Red Cross, Hiram G. Andrews Center, and various hospitals. For Mr. Lyle Stoner's and Ms. Marianne Wentworth's Communication Technology Classes, students produced video recordings, the morning announcements, made Web pages and an animated 3D studio program. These activities provided hands-on experiences for students in the world of work.

Activities in the arts included fine arts and domestic arts. Mr. John Varmecky and Mrs. Maureen Kimlin-Kinol combined all advanced arts and craft classes together in 1999 to form a studio arts class. The Home Economic Department was a creative adventure under the supervision of Mrs. Lugene Sheets and Mrs. Jeanne Hockensmith. They taught courses on clothing, nutrition, and family relations.

With the upgraded curriculum, Mrs. Jean Thompson provided a look at a different culture. In the beginning of the twentieth century the city of Johnstown was dubbed a city of foreigners, with many different languages. However, even though ethnic cultures and mores have been preserved, these languages have not. Mrs. Thompson provided an opportunity for students in her French classes to experience the French culture in French Canada. In 1999, twenty-six students and their chaperones traveled to Quebec, Canada. The students had a fun-filled adventure visiting museums, parks, and malls. Johnstown High School also participated in the Foreign Exchange Program for more than ten years. In the 1998–1999 school term, they had three foreign exchange students. The students were Aki Kobayashi from Japan, Bernardo Fonesca from Brazil, and Keith Evenson from Norway.

In-School Boot Camp

In the fall of 1999, the Greater Johnstown Middle School instituted a new type of suspension program. In previous years, students were suspended out-of-school, but this innovative program was an in-school suspension program. A police officer, Mr. Reginald Floyd ('82) from the Johnstown Police Department, was stationed full-time in the middle school. The students wore sweatshirts with GJMS on the front and the initials CSP on the back, the acronym for Comprehensive Suspension Program. The CSP sweatshirts were like a prison uniform, signaling to peers and classmates that the student had violated the rules and policies of the school district. Therefore, wearing the sweatshirt was also a form of punishment.

Mr. Floyd required students to read the definition of disorderly conduct from the Pennsylvania Crimes Code. There was a structured routine for the in-school suspension program, consisting of mandatory exercise sessions. Dr. Zahorchak, superintendent, stated that misconduct was punished in a series of steps. The steps started with a warning from the principal, to detention, and then to in-school suspension. The worst violations carried out-of-school suspensions.

In-School Suspension

First violation	One day
Second Violation	Two days
Third Violation	Five Days
Fourth Violation	Ten days

After the second suspension, a Cambria County Human Services caseworker evaluated the student to determine what may be contributing to behavioral problems. The school system also involved a district psychologist. Mr. Dino Scarton, the principal, said there was a drop in violations. The Suspension Program was a support, academic integrated program.

1999 Student Support Program
Integrated with Core Curriculum

(Augmented by Leadership)
Alternative Comprehensive Suspension Program
Social: Students complete a Social Development Assignment Kit: Provides pro-social education
Physical: Guided through group-exercise twice per day
Academic: Supervised reading writing and math prompts each day
Homework: All Assignments are completed, including quizzes and tests
Journals: Daily written reflections

Alternative to out of school suspension

First time:	One day
Second time:	Three days
Third Time:	Five days
Fourth Time:	Ten days
Fifth Time:	Recommended for expulsion

(Intervention Hearing: Administration, Guidance, SAP)

The Student Support Service was part of a Community Mentoring Project (CMP) in partnership with the Police Department personnel or trained community members. These professionals served as mentors for students who had been assigned to the Alternative Comprehensive Suspension Program (ACSP) for the third time. The CMP Project time-span was nine weeks with emphasis on behavior in classes, attendance, and achievement. The guidance program supervised the advisor program, and conducted group support sessions and crisis response. An administrator could recommend psychological screening to determine if sessions with a behavioral specialist were needed.

Community Mentoring Program

In 1998, the City of Johnstown's Police Department and the Greater Johnstown School District presented the Community Mentoring Pilot Project. The proposal for this program was submitted for the Federal Community Oriented Police Service Grant (COPS). The program was designed to prevent violence and to promote a safe, orderly, and positive learning environment at Johnstown middle and high schools. City police persons were involved with students to assist in changing negative behavior before the behavior caused his or her expulsion from school

High School Obedience Program

With the In-School Boot Camp's success in reducing suspension in the middle school, the district executed an Obedience Program in the high school in 2001. Officer Barney Solomon of the Johnstown Police Department worked with a private security contractor to supervise the halls and works with students. Students who committed minor offenses, such as repeated lateness or fighting, were referred to Mr. Solomon. Major offenses such as possession of alcohol and drugs, and carrying weapons were still classified as out-of-schools suspensions. The program was expected to reduce 50 % of the high school suspensions. The high school benefitted from the program with a police officer in the school at all times to create a safer environment. Students benefitted from the program because they became comfortable with a police officer on duty as a help to them, and not someone to be feared. However, the focus was on helping the students. The program had three components: physical workouts, life skills lessons, and makeup of class work. Mr. Solomon said that he wanted to "help students in life skills, what they can expect after high school" (*Tribune*, 9 September 1901, pp. A1–A4). Teachers were provided resiliency training to increase bonding between students and staff and to set boundaries for behavior. Within these boundaries, guidelines for discipline were established.

A $64,000 Safe Schools Grant from the commonwealth funded the program, for one-third of the cost. Johnstown Police Department allocated $50,000 and the school district provided $85,000.

Camp Trojan

Mr. Reginald Floyd, a Johnstown Police Officer who heads the Suspension Program in the school district, introduced Camp Trojan Summer Youth Program. The camp offered regular exercise sessions for participants, basic first aid instruction, cardiopulmonary resuscitation training, drug resistance techniques, and problem-solving skills, such as how to deal with peer pressure. Mr. Dino Scarton, the middle school principal, stated that the camp aimed to establish leadership skills, discipline, and a code of honor for students for dealing in negative peer pressure. Camp Trojan was offered free to all students from sixth to eleventh grades, not only in the area but even out of the district. The program included field trips to woods surrounding the city.

During the summer of 2001, Mr. Floyd partnered with Keystone Economic Development, Inc., and Pleasant Hill Baptist Church Youth Fellowship (BYF), for a field trip to Washington, D.C. Deacon Jeffrey Wilson and 38 youth from BYF participated with the group of other students. About 175 Johnstown students participated in the summer program.

Mandatory Identification Program

The Board of Education adopted a Mandatory Identification Program on November 1, 1999. The identification program promotes safety in the schools and also provides a degree of comfort to the students and the staff. The tags are similar to the tags that were worn by steelworkers in the 1950s. Hospital employees have also used staff identification tags. Today, other businesses are using the same type of safety measures. These safety measures were implemented before the terrorist attack on September 11, 2001.

The school ID tags display the name, photograph, homeroom, grade, barcode, and bus number of each student. Each paraprofessional person who interacts with students can identify the student with information from the tag; for example, the bus driver can identify the student as a rider on his bus. The cafeteria can tabulate meals that are ordered by the student. Without the photograph, students might use a false identification. Therefore, students are not admitted into the school building without ID tags.

The ID tag is also a requirement for all employees of the school district ,including the superintendent, teachers, and custodians. The tag identification extends to visitors. Each visitor to administration or the school buildings must sign in with the receptionist, with date and time of arrival. They are issued a temporary badge for the duration of their visit. In the school building, the receptionist also requests the car keys of the visitor. When five members of the American Association of University Women (AAUW) made a presentation to West Side School, all of the members received ID tags in the office before going to the classroom. At the Garfield Middle School, the president of the Johnstown Branch of the NAACP was given an ID tag and her car keys were requested. When members of the Pennsylvania Human Relations Commission meet with the superintendent, they are tagged before entering administrative offices.

The board is proactive with protecting students and providing a safe environment for learning and athletic activities.

Outstanding 1999 Athletics

Johnstown High School Golf Team

Johnstown Trojan Golf Team was undefeated in sectional play, under the skilled coaching abilities of Coach Henry Streilein. The team had only two losses in the conference play. Brad Clark and Tim Selders participated in the district playoffs.

Girls Volleyball Team

The girls volleyball team qualified to play in the District 6 AAA playoffs for the third consecutive year. Under the coaching of Denny Cruise, they had victory over Somerset in the preliminary round but lost to Central High School in the finals.

Varsity Senior Players

Stacy Blender	Christina Milazzo
Mame Parch	Crystal Probehalla
Becky Siemlok	

Wrestling

The wrestling team did not have a winning season. However, various team members had personal achievements and recognition. Anthony

Andrews made history in the school district as the only wrestler to have 100 victories in his high school career. He was also the state runner-up in Class AAA competition. Another senior, Butch Andrews, demonstrated outstanding wrestling talent.

Boys Tennis Team

The Johnstown High School's boys tennis team record was 10-4. They defeated Westmont to earn the District 6 Championship against Westmont in the title game. After playing for more than six hours, the doubles tandem of Jeff Kwiatkowski and Jan Holtzman finished the third set 6-1 and secured the first District VI title. Joe Ramirez coached this outstanding competition.

School Survey

The *Trojan Times,* the Johnstown High School newspaper, reported the results of the Communities that Cares Survey. On December 6, 1999, the newspaper reported that the Johnstown Schools were not that bad. The findings of the survey showed that the Johnstown Schools are within 2 or 3 % of the national comparison on violence. However, Superintendent Dr. Gerald Zahorchak, commented that the survey could not be a reliable instrument because of the inconsistency of reporting data. The State Department of Education concurs that each school district uses its own instrument to report incidents. However with the awareness of such incidents, schools have made steps to deal with violence in the schools. The incidents have decreased to more than half since 1995. According to the August 22, 2000, *Tribune Democrat,* in December 1998 Governor Ridge signed Act 159, that makes aggravated assault on a teacher a first degree felony. Within the guidelines of this act, youth offenders are transferred to the adult court. "Every school District in Pennsylvania has signed a memorandum of understanding with its local law-enforcement officials, outlining each entity's responsibilities when dealing with a violent incident."

Empowering Youth

On December 14, 1999, the Keystone Economic Development Corporation (KEDC) introduced a pilot program, the Neighborhood Youth Leadership Council, to Kernville Students. The Youth Neighborhood Council conducts monthly neighborhood meetings on prevention strategies. Mr. Allen Andrews, Sr. ('69), Executive Director of KEDC, introduced the council to help reduce drugs, alcohol, tobacco, and

Keystone Development, *Courtesy of Recci Patrick*

violence among neighborhood youth. The council was made up of five high school students, four middle school students, and two neighborhood adults. The council was empowered to use the school's radio station, television, and their own newsletter. Representatives from the council attended city council and Johnstown School Board meetings and also talked with the chief of police. The council had a voice in shaping the future of Johnstown and making a difference in the daily life of youth. The Leadership Program curtailed the development of cliques. Monique Johnson's national award–winning essay entitled "Cliques" was printed in the *Centralizer*. Her argument was that clique is one word that can bring about death and destruction to an entire civilized nation of American teenagers (*Centralizer*, 1 January 2000).

Division of Federal Programs– Pennsylvania Department of Education

2000–2001 Federal Title Programs

Title I

Title I is a supplemental education program that provided financial assistance to local education agencies to improve educational opportunities for educationally deprived children. The programs are designed for school buildings with an enrollment of students from families who fall in the poverty range. Fifty percent of the student body must be classified at the poverty level or below. Funds may be used in school-wide programs to upgrade the entire school curriculum. The Title I appropriation for Johnstown schools was $2,032,685 for disadvantaged students.

Title II

Title II was a federally funded program that provided financial assistance to improve the skills of teachers and the quality of instruction in mathematics and science in public and private elementary and secondary schools. Title II appropriation for the Johnstown schools was $34,648 for teachers' development.

Title VI

Title VI provided funds to implement innovation strategies. The appropriation was $31,275. Title VI also provided funds to reduce class size from kindergarten through third grades. The class size was reduced from 18 to 1. The allocation was $237,073. The Greater Johnstown School District participated in summer meal programs. The government provided federal funds to cover meals for children from low-income families.

The Johnstown School District is the largest school district in Cambria County, and one of the poorest districts in the commonwealth. The school district, located within the city limits of Johnstown, is classified as urban. According to the *Tribune Democrat* of November 23, 2000, the region has 6.3 % unemployment, the highest of any metropolitan area in Pennsylvania. Cambria County has 12.7 % of the population living in squalor. The commonwealth's median annual household income is $37,267. However, Cambria County's median annual household income is $28,786, the sixth lowest. These figures qualify the district for federal funds.

The New High School

On April 4, 2001, the Greater Johnstown School Board approved the addition of six classrooms and a $38 million design for the new high school slated for student occupancy in the fall of 2003. Building a new high school had been a controversial issue for several years. However, ground was broken for a new high school on August 31, 2001, at the Greater Johnstown High School. The *Tribune Democrat* reported that the Johnstown Renaissance Partnership wrote a letter to the district superintendent expressing its concern about the direction of the project. Mr. Orlando Hasselman, chairperson of USBancorp (Ameriserv) was concerned that services would be duplicated in the area, notwithstanding a sizable tax increase. The Renaissance Partnership stated that they supported a modern school, but called for adjustments. Some of the adjustments were to have the construction managed within the approved budget, with assurance of no new tax increases. They stated that the district should cooperate regionally to avoid duplicating athletic fields, auditoriums, and other facilities and to develop vocational training programs geared toward new technology.

Dr. Donato Zucco ('58), Mayor of the City of Johnstown, pointed out that property taxes had not been raised since 1994 and that the district is suffering from unemployment. Mr. Ed Cernic ('50), a descending board member, described the project as a "Taj Mahal" around Cochran Auditorium. The comment was referring to the aging concert hall that the school district incorporated in the building plans. In spite of the overwhelming opposition, the school board approved the design to replace the seventy-six-year-old school building on Central Avenue.

The board vice president, Mrs. Mary Beth Stern, stated, "As we break ground today, I feel we have won and more importantly, our children have won."

Dr. Clea Hollis, president of the local Johnstown Branch of the NAACP, was one of the participants in the groundbreaking ceremony, with remarks. She said:

> It is an honor to be asked to speak. My late husband, Dr. Levi Hollis, was the fifteenth superintendent of the Greater Johnstown School District. He built his administration on the backs of other superintendents. Dr. Gerald Zahorchak can move the district forward, because of the accomplishments of other superintendents. Today we break ground to share in this gift to our Johnstown students. This is a gift of advancement to the high tech world and to better economic horizons for each student, for the prosperity of Johnstown. A community is only as good as its schools.

Father Christian Oravec ('55), president of Saint Francis University, Loretto, Pennsylvania, also participated. The NAACP acknowledged him in 2001 for his outstanding campus-wide Diversity Program. St. Francis University actively recruits students from the Johnstown Schools and has maintained an Upward Bound Program for high school students for more than a quarter of a century.

The Greater Johnstown School District is in the city and has been a part of the city family, like a child belongs to his or her family. The Johnstown Public schools have been fortunate to be located in the city and be able to use the city facilities, such as Point Stadium and the Cambria County War Memorial. However, maturation has occurred and some alumni and some students, hopefully wanted their own athletic facilities, like their smaller, neighboring, suburban schools. Unfortunately, the budget of the new school could not support the building of a sizable football stadium with field lights.

Comprehensive School Reform Model

The comprehensive new high school building was designed with progressive programs for students. The design emerged from an educational program that stressed a strong fundamental background and career planning. The educational program is a movement toward a curriculum based on developing each student for proficient career development. The Johnstown School program ensures that students will develop core academic skills combined with real-life experiences focused on moving to post-secondary education and careers. Reading, writing, and mathematics have career-based knowledge and experience akin to the twenty-first century's world of work. The comprehensive school reform model is developed by Johns Hopkins University. Dr. Zahorchak, the superintendent, stated that the Johnstown Schools would be in partnership with Johns Hopkins University's Talent Development. Talent Development is one of the U.S. Department of Education's touted comprehensive school reform models. The Talent Development Program with career paths will serve as the foundation of the new educational program, which emphasizes school-to-work. The program will force organization and curriculum innovations for the new school.

The career path model will include a ninth-grade academy and freshman seminar as a year-long integrated orientation for new students. Tenth graders will select a career path. Each career path will consist of a committee that will include a principal or assistant, a guidance counselor with a support staff, and an interested team of vocational and academic professionals.

Talent Development Program
1. High Academic Standards
2. Complete School Reform
3. Smaller Organizational Units
4. Post Secondary and Career Focus
5. Establishment of a Ninth Grade Pathway
6. An Evening School for Older Drop-out Students
7. Supportive Interventions for All Students.

The Talent Development Program, as the new curriculum for the new school, will enhance the students' employment college opportunities. The Talent Development Program appears to be in tune with the National Education Association's top policy priorities.

NEA's Top Priorities for Public Schools

1. Lifting up Low-Performance Schools, through full funding of Title 1. No child will be left behind.

2. Ensuring qualified teachers through a partnership of state and local school districts.

3. Modernizing America's Public Schools. Through an innovative initiative combining the use of tax credit bonds education and the federal government. Creating an environment that supports excellence.

4. Making a lifelong difference through early childhood education, with universal preschools to the expansions of the childcare block grant and Dependent Care Tax Credit. Entering school ready to excel.

5. Funding, fully, the Individuals with Disabilities in Education Act (IDEA) within five years.

6. Holding schools accountable for student performance by helping school districts align goals, curriculum, standards, professional development and assessments, into a powerful weapon to raise student performance.

Dr. Zahorchak's report indicated that the aforementioned priorities by NEA have been incorporated into the Greater Johnstown School Program. The American public schools have always been under local control. However, his report suggests that every child has an opportunity to excel with an equal opportunity. The report also recognizes and provides for barriers that may inhibit school performance.

Superintendent's Report

1. A High School building program
2. Achievement scores rose significantly in half of the district's schools
3. West Side Elementary School is recognized by the U.S. Department of Education as a distinguished school.
4. A deficit budget of four years reports a 20% fund balance
5. Budget does not include a property-tax increase
6. Creative funding permitted class reduction
7. The district adopted new language arts and math standards and assessments.
8. Resiliency training efforts and system reform
9. Middle School reform reduced 50% of the school suspensions
10. Increased general fund budget over $400,000
11. New federal and state grant funds totaling $1406,000
12. Title 1 funds used to augment salaries
13. Community involvement organizations

Dr. Gerald Zahorchak
March 29, 2000

Technology Grant

On February 9, 2001, Dr. Zahorchak announced that the Greater Johnstown School District received a State Grant for the Link-to-Learn Program. Representative Edward Wojnaroski was instrumental with helping schools in his Seventy-first District receive grant money. The Greater Johnstown School District and the Greater Johnstown Vocational-Technical School received these funds. Greater Johnstown received $146,080. The funds will be used to strengthen reading, writing, and math skills. The skill levels are customized for each student's success with an evaluation on progress. Technology is the vehicle used to share progress results with parents. Link-to-Learn is a multi-year initiative designed to expand the use of technology in Pennsylvania's classrooms.

The program involves buying updated computers and also providing technology training for the teachers. More than $240 million were invested in education technology.

In 1991, the Pennsylvania Department of Education (PDE) began restructuring the Vocational Education Program to meet requirements to be classified as technical education (Greer, 1991, p. 9). PDE restructuring can be linked to "consumerism" that might create another group of high school students aspiring to attend college. With societal changes and demands, high schools have had to become more responsive to "consumerism," attempting to meet the needs of all students. However, the country is in a state of recession that may cause some students to postpone college; a technical background may put graduates immediately in the job market.

School Finance

The survival of our democracy depends on the quality of education in our schools. That quality is unequivocally bound with educational standards established by leadership. However, educational programs survived on the financial plan adopted by the Board of Education. The Board of Education was primarily established to supervised state and local funding for education. Unfortunately, education is an indescribable value. Therefore, it is difficult to persuade parents and residents to support education at a meaningful level, because it often means increased taxes. Public schools are essential for acquiring Americanization to move our youth into productive roles to enhance the global community.

Public school financing is not easy for most school communities. The finance program reflects the degree of cultural progress and understanding the board of education has been able to achieve in the community to address existing educational problems. Each community is unique, with its own problems and peculiar economic strengths or weaknesses. Each community has its own standards for the schools and its own perceptions of values and mores to be promoted. The Greater Johnstown School System's challenge is gaining and maintaining financial support for educational programs. Students from the Johnstown School System should be able to compete on equal terms with students educated in schools anywhere in the country.

The 2000 presidential election had a strong emphasis on education. Consequently, President Bush presented his education plan three days after taking office. He underscored his commitment to the well being of current and future generations of students. His proposal included annual testing of students from third through eighth grades and early reading programs. The greatest controversy is the use of federal funds for private schools. According to the January 27, 2001, *Tribune Review*, low-income families would be able to use $1,500 per student for financial assistance to private and public schools if their local schools do not meet the standards in three years. Ted Kennedy, the senior Democrat on the education committee and a supporter of teachers' unions, stated, "I don't think that we ought to abandon the schools by taking money away from public schools in order to save them." Political economist, James Bauchanan, points out that reform is not possible unless the rules change. The voucher is a way of changing the rules and forcing accountability. At the 2001 NAACP National Convention in New Orleans, the organization came out in opposition to the charter schools or the voucher system. Most underrepresented students are enrolled in public schools. Taking revenue from the schools makes the public school weaker and provides even a lesser education for minority students.

The Pennsylvania Voucher Plan died amid "Mean Spirited" attacks on June 17, 1999. Pennsylvania Governor Tom Ridge abandoned his efforts to get a voucher proposal through the General Assembly. This was his second attempt in five years to pass such a bill, but the teacher union was strong enough to persuade opposition to the bill. The Pennsylvania State Education Association (PSEA) 147,000 members were more influential than the commonwealth's 3.5 million Catholics. Catholicism is 30 % of the population.

The National Education Association (NEA) is the nation's largest professional employee organization, representing more than 2.3 million educators. In a lawsuit, NEA challenged the Southeast Delco School Board for vouchers to be unconstitutional *(Giacomucci v. Southwest Delco School District,* 742A.2d 1165). The suburban Philadelphia School Board adopted a voucher scheme that granted $250 per student in private kindergarten, $500 per student in private school grades one through eight, and $1,000 for private high school. No income requirements were attached to voucher eligibility. On October 14, 1998, the Court of Common Pleas in Delaware County ruled in the plaintiff's favor, stating that the school board lacked authority to create a voucher scheme under the Public School Code. NEA's recommendations on low-performing schools are designed to eliminate the gap by raising all students to the highest levels.

The National School Board Association (NSBA) commissioned a poll of the voucher system. The findings from the poll conducted by Zogby, an international research group, was contrary to a poll taken by the Joint Center for Political and Economic Studies. They argued that the conflict was caused by responses to the design of the questions, as is the case with most surveys. Opponents say school vouchers siphon public school funds, leaving less money for academic programs that are built around already dwindling resources. Minority students or underrepresented students are at the crux of the issue. Inner-city schools often suffer because state funding is allocated based on property taxes. Schools in poor areas with low property values receive less funding than more affluent areas, sometimes in the same county (http://www. diversityinc. com).

On October 7, 2001, the Supreme Court heard arguments on the constitutionality of the Cleveland Schools' voucher system. Supporters of the voucher program claim that students improve on test scores because they are able to gain assess to a greater amount of knowledge. Therefore, they receive a higher quality of education, with a smaller teacher-to-student ratio. Currently 4,266 Cleveland children use vouchers to attend 56 private schools, with 96 % of the children in religious schools. Sixty percent of the families in Cleveland are below the poverty line. The vouchers are up to $2,250 toward tuition in Ohio for participating schools. Currently, vouchers are used in Dayton and Cleveland, Ohio; New York, New York; Washington, D.C., and Milwaukee, Wisconsin. The Supreme Court Decision will have an effect on Pennsylvania schools. Johnstown Schools have been affected by the various laws and acts since the beginning. In 2001, the Greater Johnstown School District has been condensed from fifty schools to four schools in the district.

Greater Johnstown School District—2001
Board of School Directors

Ruth Jenkins	President
Beth Stern	Vice President
Donald Irwin, Jr.	Treasurer

Debra A. Crowder	Secretary
Edward Cernic, Jr.	Robert Miller
Derrick Nash	Robert Roseman
Loretta Stumpo	Doris Todorich
Joseph Yeager	David Andrews, Esq.

Administrative Office

Dr. Gerald Zahorchak	Superintendent
Dr. Steven Greenfield	Director of Education
Donald Irwin, Jr.	Business Manager
Charles McCabe	Federal Program Coordinator
Ralph Osmolinski	Technology Coordinator
William Geisweidt	Food Service Director

Greater Johnstown High School
Grades: Ninth–Twelfth

Alan Johnson	Principal
Donald Civis	Assistant Principal
Anita Sukenik	Guidance Counselor
Patricia Noon	Guidance Counselor
Lisa Miller	School Nurse
Connie McClain	Librarian
65 Classroom Teachers	

Greater Johnstown Middle School
Grades: Sixth–Eighth

Dino Scarton	Principal
Theresa Ritter	Principal
James Reiser	Guidance Counselor
Maureen Yost	School Nurse

30 Homerooms
56 Teachers in Six Core Teams

East Side Elementary School
Grades: Kindergarten–Fifth

Robert Beatty	Principal
Dr. John Jubas	Assistant Principal

West Side Elementary School
Grades: Kindergarten–Fifth

Barbara Parkins	Principal
Rita Redden	Assistant Principal
Ruth Ann Ficco	Instructional Support Leader

(Appalachia Intermediate Unit 8, pp. 39–40).

* Greater Johnstown School District Community Report Card (June 29, 2001)

2001 Greater Johnstown School District Statistics

Schools	Number	Enrollment
Elementary	2	1809
Middle	1	788
High School	1	956
Total District Enrollment		3553

Average Class Size

Grade 1	20
Grade 8	25

Student to teacher ratio 12-1, including special teachers

Beginning special instruction	Grade
In-class Computers	1
Band Instrument Lessons	6
Gifted pull-out Programs	2
After School Day Care Program	

High School

Interscholastic Sports Programs	14 (8 = Boys–6 = Girls)
Foreign Language Classes	4
Advanced Placement Classes	5
Seniors receiving Diplomas	99 %
Graduates going to Higher Education	65%

(http:list.realestate.yahoo.com/re/schools/district/pa/506.html assessed Dec. 9, 2001)

In 2002 the Greater Johnstown School District remains the largest of twelve school districts in Cambria County, Pennsylvania.

2002 Cambria County Schools

School District	Student Population	Student Ratio	Class size First Grade	Percent of Graduates	Percent to College
Blacklick Valley	751	13	17	95	72
Cambria Heights	1693	16	23	99	76
Conemaugh Valley	974	15	20	97	66
Central Cambria	1984	15	16	92	68
Ferndale	804	13	21	100	69
Forest Hills	2382	19	17	99	72
Greater Johnstown	3429	12	25	99	41
Northern Cambria	932	9	20	98	34
Penn Cambria	1933	16	23	100	55
Portage	1073	13	21	100	75
Richland	1552	15	24	99	69
Westmont Hilltop	1640	13	23	100	77

(http:/list.realestate.yahoo.com/re/schools/search.html?c=Johnstown&s=PA assessed Dec. 9, 2001)

Family Center *

Director–Mary Schroyer

Component:	Cambria County Resource Initiative
Location:	East Side Elementary School
Staff:	5
Students:	125+ Basic Computer Instruction
	500+ during 2000–2001

Support Groups

Fatherhood Initiatives 11 Groups = 90+ male students
Up with Downs
Parents United for Making Progress Together
Endometriosis
ALS
Grandparents as Parents
Brownies
Cub Scouts
Girl Power 230+ female students
Tiger Scout

Co-Sponsored Activities

East Side Elementary School	Spring Fling, Oktoberfest
	Valentine Day Dance
1st Summit Bank	Playground Project
Sears	H.O.P.E. (Helping one person excel)
Trinity Evangelical Church	Clothing Drive
Westmont Key Club	December Coat Drive
NAACP	MLK Weekend

* 2001 Community Report Card

Greater Johnstown School District Business Office *

Mr. Donald Irwin, Jr.–Business Manager
Expenditures: $32.5 Million
Fund Balance: $3.3 Million
Savings: $2.5 Million
96 mils/tax–(no tax in crease for 6 consecutive years)

* 2001 Community Report Card

Transportation Department *

Mr. Dave Taylor–Director
Annual Budget: $1.2 Million
Bus Contract   McIlwain's Bus Line
Buses: 46 Regular
                   6 Mini
Service: District Students
                   Non-Public
                   Alternative Education
Passengers: 2800 students daily
Route: Tanneryville, Belmont, Riverside, Roxbury

* 2001 Community Report Card

2001 Community Report Card Breakfast

One of the authors had the opportunity to attend the Greater Johnstown School District's First Annual Community Report Card Breakfast with about eighty other community leaders on June 29, 2001, at East Side Elementary School. East Side is the former Meadowvale School Building. The Reverend Christian Oravec, president of St. Francis University, recognized Superintendent Gerald Zahorchak with the Distinguished Alumnus in Education Award from St. Francis University, Loretto. Father Oravec spoke about Dr. Zahorchak's roots as a student at Greater Johnstown and at St. Francis University.

Greater Johnstown Administration Building, *Courtesy of Judy Browne Photography*

Dr. Zahorchak informed the audience about the achievements in the district. He stated that all schools in the district had increased their student assessment scores with West Side Elementary leading. (Westside is the former Westwood School.) He mentioned that East Side had been honored by the U.S. Department of Education with the Distinguished School Award in 2000. East Side is engaged in a program developed by Johns Hopkins University, titled the Comprehensive School Reform model and the Success for All. (See CSP). East Side was only one of ninety schools in the United States to be recognized as a "Distinguished School."

Other schools had also received awards. The Johnstown Middle School had received the Pennsylvania System of School Assessment Incentive Award for the past two years in recognition of rising assessment scores. Greater Johnstown High School and East Side Elementary School both received incentive awards for attendance improvement and rising student assessment scores for the past three years. In essence all four schools in the district were recognized for student achievements.

U. S. Representative John Murtha was presented the "Friend of Education Award,' because of his continued support of the district's programs, especially funding for the summer in the city program.

Joyce Murtha Breast Care Center, *Courtesy of Ted Hollern*

Congressman Murtha has displayed his friendship to the area by funding many projects. The Windber Research Institute, in nearby Windber, is one such initiative. The Institute will attract scientists to the area and also keep some local graduates in the area.

2001 Community Report Card

Mission Statement

Through a shared vision, the Greater Johnstown School District, supported by pride and tradition, is committed to creating and sustaining a community of learners who will pursue high standards to succeed in a diverse, global society.

Support, Grow, and Succeed.

Superintendent's Message

I am proud to be the Superintendent of the Greater Johnstown School District for many reasons. Mostly because I belong to this District as a former student, life-long community member and as a school leader.

Our community takes pride in its history. Today we meet to check progress of our current status and to discuss plans for our future. The Greater Johnstown School district "Community Report Card" is one of our many attempts to keep parents, students, and all community members informed about the progress and development of our school district.

As citizens of Johnstown, we know the strength and determination of our citizens. We have come back after three floods and many other challenges. Your attendance today at our Community Breakfast is so greatly appreciated. It shows us your support and interest in our district. I am especially proud of the county and city governments, along with dozens of active partners here today, who play a key role in the healthy development of our children.

Thank you for being part of our school community and for being instrumental in the growth of our students. Together, we are building a strong community with skilled individuals who are needed to stay and work in Johnstown.

Yours in education,

Gerald L. Zahorchak, D.Ed.
Superintendent of Schools

Safe Schools in a Safe City

The Johnstown Schools are nestled in one of the top ten safest cities in the United States. "Morgan Quitno Research Company ranked Johnstown ninth in a study of 254 metro areas, by crime data reported by the FBI for six basic crime categories: Murder, rape, robbery, aggravated assault, burglary and car theft" (*Tribune*, 20, January, 2002). Chief of Police William Clark said, "For our population rate, our violent crime is very low." Morgan Quitno's comparison results are published in the "City Crime Rankings." The findings support Johnstown's motto, "Friendly, Safe and Clean." Apparently, these values are upheld by the citizens of Johnstown and elected officials.

School board members are officials elected to serve in the best interest of the students. When the newly elected board takes office, they have visions and most of these visions are revisions to complement the mission of the school district. The mission should be student-driven, based on the culture to transcend traditional values cast in a changing world. Therefore, the progress of Johnstown is, to some extent, embedded in the progress of the Greater Johnstown students, which is in turn controlled by an elected board of school directors who approve budgets and programs.

Epilogue ❖

The purpose of writing *The Saga of the Johnstown City Schools: Echoes from the Halls* was twofold. The first purpose was to compile data collected by one of the superintendents of the Greater Johnstown School District, the late Dr. Levi B. Hollis, Jr. Of course, his collection of data was enhanced with additional research and extended to 2002. The second purpose was to illustrate academic milestones and contributions of Johnstown's African-American Community with the development of the Johnstown Schools. With the Americanization theme that wove the pages together, isolated ethnic communities are also woven together to accept and appreciate differences in an educational arena of a holistic community. In 2002, the Americanization theme is as great a need as it was in the 1800s and 1900s.

Greater Johnstown students ride off into the future.

Jamal Ellerbe, *Courtesy of Ralph J. Patrick*

Greater Johnstown School District Newsletter

(see following pages)

February, 1995.

Teacher and Students Enjoy "English as Second Language"

Mrs. Marcia Kissel teaches reading to Sun Hin and Chang Uk Lee.

Although it doesn't happen in Johnstown with the frequency it does in many larger cities, each year there are a few children attending school here for whom English is a foreign language. This year Mrs. Marcia Kissel, a reading teacher at Johnstown High School, has two students from South Korea.

Chang Uk Lee, 19, is a junior at JHS. His sister Sun Hin Lee, 16, is a sophomore. Both are studying reading from Mrs. Kissel. The Lee's came from Korea to the U.S. last October and are living in Johnstown with their parents, a younger brother, and an aunt's family.

Mrs. Kissel has taught students from Vietnam and Guatemala at JHS, and while at Meadowvale she had two students from Argentina. Since learning

English is so vital for a foreign student's success, Mrs. Kissel has a number of techniques to help them. In the elementary grades, when they are just beginning to learn any written language, students respond well to flash cards. At the high school level, they use dictionaries as invaluable.

Mrs. Kissel says there are some major differences between students learning English as a second (or third or fourth) language and those who speak it as a native tongue. For one thing, students from foreign countries are generally more precise in following the rules of grammar, possibly because they haven't heard English misused all their lives. She says foreign students work extremely hard to learn proper English because they're highly-motivated and realize they must be proficient in English to succeed in their adopted country. Mrs. Kissel has found her foreign students to be polite, disciplined, and

prompt. Both Chang and Sun Lee plan to attend college, and both seem to be adapting well to the culture of America. Strong academic discipline has been a part of their lives. In Korea, they attended school from 7:30 in the morning until dinner, then returned to classes until 9:00 P.M. On Saturdays they got a break. School was not in session in the evening. They came to this country with some knowledge of our language, since in South Korea all students study Korean, English, Chinese, and a <u>fourth</u> language.

ARTISTS VISIT JHS

Mrs. Kathy Samay with Rick Fuge

During the fall semester, Mrs. Kathy Samay, the coordinator of the Johnstown Extension of the Southern Alleghenies Museum of Art, demonstrated the art of papermaking to John Yarmecky's Advanced Art students at Johnstown High School.

Mr. Yarmecky has been asking community artists to speak to his advanced art classes for the past six years.

In addition to Mrs. Samay, his classes have been visited this year by Kevin Kurtz, a "plein-air" painter from Everett; Robin Green, a wood-block printmaker from Johnstown; and Walter Smith, a chain-saw sculptor from Mineral Point. Artists and craftsmen from Indiana and surrounding communities have also taken part in the visiting artist program.

This year the parents of the art students have been invited to join their children in the visiting artists' presentations.

KNOWLEDGE IS THE KEY
TO ENLIGHTENMENT

February, 1985

Teacher and Students Enjoy "English as Second Language"

Mrs. Marcia Kissel teaches reading to Sun Min and Chang Uk Lee.

Although it doesn't happen in Johnstown with the frequency it does in many larger cities, each year there are a few children attending school here for whom English is a foreign language. This year Mrs. Marcia Kissel, a reading teacher at Johnstown High School, has two students from South Korea.

Chang Uk Lee, 18, is a junior at JHS. His sister Sun Min Lee, 16, is a sophomore. Both are studying reading from Mrs. Kissel. The Lee's came from Korea to the U.S. last October and are living in Johnstown with their parents, a younger brother, and an aunt's family.

Mrs. Kissel has taught students from Vietnam and Guatemala at JHS, and while at Meadowvale she had two students from Argentina. Since learning

English is so vital for a foreign student's success, Mrs. Kissel has a number of techniques to help them. In the elementary grades, when they are just beginning to learn any written language, students respond well to flash cards. At the high school level, they see dictionaries as invaluable.

Mrs. Kissel says there are some major differences between students learning English as a second (or third or fourth) language and those who speak it as a native tongue. For one thing, students from foreign countries are generally more precise in following the rules of grammar, possibly because they haven't heard English misused all their lives. She says foreign students work extremely hard to learn proper English because they're highly-motivated and realize they must be proficient in English to succeed in their adopted country. Mrs. Kissel has found her foreign students to be polite, disciplined, and prompt.

Both Chang and Sun Lee plan to attend college, and both seem to be adapting well to the culture of America. Strong academic discipline has been a part of their lives. In Korea, they attended school from 7:30 in the morning until dinner, then returned to classes until 9:00 P.M. On Saturdays they got a break. School was not in session in the evening. They came to this country with some knowledge of our language, since in South Korea all students study Korean, English, Chinese, and a <u>fourth</u> language.

ARTISTS VISIT JHS

Mrs. Kathy Samay with Rich Fuge

During the fall semester, Mrs. Kathy Samay, the coordinator of the Johnstown Extension of the Southern Alleghenies Museum of Art, demonstrated the art of papermaking to John Varmecky's Advanced Art students at Johnstown High School.

Mr. Varmecky has been asking community artists to speak to his advanced art classes for the past six years.

In addition to Mrs. Samay, his classes have been visited this year by Kevin Kurtz, a "plein-air" painter from Everett; Robin Green, a wood-block printmaker from Johnstown; and Walter Smith, a chain-saw sculptor from Mineral Point. Artists and craftsmen from Indiana and surrounding communities have also taken part in the visiting artist program.

This year the parents of the art students have been invited to join their children in the visiting artists' presentations.

DR. LEVI HOLLIS
-NEW MAN IN CHARGE

In the fall of 1984, veteran District Superintendent Dr. Donato Zucco resigned his school position to enter private business. The Greater Johnstown School Board conducted a wide-ranging search to find a successor to Dr. Zucco. The candidate they selected decided at the last minute not to accept the Johnstown position. Rather than fill the vacancy hurriedly, the Board chose to wait until after the current school year, when qualified candidates would be able to leave their current assignments more easily. Dr. Levi Hollis was named Interim Superintendent, to serve until a permanent nomination is made. Here is a look at the "new man in charge."

DR. LEVI HOLLIS
INTERIM SUPERINTENDENT

Newsletter: Dr. Hollis, where are you from?
Dr. Hollis: I came here from Warren, Ohio, and prior to that I was in New Kensington, Pennsylvania, or a suburb of New Kensington called Lower Burrell Township. I am a native Pennsylvanian.

Newsletter: Tell us a little about your family.
Dr. Hollis: I am married, of course, and I have two terrific children, both of whom are teenagers now. My oldest turned sixteen this fall. She is an excellent student, and we're all proud of her volleyball participation; and she's also interested in music and has played in the band. My son is a freshman. My daughter is a junior. He is very much interested in music. He's in the WJAC-TV Heartland Band and in the Indiana University Honors band. What's more important to me is that they're very good students and I think they're good citizens.

Newsletter: How did you select education as a profession?
Dr. Hollis: My first choice was opthomology. However, I have a brother who is two years younger than I am, and my brother and I were in college at the same time. My parents really

----
"MY FIRST CHOICE WAS
OPTHOMOLOGY."
----

didn't have the money to send me to opthomology school. The nearest one at that time was the University of Pennsylvania. I recall looking at the brochures for tuition costs, and it was beyond our means, really, to have me go there. My mother had taught many years before, so we both went into education. When we graduated, I continued in education, but my brother went into another line of work because he could earn more money.

Newsletter: Where are your college degrees from?
Dr. Hollis: My degrees are from Duquesne University, Ohio State University, and Kent State University. But I've also done additional work at the University of Pittsburgh and St. Bonaventure University in New York.

Newsletter: How did you originally learn about the position in Johnstown and why did you apply here?

Dr. Hollis: That's an interesting story. I do some public speaking, and at this time I was invited to give a speech in New Kensington. I had driven over from Warren, and the man who introduced me that evening was from the New Kensington School District. As we were having dinner, he told me about the job in Johnstown. I didn't even know where Johnstown was. When I got back to Warren I forgot about the job. Some days later I wrote a letter to the personnel director in Johnstown, who turned out to be Dr. Melleky. He answered the letter and sent me an application. I completed the application and sat it on my desk at home. It laid there a couple of weeks, at least a couple of weeks. Finally my wife said, "Either mail it or throw it away." So, I went back in the house, got it, put a stamp on it, and put it in the mailbox. That led to my getting an interview. The position was mentioned to me at a speech I was giving. I never saw it in the newspaper or anywhere else.

"I'D LIKE TO THINK I'VE MADE
SOME IMPACT ON THE
CURRICULUM."

Newsletter: What do you think have been your major contributions since you've been here?
Dr. Hollis: I'd like to think I've made some impact on the curriculum. One of the first things that we tackled when we came here was to develop the Scope and Sequence. Another thing that we did early on was to develop the Alternative Program. We initiated the TESA Program. Summer school is another thing that we've developed since we've been here.

Newsletter: When the position of Superintendent became vacant last fall, why didn't you apply when you had the credentials?
Dr. Hollis: I felt that the timing just might not be right.

"I HAVE A TIME-LINE THAT I WANT TO FOLLOW IN MY CAREER."

I have a time-line that I want to follow in my career and I wasn't certain that I wanted to apply at that time. The current situation will give me a chance to make a better assessment.
Newsletter: What do you feel are the major weaknesses in Johnstown Schools?
Dr. Hollis: Well, like other districts, I think we have a cash flow problem. We sometimes run the danger of losing sight of our mission because we are always hemmed in by a finite amount of money which must be spent, it appears to me, on an infinite amount of District needs. So, we're always trying to balance our needs against our resources. That's our weakness. And it's a weakness that I think is shared by a lot of school districts. I think we need to do more to personalize the profession in our district. We need to do what we can to try and have the teacher believe that the administration and the Board and the community really have a personal interest in what he is doing. By the same token, I think the teacher

needs to try and personalize, in a professional manner, his work with the students. I think the students need to feel that the teacher views them with worth and respect and is willing to

do everything within reason to help them achieve.
Newsletter: What about our strengths?
Dr. Hollis: I think we are reflective of a strong community resiliancy. Our district has been beset with a lot of moves, has been beset with staff reductions, but I think our people have been able to face these adversities with a good deal of strength and resolve, which is reflective of the community. It faces mill closings and mill cutbacks and floods and bounces back. Our teachers do the same thing.
Newsletter: Very often we're accused of being rather parochial here in the Johnstown area. Do you feel you've been accepted as a member of the professional community since you moved here?
Dr. Hollis: I think that would be something that would be viewed in different degrees by whoever is discussing it. Personally, I think I have been able to become quite active in the community. I've been chairman or president of three community boards, major boards. I currently sit on three or four

---
"I THINK ACCEPTANCE IS A MATTER OF HOW MUCH YOU CAN CONTRIBUTE."
---

boards in town. I think acceptance is a matter of how much you can contribute. What I try to do is make a worthwhile contribution. It's the contribution, I think, not necessarily the person. If you make a good contribution, then you're accepted for that contribution.
Newsletter: If you picture yourself down the road, say, ten years from now, where would you like to be?
Dr. Hollis: I would like to stay in education. In ten years I would like to have served as a superintendent, and I would like to be either in, or seriously considering, a position in a college or university, teaching educational administration. I think my

time here in Johnstown and the experience I had in Warren, Ohio, are rich resources that I can draw on to teach such a course. A lot of things have happened to you when you are in the position, which are never really printed in textbooks. One thing I have in mind is I'd like to do a book. I have collaborated with two professors and we have done one book, which

"ONE THING I HAVE IN MIND IS I'D LIKE TO DO A BOOK."
---

was used at a couple of universities for some time, and I did publish a research guide myself. I'd like to look again at publishing; I'd like perhaps to do something on matching the superintendent with the school district. I think that there's perhaps nothing written about that at this time. When a person is seeking a superintendency, I think it's important for him to try to match his background and personality with the district.

DR. HOLLIS JOINED THE GREATER JOHNSTOWN SCHOOL DISTRICT AS THE DIRECTOR OF SECONDARY EDUCATION IN 1975. HE IS A NATIVE OF NEW KENSINGTON, PA.

HAPPENING IN OUR SCHOOLS...

Chemical People Fight Drug, Alcohol Abuse

Throughout the nation, school children are becomming more and more aware of the dangers of drug and alcohol abuse. Public service announcements on radio and television and warnings from famous sports and entertainment personalities continuously point out the harm that drugs and alcohol can do to young bodies. Warnings against driving under the influence of drugs and alcohol are graphically portrayed on television.

Helping to localize these national messages for students in our schools is the Greater Johnstown School District Chemical People Task Force, a group of about twenty-five concerned citizens formed just over two years ago.

At Roxbury Elementary School, the P.T.A. presented ribbons to students who made the honor roll. Above, fourth graders Ryan Blough and Lori Rowzer, who both had all A's, were among 31 fourth and fifth graders to receive awards from Principal Barbara Casavant. Both Ryan and Lori scored in the 95th percentile on the California Achievement Test. Mrs. Casavant reports that of the 34 pupils in fourth grade at Roxbury, 16 scored in the 80th percentile or higher on the C.A.T.

Rosalie Danchanko, Director of Victims' Services, visits children at Chandler Elementary School in the photo above. Ms. Danchanko talked to students in grades kindergarten through five at Chandler, Meadowvale, and Roxbury Schools. Using audio-visual aids and her own message, she provided the children with a program aimed at preventing child sex abuse. Her visits were arranged by John Sholtis, an elementary guidance counselor.

Mrs. Josephine Romani helps plan a new project with the Chemical People.

The Chemical People meet the second Wednesday of each month at 7:00 P.M. at the Meadowvale Conference Room. Under the leadership of Mrs. Josephine Romani, the local group has sponsored wholesome dances for area young people and has supported efforts to encourage alcohol-free graduation parties.

The job of educating students to the dangers of drug and alcohol abuse can be accomplished even more effectively if a larger number of concerned adults get involved. The Greater Johnstown Chemical People task Force next meets at 7:00 P.M. on Wednesday, March 13, at Meadowvale. You are invited!

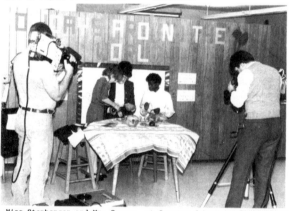

Miss Stephenson and Mr. Corona at Greater Johnstown Junior High had speakers into their classes to explain holiday traditions from throughout the world. Here, Dawna Hahl tells Lynn Beppler and Greta Carter about festivities in Germany. The presentations were taped by WJAC Television. They were also recorded by Wally Leech (on the right), Director of GJSD Media Services.

Photograph Collection
Bruce Haselrig
Burns Photography
Cover Studio
Dorothy Thomas
Hoss's Family Steak and Sea House Historical Collection
Jessie Crawley-Grigsby
Jonathan Darling
Johnstown Area Heritage Association
Judy Browne Photography
Ralph Patrick
Recci Patrick
Ted Hollern
William L. Glosser

Qualitative Research
Oral history for this publication was offered by many graduates and former residents of Johnstown. Some of these persons were Allen Andrews, Sr.('69), Gladys Andrews ('59), Deanna Fisher ('75), Jessie Crawley-Grigsby ('47), Bruce Haselrig, Sr. ('62), Burrel Haselrig ('39), William Jackson ('45), Cora Jarvis-Redden, Walter Jeffers ('59), Hope Johnson, Joyce Johnson ('59), Claudia Jones, Victoria King ('75), John Kovac ('67), Dorthea McCray ('62), Mike Messina ('75), Daniel Perkins ('69), Kathleen Stewart, Jeffrey Wilson, and Alvena Wright.

The media and the school board minutes provided detailed information about racial, sports, music, and curriculum issues pertaining to the schools and the community. For qualitative data, persons in the community were interviewed to provide more insight to some of the issues. *The Saga of the Johnstown City Schools* also provided a written history of the development of the African-American Community with the Johnstown Schools. On January 27, 2002, Dr. Lamar Lee, Jr., Pastor of First Cambria A.M.E. Zion Church, said, "Every year the country stands aside to gyrate African-American history into the agenda, for one month. African-Americans are not a one month stand, nor were African-Americans standbys and observers of history; they were participants."

Annotated Bibliography ❖

American Association of University Women (AAUW) Johnstown Branch, *Women of Cambria County, Their Work—Their History—Their Contributions 1770–1987.* (1988). Indiana: A.G. Hallidin Publishing Co. *Women of Cambria County* is a book about local Johnstown Women authored by local American Association University Women. (Clifton, G.; Cooper, E.; Fattman, A.; Himes, M.; Johnson, J.; Redden, R.) The book lends itself to the study because women of the area have been the backbone of many school projects and have served in the teaching profession since the establishment of the first Johnstown School.

Appalachia Intermediate Unit 08, 2000–2001 Directory. Ebensburg: Educational Services. Appalachia Intermediate Unit 8 Directory is an official document that provided information about the administrative teams of each school district in Intermediate Unit 08 and the members of the board of directors of these districts. The directory is compiled each year.

Astin, A. W., Green, K. C., Korn, W. S., and Schalit, M. (1985–1990). American Freshman: National Norms. Los Angeles, CA. Higher Education Research Institute. Graduate School of Education. University of California. For the purpose of this study the "Weighted National Norms for All Men" sections were analyzed. The study was compared with findings of the Deremer Study.

Berger, Karl (ed). *Johnstown, the Story of a Unique Valley.* (1985). Johnstown: Johnstown Flood Museum. Coleman, N. "History of Public Transportation"; Cooper, E. M. "Underground Riches: The Story of Johnstown's Coal Industry"; Johnson, G., Giles, E., and Michaels, R. "Johnstown and the Pennsylvania Canal"; Johnson, H. B. and duPont, B. T. "The Black Community"; Morawska, E. "Johnstown's Ethnic Groups"; Pawlowski, E. "The History of City Planning"; Robson, J. G. "Indians of the Conemaugh"; Williams, B. and Yates, M. "Labor in Johnstown"; Burkett, R. A. "Iron and Steel Making in the Conemaugh Valley." The book was written and illustrated by people who live in the Johnstown Community. These residents had the expertise and knowledge about the contents of their chapters.

Blackington, F. H. *University of Pittsburgh at Johnstown, Alumni Directory, 1994.* (1993). White Plains: Bernard C. Harris Publishing Co. The directory provided biographical data of graduates of the Johnstown Campus and the Asphalt Campus.

Blockson, C. L. *African-Americans in Pennsylvania. Above Ground and Underground.* (2001). Harrisburg: RB Books. Mr. Blockson wrote this historical book as a response to a teacher's statement, "Negroes have no history…They were born to serve white people." Even with negativism, teachers have a way of motivating students to produce something positive. Mr. Blockson was motivated to research and record the neglected history of African-Americans in Pennsylvania. This same motivation also occurred with the writing of *The Saga of the Johnstown City Schools.* The authors of the *Saga* discovered the same findings with their research as Mr. Blockson. The major findings were a void or delayed academic diversity in the development of the schools. The second thread of African-American life in Johnstown has been the ongoing struggle against oppression for equality, freedom, and education.

Blue and the Gold, Cochran Junior High School, October 1978. An editorial student staff at Cochran Junior High School published the regular school news.

Buck, S. J. and Buck, E. H. *The Planning of Civilization in Western Pennsylvania.* (1995). Pittsburgh: University of Pittsburgh Press. Historically, the authors placed Johnstown in the development of the Commonwealth of Pennsylvania. The City shared in the growth and is similar to other small towns.

Burkert, R. *Pictures from Our Past—A Visual History of Johnstown.* (2000). Johnstown: Johnstown Heritage Association. Historical pictures are organized in this book to tell the Johnstown story, starting with a copy of the original land grant deed. On a small scale, the book wove the community together, including the Johnstown Public Schools.

Deremer, R. Comprehensive School Survey. (May 1969). University of Pittsburgh Associates. Pittsburgh, Pennsylvania. Dr. Deremer conducted a study in the Greater Johnstown School District to ascertain the attitudes of the community. He used parents and neighbors of six grade students for the study. The study provided information for the Board of School Directors and administrators to shape programs for the district's students.

First Cambria A.M.E. Zion Church (booklet). The Pennsylvania Historical and Museum Commission, Bureau of Archives and History, Division of History presented the Historical Marker to First Cambria A.M.E. Zion Church, Johnstown, Pennsylvania, on May 10, 1997. The church organized in the spring of 1873 as Cambria Chapel, and was recognized as the oldest black church in Johnstown. Since establishment, the church has served a dual purpose for religion and as a meeting place to discuss issues pertaining to equality and unity in the community. Over the years, the NAACP has met in Fellowship Hall of the church.

Greater Johnstown High School Alumni Directory. (2000). Johnstown, PA. White Plains: Bernard C. Harris Publishing Company. The alumni directory is a handbook of all graduates of Johnstown High School from 1922 through 2000. The directory listed the careers and location of each member of the senior class.

Greater Johnstown High School Course Descriptions. Johnstown: Greater Johnstown School District. The Greater Johnstown School District periodically published a course description booklet. Several booklets were used for this study.

Greater Johnstown High School In-Service Report. Dr. M Wayne Vonarx, superintendent (June 10, 1974), presented reports to the board of directors. Superintendents' reports were used throughout this study.

Greater Johnstown Minority Scholars Club, (Brochure) 2000. The *Greater Johnstown Minority Scholars Club was* organized in 1984. Every year Greater Johnstown guidance counselors refer students from ninth through twelfth grades for consideration of membership.

Greater Johnstown School Board minutes. The greater Johnstown School Board has met on a regular schedule. The school board minutes are recorded and are public documents. Selected school board minutes from 1834 through 2000 were perused for much of this study.

Greater Johnstown School District Community Report Card, June 29, 2001. The booklet was circulated at the first annual Community Report Card breakfast, held at East Side Elementary School. It contained information about the schools and updated plans for the new high school.

Greer, D. G., "The Leadership Role of Today's Colleges," *The Chronicle of Higher Education.* October 2, 1991. Greer argued that with a differential cost of education, middle-income people would carry the burden of paying the most for education. Further, he argued that differential pricing would also perpetuate more inequalities among socioeconomic groups.

Hollis, C. P. *A Study of the Influence of Affirmative Action.* (2000). Ann Arbor: Bell & Howell Co. The study was conducted to ascertain if current legislation has been applied to disparage practices and behavior. The study was applicable to some of the EEO cases presented in *The Saga of the Johnstown City Schools.*

Hollis, L. B. *Greater Johnstown School District: Long Range Plan.* (1984–1989). Johnstown, (PA): Johnstown School District. (Cambria County). The Long Range Plan was a strategic Five Year Plan to advance student achievement in the Greater Johnstown School District.

Hollis, L. P. *Equal Opportunity for Student Athletes.* (1998). Ann Arbor: Bell & Howell Co. All students are guaranteed equal opportunity in education by the Fourteenth Amendment of the Constitution and interpretations from the 1954 Supreme Court Decision, *Brown Versus the Board of Education.* The Greater Johnstown Schools have always had a very active athletic program and the text was used as a guide when reviewing policies and practices.

King, V. (1998). Church Historian. Bethel A.M.E. Church was founded in Rosedale Borough and was closely involved with the early history of the Johnstown Schools.

(http://list.realestate.yahoo.com/re/schools/search.html?c=Johnstown&s=PA assessed Dec. 9, 2001) Johnstown, Pennsylvania, website provided updated in formation on the city and the schools.

Literary Herald. Before the *Spectator*, students at Johnstown High School published a weekly paper called the "Literary Herald." Articles were written in the Literary Herald about the Johnstown High School.

McCullough, D. *The Johnstown Flood.* (1968). New York: Simon & Schuster. The book is an historical account of the Great 1889 Flood. The environmental climate of the Johnstown community is revealed in a chain of events from before, during, and after the flood. Mr. McCullough depicted the flood as a national scandal.

Memories of Johnstown, PA. (2001). Johnstown: Windber–Johnstown Area Genealogical Society. Gary Beuke, Carolyn Clark, V. Gwynne (Hamer) Fetsko, Nancy L. Hoover, Nancy Scrudders Miller, Mary Louise Wagner, John Wilson. Memories is a book of reminiscences and photographs from the people of Johnstown, compiled by the Genealogical Society. The section titled "Where We Learn," about the Johnstown Schools, was used for this study.

Morawska, E. *For Bread With Butter, Life Worlds of East Central Europeans in Johnstown, Pennsylvania, 1890–1940.* (1985). Cambridge: Cambridge University Press. This study is about the process of European immigrants coping in the new environment of Johnstown, Pennsylvania. In a social environment, adaptive options are presented.

Morawska, E. *Insecure Prosperity: Small-Town Jews in Industrial America, 1890–1940.* (1995). Princeton: Princeton University Press. The book is an historical narrative of development of ethnic communities in Johnstown. Although the focus is on the Jewish ethnic community, the development of Johnstown follows the Americanization theme and educational reform.

Pittsburgh Post-Gazette is a daily and Sunday Newspaper. Often Johnstown news is reported in the *Pittsburgh Post-Gazette.* News articles were documented as related to the study of the Johnstown Schools.

Riggenbach. E. M. *A Bridge to Yesterday, An Early History of Monte Vista, Colorado.* (1982). Monte Vista: High Valley Press. The early history of Monte Vista was interestingly compared with the early history of Johnstown. The one-room schoolhouse was consolidated to offer a more comprehensive school program.

The *Spectator.* The *Spectator* was a literary paper published by the schools, starting about 1898. Data for *The Saga of the Johnstown City Schools* were obtained from various issues of the *Spectator* and other publications. The *Spectator* also became the name of the senior yearbook.

Strayer, H. H. and London, I. L. *A Photographic Story of the 1889 Johnstown Flood.* (1999). Johnstown: Johnstown Area Heritage Association. The story is a documentation in pictures of the devastation of the city of Johnstown by the 1889 Flood.

Thompson, K. and MacAustin, H. *The Face of Our Past.* (1999). Bloomington: Indiana University Press. This photographic tome is a portrayal of the historical struggle of black women in America.

Tribune-Democrat Newspaper, Johnstown, Pennsylvania. The *Tribune-Democrat* is a Community Newspaper Holding, Inc. The Newspaper serves the residents of Johnstown and west central Pennsylvania. The *Tribune* and *Tribune-Democrat* newspaper articles were perused for a major part of the research of *The Saga of the Johnstown City Schools.* The Cambria *Tribune* Newspaper was started in 1853 as a weekly newspaper and began reporting Johnstown School news. Twenty years later, in 1873, the newspaper was renamed the *Johnstown Tribune.* With the coverage of the expanded population, the *Tribune* became a daily newspaper. The Johnstown Democrat was founded as a weekly newspaper in 1863 and changed to a daily newspaper in 1888. The *Johnstown Tribune* published in the afternoon and the Johnstown Democrat published in the mornings until a merger of the two papers occurred. They published daily with a combined named of *Tribune-Democrat.* In 1952, the two papers were merged into an all-day paper called the *Tribune-Democrat.* The Sunday edition started March 6, 1977, before the 1977 flood. After the flood, the *Tribune-Democrat* became a daily seven-day morning newspaper.

Trojan Centralizer, Volume one, Number one, October 1980. The Trojan was a newsletter published by students at Johnstown High Schools. The *Centralizer* reported issues and programs of interest to the student body.

Dr. Clea P. Hollis

Dr. Clea Patrick Hollis earned her Bachelor of Science Degree, cum laude, from Youngstown State University, Youngstown, Ohio. She taught in the Warren City Schools prior to moving to Johnstown, Pennsylvania. She earned her Master's Degree in Education and her Doctorate in Higher Education Administration from the University of Pittsburgh. She holds Preschool, Elementary and Reading Specialist Certifications from the Pennsylvania Department of Education. She also taught in the

Dr. Clea P. Hollis, *Courtesy of Cover Studio*

Richland Township and the Westmont Hilltop School Districts, Johnstown, Pennsylvania. She was the first African-American and the first female to serve in the president's cabinet at the University of Pittsburgh, Johnstown Campus. She is currently a consultant for the U.S. Department of Education.

In 2001, Dr. C. P. Hollis was honored by the YWCA's Tribute to Women for Community Service and the National Organization for

Women (NOW) as Woman of the Year. She holds membership in the American Association for Affirmative Action, Unity Coalition of the Southern Alleghenies, and is a Life Member of the NAACP. She is chairperson of the Board of Trustees at First Cambria African Methodist Episcopal Zion Church, secretary of the Greater Johnstown Minority Scholars Club, and was the executive director of the Greater Johnstown Enrichment Program. She also serves on the board of directors for the Windber Medical Center, Windber, Pennsylvania; the 1001 Advisory Board for Hiram G. Andrews Rehabilitation Center; and the Advisory Board of the Pennsylvania Human Relations Commission (PHRC). In 2002, she serves as the president of the Johnstown Branch of the National Association for the Advancement of Colored People (NAACP), vice president of the American Association for University Women (AAUW), and vice president of the Elizabeth Lindsay Davis Club.

Dr. Leah P. Hollis

Dr. Leah Patricia Hollis, as the daughter of one of the superintendents, grew up among school board directors and was a voice in the *Echoes of the Halls*. After she graduated from Richland Township High School, Johnstown, Pennsylvania, she earned her Bachelor of Arts Degree in English as a Henry Rutgers Scholar, from Rutgers University, New Brunswick, New Jersey, and her Master's Degree in English from the University of Pittsburgh, Pittsburgh, Pennsylvania. She continued her academic studies to earn a Doc-

Dr. Leah P. Hollis,
Courtesy of Cover Studio

torate of Education in Higher Education Administration from Boston University, Boston, Massachusetts. Dr. L. P. Hollis has been an administrator at the University of Pittsburgh and Northeastern University, Boston, Massachusetts. She has also taught Racial Ethnicity at New Jersey Institute of Technology and English at Northeastern University. Formerly the Director of the Learning Resource Center, Rutgers University, Newark Campus, Dr. L. P. Hollis is a presidential appointee to her current position, Director of Academic Support Services for Student Athletes, Rutgers University, New Brunswick, New Jersey.

Dr. Leah Hollis' publications include Service ACE: Which Academic Services and Resources Truly Benefit Student Athletes (2001), Equal Opportunity for Student Athletes (1998); "The Ultimate Triple Jump: The Psycho-Social, Historical, and Current Dynamics Affecting African-American Female Athlete's Identity and Success," (Athletic/Academic Journal—1997); Out of Line and Cleo Patrick Stage Plays, Ensemble Theatre, Newark, New Jersey (1990–1992); In and Around Rutgers University: A Student Guide, Thunder Road Press, New Brunswick, New Jersey, (1990); and EEO Bulletin, Johnson & Johnson Inc., Newsletter, New Brunswick, New Jersey (1989–1990).

Index ❖

Give the Gift of
The Saga of the
Johnstown City Schools
to Your Friends and Colleagues

CHECK YOUR LEADING BOOKSTORE OR ORDER HERE

❑ **YES**, I want _____ copies of *The Saga of the Johnstown City Schools* at $29.95 each, plus $4.95 shipping per book (Pennsylvania residents please add $1.80 sales tax per book). Canadian orders must be accompanied by a postal money order in U.S. funds. Allow 15 days for delivery.

❑ **YES**, I am interested in having Clea P. Hollis and Leah P. Hollis speak or give a seminar to my company, association, school, or organization. Please send information.

My check or money order for $_____ is enclosed.

Name _____

Organization _____

Address _____

City/State/Zip _____

Phone_____ E-mail _____

Please make your check payable and return to:
Patllis Press
P.O. Box 5336
Johnstown, PA 15904